HUMAN RIGHTS
IN CHINA

China Today Series

Greg Austin, *Cyber Policy in China*

Jeroen de Kloet and Anthony Y. H. Fung, *Youth Cultures in China*

Steven M. Goldstein, *China and Taiwan*

David S. G. Goodman, *Class in Contemporary China*

Stuart Harris, *China's Foreign Policy*

William R. Jankowiak and Robert L. Moore, *Family Life in China*

Elaine Jeffreys with Haiqing Yu, *Sex in China*

Michael Keane, *Creative Industries in China*

Joe C. B. Leung and Yuebin Xu, *China's Social Welfare*

Hongmei Li, *Advertising and Consumer Culture in China*

Orna Naftali, *Children in China*

Eva Pils, *Human Rights in China*

Pitman B. Potter, *China's Legal System*

Pun Ngai, *Migrant Labor in China*

Xuefei Ren, *Urban China*

Nancy E. Riley, *Population in China*

Judith Shapiro, *China's Environmental Challenges 2nd edition*

Alvin Y. So and Yin-wah Chu, *The Global Rise of China*

Teresa Wright, *Party and State in Post-Mao China*

Jie Yang, *Mental Health in China*

You Ji, *China's Military Transformation*

LiAnne Yu, *Consumption in China*

Xiaowei Zang, *Ethnicity in China*

HUMAN RIGHTS IN CHINA

A Social Practice in the Shadows of Authoritarianism

Eva Pils

polity

Copyright © Eva Pils 2018

The right of Eva Pils to be identified as Author of this Work has been asserted in accordance with the UK Copyright, Designs and Patents Act 1988.

First published in 2018 by Polity Press

Polity Press
65 Bridge Street
Cambridge CB2 1UR, UK

Polity Press
101 Station Landing
Suite 300,
Medford, MA 02155 USA

ISBN-13: 978-1-5095-0069-7
ISBN-13: 978-1-5095-0070-3(pb)

A catalogue record for this book is available from the British Library.

Typeset in 11.5 on 15 pt Adobe Jenson Pro
by Toppan Best-set Premedia Limited
Printed and bound in Great Britain by CPI Group (UK) Ltd, Croydon.

The publisher has used its best endeavours to ensure that the URLs for external websites referred to in this book are correct and active at the time of going to press. However, the publisher has no responsibility for the websites and can make no guarantee that a site will remain live or that the content is or will remain appropriate.

Every effort has been made to trace all copyright holders, but if any have been inadvertently overlooked the publisher will be pleased to include any necessary credits in any subsequent reprint or edition.

For further information on Polity, visit our website: politybooks.com

Contents

Map	vii
Chronology	viii
Acknowledgements	xii
Abbreviations	xiv

Introduction — 1

1. Human Rights and Competing Conceptions of Justice, Law and Power — 9
The *yuan* tradition of righting wrongs — 13
The rights tradition — 16
Official counterdiscourses — 20
Conclusion — 31

2. Institutional Avenues of Human Rights Advocacy — 32
The place of human rights in the normative framework — 33
Institutional avenues: the judiciary — 43
Institutional avenues: 'letters and visits' and the media — 47
Advocacy as resistance — 51
Conclusion — 54

3. Liberty and Life 55
Restrictions of personal liberty 57
Torture 64
The right to life and the death penalty 69
Conclusion 75

4. Expression and Thought 77
The limits of the right of free expression 79
Censorship and crimes of expression 82
'Smart' technologies of expression vs 'smart'
control technologies 87
'Public opinion guidance', 'thought work' and
'social credit' governance 92
Conclusion 98

5. Inequality and Socio-economic Rights 100
The impact of urbanization on land and
housing rights 103
Education rights of rural and migrant worker
children 108
The human rights effects of environmental
degradation 114
Conclusion 117

6. Rights Defenders 121
The emergence of civil society advocates 123
The consequences of authoritarian revival 135
Conclusion 143

Conclusion 145

Notes 153
Index 215

Map

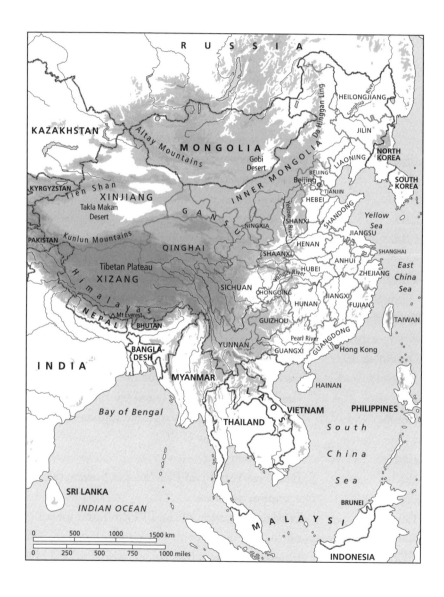

Chronology

1894–5	First Sino–Japanese War
1908	Draft Constitution incorporates individual rights
1911	Fall of the Qing dynasty
1912	Republic of China established under Sun Yat-sen
1927	Split between Nationalists (KMT) and Communists (CCP); civil war begins
1934–5	CCP under Mao Zedong evades KMT in Long March
December 1937	Nanjing Massacre
1937–45	Second Sino–Japanese War
1945–9	Civil war between KMT and CCP resumes
October 1949	KMT retreats to Taiwan; Mao founds People's Republic of China (PRC)
1950–3	Korean War
1953–7	First Five-Year Plan; PRC adopts Soviet-style economic planning
1954	First Constitution of the PRC and first meeting of the National People's Congress
1956–7	Hundred Flowers Movement, a brief period of open political debate

1957	Anti-Rightist Movement
1958–60	Great Leap Forward, an effort to transform China through rapid industrialization and collectivization
1958	The household registration (hukou) system is introduced
March 1959	Tibetan Uprising in Lhasa; Dalai Lama flees to India
1959–61	Three Hard Years, widespread famine with tens of millions of deaths
1960	Sino–Soviet split
1962	Sino–Indian War
October 1964	First PRC atomic bomb detonation
1966–76	Great Proletarian Cultural Revolution; Mao reasserts power
February 1972	President Richard Nixon visits China; 'Shanghai Communiqué' pledges to normalize US–China relations
September 1976	Death of Mao Zedong
October 1976	Ultra-Leftist Gang of Four arrested and sentenced
December 1978	Deng Xiaoping assumes power; launches Four Modernizations and economic reforms
1978	One-child family planning policy introduced
1979	US and China establish formal diplomatic ties; Deng Xiaoping visits Washington
1979	PRC invades Vietnam
1982	Census reports PRC population at more than one billion
1982	Fourth Constitution of the PRC

December 1984	Margaret Thatcher co-signs Sino–British Joint Declaration agreeing to return Hong Kong to China in 1997
1988	PRC ratifies the Convention Against Torture
1989	Tiananmen Square protests culminate in June 4 military crackdown
1991	First government White Book on Human Rights
1992	Deng Xiaoping's Southern Inspection Tour re-energizes economic reforms and drive to urbanization
1993–2002	Jiang Zemin is president of PRC, continues economic growth agenda
1998	PRC signs the ICCPR (not yet ratified)
2001	PRC ratifies the ICESCR
November 2001	WTO accepts China as member
2002–12	Hu Jintao, General-Secretary CCP (and President of PRC from 2003)
2002–3	SARS outbreak concentrated in PRC and Hong Kong
2003	Sun Zhigang Incident and founding of NGO Gongmeng
2004	Constitution includes phrase 'the state respects and protects human rights'
2004–5	Lawyer Gao Zhisheng publishes open letters on Falun Gong torture
2006	PRC supplants US as largest CO_2 emitter
December 2006	Founding of anti-discrimination NGO Yirenping
August 2008	Summer Olympic Games in Beijing

December 2008	Publication of Charter 08, imprisonment of Liu Xiaobo
2010	Shanghai World Exposition
2011	The 'Jasmine Crackdown' targets human rights defenders
2012	Xi Jinping appointed General-Secretary of the CCP (and President of PRC from 2013)
2013	Abolition of RTL
2013	Document No. 9 rejects 'so-called "universal values"'
2014	CCP Central Committee Decision Concerning Some Major Questions in Comprehensively Moving Governing the Country According to the Law Forward
2015	National Security Law, Counterterrorism Law, Anti-Espionage Law
July 2015	'709' crackdown on human rights lawyers begins amidst intensified civil society persecution
2016	Cybersecurity Law, Foreign NGO Management Law, Charity Law
July 2017	Death of Liu Xiaobo

Acknowledgements

I would like to thank the two External Readers for their most helpful and encouraging comments on the draft manuscript, Helin Laufer Gencaga for her excellent research assistance, and Jonathan Skerrett and Neil de Cort at Polity for the excellent work on the book's production. I am greatly indebted to the Law School at King's College London for giving me an academic home to work from and for its generous support for my fieldwork research through the 2015–16 PC Woo Fellowship. I am also deeply grateful for conversations about the issues discussed in this book while I was working on it, with many colleagues and friends in academia, the media, and human rights NGOs. Among them are – with apologies for any negligent omissions – Björn Ahl, Stéphanie Balme, Jean-Philippe Béja, Jérémie Béja, Mayling Birney, Michel Bonnin, Alain Bouc, Chris Buckley, Albert Chen, Chen Weitseng, Chen Yongxi, Alvin Cheung, Jerry Cohen, Elena Consiglio, Rogier Creemers, Jeremy Daum, Jacques DeLisle, Matthew Erie, Harriet Evans, Octavio Ferraz, Corinna-Barbara Francis, Fu Hualing, Guo Yicong, Stephen Guest, Terry Halliday, Kathrin Hamenstädt, He Weifang, Jane Hendersen, Marie Holzmann, Jiang Jue, Perry Keller, Tom Kellogg, Katrin Kinzelbach, Ben Liebman, Sida Liu, Darius Longarino, Elizabeth Lynch, Nicola Macbean, Aruna Nair, Elisa Nesossi, Will Partlett, Tom Phillips, Tim Pringle, Kathryn Rand, Sophie Richardson, Stein Ringen, Joshua Rosenzweig, Flora Sapio, Ewan Smith, Marina

Svensson, John Tasioulas, Teng Biao, Frank Upham, Sebastian Veg, Sophia Woodman, Zeng Jinyan, and Zhang Yihong. Some of those whose contributions have been particularly important unfortunately cannot be named, including the anonymized interlocutors quoted here. I am deeply grateful to them, too. All errors are of course my own.

Eva Pils
London, April 2017

Abbreviations

ABA	American Bar Association
ACFTU	All China Federation of Trade Unions [中华全国总工会]
ACLA	All China Lawyers' Association [中华全国律师协会]
ACWF	All China Women's Federation [中华全国妇女联合会]
CAT	Convention Against Torture
CCP	Chinese Communist Party [中国共产党]
CEDAW	Convention on the Elimination of All Forms of Discrimination against Women
CECC	Congressional-Executive Commission on China
CERD	Convention on the Elimination of All Forms of Racial Discrimination
CHRD	Chinese Human Rights Defenders
CL	People's Republic of China Criminal Law [中华人民共和国刑法]
CPL	People's Republic of China Criminal Procedure Law [中华人民共和国刑事诉讼法]
CPPED	Convention for the Protection of All Persons from Enforced Disappearance
CPRM	Convention on the Protection of the Rights of All Migrant Workers and Members of Their Families
CRC	Convention on the Rights of the Child

CRPD	Convention on the Rights of Persons with Disabilities
GONGO	Government-Organized Non-Governmental Organization
ICCPR	International Covenant on Civil and Political Rights
ICESCR	International Covenant on Economic, Social and Cultural Rights
ILO	International Labour Organization
NGO	Non-Governmental Organization
NPC	National People's Congress [全国人民代表大会]
NPCSC	Standing Committee of the National People's Congress [全国人民代表大会常务委员会]
OHCHR	Office of the High Commissioner for Human Rights
PRC	People's Republic of China [中华人民共和国]
RTL	Re-education Through Labour [劳动教养]
SPC	Supreme People's Court [最高人民法院]
US	United States
UDHR	Universal Declaration of Human Rights
UN	United Nations
UPR	Universal Periodic Review

Introduction

In 1991, the Chinese government published a White Book on Human Rights which declared its commitment to the 'lofty goal' of human rights, as well as support for the United Nation's treaty framework.[1] Two years after its violent suppression of the June Fourth movement for democracy, and at a time of major political transitions around the world, China found itself under some pressure to overcome its global image as a dictatorship prepared to murder its young. It needed to reconnect to the international community.[2] This community, in turn, expected it to change and, eventually, conform to a liberal model. China was already then a signatory to some United Nations (UN) human rights treaties and was to sign (and in most cases ratify) several more in years to come.

As of today, China takes an active part in some of the United Nations based mechanisms, notably the Universal Periodic Review (UPR) process.[3] It has written 'respect and protection of human rights' into its Constitution, and produced two five-year Human Rights Action Plans (the most recent one for 2016–20).[4] It also argues that it has greatly furthered human rights goals by 'lifting millions out of poverty'[5] and that, anyway, there is no universal idea of human rights.[6]

These claims have met with criticism from many quarters. The catalogues of Chinese human rights violations are long. They include torture and other abuses in the criminal justice system, the lack of media and internet freedom; land rights, labour rights, 'birth planning' policies; and various kinds of discrimination, including against the physically or mentally disabled, the persecution of dissidents, communities of faith and minorities.[7] The news media, reports by non-governmental organizations' (NGO), reports generated by UN bodies and processes and foreign governments' commentary on human rights in China[8] testify to a strong interest in how and why human rights in China are violated, and how they can be defended and protected. Their comments on human rights issues in China are complemented by scholars, domestic and international, journalists, artists, and so on; and these comments often draw attention to the bleak and dire.[9]

Yet, even the bleakest comments tend to be framed in a language of reform, of potential, expected, and on the whole likely, albeit sometimes obstructed or thwarted, improvement. There has long been a widely held belief that China is − must be − on a path of slow transition towards improved rule of law.[10] The magic word appeared to be 'engagement' − through engaging China at governmental and non-governmental levels, it would be possible to bring the relevant actors round to the ideas inspiring rule of law and human rights, thus preparing the ground for a liberal transition. Complementing and, arguably, nurturing this expectation, a large industry of governmental and academic programmes led by NGOs or government-organized NGOs (GONGOs), working with Chinese institutions to promote rule of law and civil society, sprang up.

Some versions of the 'incremental reform' argument went even further, asserting that Party-State leadership was in fact best suited to achieve the difficult transition towards rule of law.[11] The continued violation of certain human rights seemed to be a regrettable but necessary evil attendant on China's slow, incremental transformation. It required acceptance of certain domestic taboos around 'sensitive' human rights topics, such as the topic of persecuted 'enemies of the People'. 'Economic reforms first, political reforms later', in the words of one of the Chinese scholars of the 'Chinese model'.[12] The claim that China was undergoing a gradual, incremental reform process appeared to solve some problems of engagement, allowing transnational actors to stay clear of downright political issues,[13] and domestic ones to stay safer. In some ways, it might be said to suit everybody.

Almost everybody. In the earlier years, the victims of human rights violations did not have much of a voice; and the more 'sensitive' their cases, the less they could be discussed domestically. But throughout the post-Mao reform era, and especially from the 1990s onwards, victims – or survivors – of rights violations grew more vocal. The ideas, the vocabulary, arguments and techniques of rights advocacy these programmes disseminated reached those who needed them through oblique and serendipitous channels. Networks inside and outside of China developed and overcame some of the divides induced by control and self-censorship; and gradually, they also changed how victims saw themselves, and how advocates related to them and to the system surrounding them. They started disrupting the 'incremental reform' narrative.

Both the paradigmatic claim that China is transitioning to better rule of law through top-down reform and human rights protection, and the arguments for authoritarian governance call for a critical assessment. This book discusses human rights in China in the light of this need. It challenges the paradigmatic, predictive expectation of transition through top-down reform as increasingly untenable. But it also argues that human rights' enduring importance and vibrancy is demonstrated by human rights advocates who challenge the system's authoritarian practices and principles.

We can only understand the bottom-up dynamic of human rights if we are not imprisoned in too narrow and authority-driven a conception of rights, and if we are sensitive to political context. In Nickel's introductory definition – helpful as a starting point – human rights are 'norms that help to protect all people everywhere from severe political, legal, and social abuses'.[14] The discussion in the following chapters will focus on a few of these rights, here considered as central nodes in a web of interconnected human rights principles – expression and thought, liberty and life, and socio-economic and anti-discrimination rights. It will engage with rules and principles that have been created to safeguard these rights through international treaties and domestic legal norms, and use the further definitions contained in these texts. But it will not claim that these or any other definitions close down disagreement over the rights they safeguard. Treaties and national constitutions have given us a shared language and some basis of consensus, of recognition-in-principle;[15] but they give rise to interpretive social practices that sustain deep disagreement.[16] State governments, courts and legislatures, and international bodies may get to decide about legal human rights norms; but according to the view adopted here, they too do not have a monopoly on defining what human rights are or how they ought to be understood, just by virtue of holding power or status.

Conversely, while international human rights treaties create institutional obligations the concluding state parties did not previously have, whether the people in these states have human rights does not depend on their governments' signing of treaties – rather, there is a moral argument for 'human rights universalism' (such as is expressed in Nickel's definition). Once a state has acknowledged obligations under human rights law, it is generally 'not necessary to argue the moral issues from the ground up';[17] generally – but not always. As will be seen in the chapters to come, acceptance of the authority of international human rights law can turn out to be especially weak in China's authoritarian environment, and rights defenders keep having to make the argument that human rights ought to be respected.

A non-positivist, non-voluntarist approach to human rights does not mean that human rights is a hopelessly 'subjective' idea that cannot be defended against criticism. It means, rather, that human rights is a contested concept;[18] that the argument for human rights is persuasive rather than peremptory; that 'the authorities' interpreting human rights, whoever they are, may get it wrong just like anyone else; and that any textual expression of human rights or constitutional principles is not conclusive of what these rights and principles mean. As discussed throughout this book, the textual basis for a human rights argument may in fact be thin or contradictory; it may consist in no more than a sentence in the Constitution, or a clause in a treaty that is routinely ignored; and it may be buried underneath language that is in tension with human rights; or made to an institution downright hostile to the very idea of rights.[19] Human rights defenders' claims here discussed as part of the social practice of human rights include many instances where the defenders cannot get access to the institutions, because the Party-State will not let them, or where even when they do get access, their human rights arguments go unheard.

The chapters to follow therefore track ways in which rights defenders in contemporary Chinese society use the concepts of human rights (*renquan*) and rights (*quanli*), as well as official or establishment discourse about rights. They draw interpretively on fieldwork,[20] as well as a variety of textual and audio-visual resources, including legal instruments, scholarly literature, NGO reports, media reports and commentary, conversations and documentaries. They emphasize the importance of engaging with the 'vernacular' human rights discourse; and they are intent on understanding the political dimensions of different human rights arguments. The idea that there is a justifying connection between rights protection and the coercive actions of the state is particularly important to the argument developed here. For example, the recognition and protection of a right to be treated as a 'human being whose dignity fundamentally matters'[21] can be taken to be central to any justification. A human rights violation, on such an account, violates a state's duty towards its citizens in a way that upsets the state's authority, or the political obligation of citizens to obey the law; and it is connected to a right of resistance. Other accounts are less immediately concerned with human rights' political justification;[22] they might, for example, focus more on the interests that human rights are central to protecting.

An examination of how relevant actors in China discuss human rights reveals a great diversity of attitudes and arguments. The authorities sometimes – for example when employing utilitarian arguments about welfare – gesture in the direction of an 'interest' theory of rights; but as argued in chapter 5, they do not commit to any coherent version of the interest theory. Their claim to govern in accordance with laws that protect rights, insistence that central authorities respect the law even when local authorities do not, and the wider 'liberal transition' argument mentioned earlier, seem to assume that human rights will become increasingly central to the justification of its power. Yet on some occasions, the authorities advocate some version of human rights particularism or relativism, or simply reject human rights. Overall, the discussion in this book shows that it is not possible to identify one coherent position taken by the Party-State; rather, the authorities employ arguments that seem convenient in the moment without recognizing any need to provide a coherent account, and without having to adopt a coherent position in the disciplining setting of a judicial process. Rights defenders, in turn, often emphasize the political dimension of human rights;[23] they engage in advocacy whose point is to demand systemic change as a political human rights requirement.[24] As discussed in chapter 1, they do not always do so to the exclusion of other conceptions of justice, including some that are not compatible with rights; and the positions they advocate are not always coherent. But broadly speaking, rights defenders' arguments are based on liberal ideas of every person's entitlement to protection against abuse of (public) power.

While the discussion in this book shows human rights in China to be a vibrant and important social practice, it also portrays it as a practice in the shadows of an authoritarian system, in which victims like the one depicted on the cover of this book may hide their face while seeking justice; in which some systematic rights violations cannot be discussed in the media, effectively challenged in the courts, or addressed by reform efforts in legislation and law enforcement; and in which many rights advocates live in peril. Even theoretical accounts of human rights produced by scholars in China, while they have their independent value and importance,[25] meet with directives and exhortations such as, for example, to produce accounts that will 'strengthen China's international image';[26] and the most important arguments and practices undermining human rights come from authoritarianism.

Authoritarian conceptions and practices of governance privilege state sovereignty and security over individual rights, and treat the universality of liberal and democratic values with relativistic scepticism. Such ideas and practices can also be found in nominally liberal-democratic systems; but it will be argued here that the Party-State has in recent years turned to more authoritarian positions, supporting law (or 'legal governance', *fazhi*) but opposing human rights, or rights liberally conceived. It is increasingly using claims of systemic superiority over liberal democracy, becoming increasingly repressive, and more often invoking Maoist legacies. For some, this has raised the question whether China today should be characterized as totalitarian or neo-totalitarian,[27] i.e. using labels that would more clearly bring out the incompatibility between the Chinese system and respect for human rights.[28]

Yet, while the claim of superiority over other systems is arguably typical of totalitarian dictators,[29] characterizations as totalitarian would capture an intention more than the reality of the current system. The system hardly meets all of the criteria political scientists have come up with to describe totalitarian systems: it does not have a 'state monopoly on information' and a 'concentration of all of the means of domination in the hand of the party and the state, so that finally the economy becomes subordinated to bureaucratic coordination and central control', in Brzezinski's definition;[30] and it would be hard to describe it, with Juan Linz, as having 'an ideology, a single mass party and other mobilizational organizations, and concentrated power in an individual and his collaborators or a small group that is not accountable to any large constituency and cannot be dislodged from power by institutionalized, peaceful means'.[31] As its responses to public protest in some instances show, the current system in China is somewhat responsive to popular demands, and in that sense sometimes held politically accountable.[32] It would also be hard to describe Chinese society as 'atomized' in the sense coined by the philosopher Hannah Arendt;[33] indeed, showing how Chinese civil society coordinates human rights based action is one of the aims of this book. Similar considerations could apply to the perhaps even more problematic term 'fascism'.[34] Against the background of such taxonomical quandaries,[35] the term 'authoritarian' will be used here in consciously broad fashion: it is well suited to a language of gradation that seems appropriate to the present discussion, not only of China but also of the global trends toward authoritarianism.[36]

The following chapters begin by situating human rights discourse within a plurality of competing justice traditions and discourses, and provide an initial examination of the chief counterdiscourses used to reject human rights (chapter 1). This provides the background for an outline of the place of human rights within the legal-political system, and an initial account of institutional avenues for access to justice (chapter 2). The next three chapters address the substantive rights of liberty and integrity of the person (chapter 3), freedom of thought and expression and cognate rights (chapter 4), and economic and social rights (chapter 5). A concluding chapter discusses human rights advocates, human rights defenders and wider civil society (chapter 6). Each of these chapters observes a current trend to reconceptualize and redesign the legal-political process in ways that further undermine human rights and, ultimately, law itself. Each chapter also tries to identify the peculiar and characteristic way in which China's version of authoritarianism shapes its systemic rights-violating practices. In conclusion, this development is briefly considered in the light of its wider, transnational implications, and of a global trend of 'democratic recession' and 'authoritarian resurgence'.

Human Rights and Competing Conceptions of Justice, Law and Power

In the 2010 documentary film *Emergency Shelter*, a group of friends gather in a park in downtown Beijing. The friends are there to support a couple temporarily rendered homeless by a long-term fight with local authorities against the demolition of their house. Seated on park benches around the wheelchair-bound rights defender Ni Yulan and her husband, the small group chat about their own experience of petitioning and complaining against the authorities. Their conversation reflects the presence of history in contemporary Chinese discourses about law, rights and justice: the words people use, the ideas they draw on, some of the assumptions they make. Zhang Aixiang, a middle-aged woman who has brought her friends clothes and food, thinks that the officials of the legal system are all in collusion, and that this is why the authorities fail to handle complaints properly.

> If you infringe ordinary people's rights (*quanli*), you should correct your mistake without delay. If you correct it, they will not complain against you, right? But the longer you fail to correct it, the more they will complain.[1]

Wang Guihua, who points out that she has some teeth missing from an encounter with the authorities, says,

> Are they afraid of you, or are you afraid of them? Why is it that people with grievances (*yuanqing*) have no recourse, that the courts cheat us,

and that staff of the Supreme Procuratorate[2] beat me into this condition? The Police won't even file your case. They say, we're all under the control of the Supreme Procuratorate, none of us dares to handle this case. That means there's no respect for law or heaven. They can beat people for nothing.[3]

And Ye Guozhu cites the proverb, 'No injustice (*yuan*) without perpetrator, no debt without creditor.'[4] Clearly he thinks that corrupt and undutiful officials will get what was coming to them one day.

We do not learn much about the individual stories behind their comments, and we do not get to hear the government's argument in their respective cases. Only Ni's and her husband's story is told in some greater detail in the film: old Beijing residents, they lost their home along with thousands of others in the great construction wave in the early 2000s; and Ni – disabled as a result of earlier police brutality, she explains – was sent to prison for her attempts to advocate on behalf of their own and other families. At the time of the film, she has just been released, and she and her husband are camping out not far from where their home once stood. Focusing away from this individual story, the conversation with their friends shows how her experience is mirrored in theirs. We are given a glimpse of the way citizens are complaining to and reasoning with the government, and see them explaining their situation to the invisible videographer, and to us. They are deeply critical, for example when Zhang Aixiang comments on the official jargon of 'social stability maintenance' that is typically used to justify coercive measures against petitioners like herself:[5]

It's you who are responsible for 'social instability'. Not your victims.[6]

They are also sceptical about getting anywhere with their complaints, but nevertheless defiant: one can sense that, regardless of how difficult it may be, they are not going to give up easily. They have a sense of their own power: they know that even if they won't get justice (whatever this might mean) they can at least make life difficult for the officials supposed to deal with them and keep them in check. In Havel's phrase, one might call it a form of 'power of the powerless'.[7] It is a power connected to people's experience of injustice and their willingness to seek justice.

Through the individual chapters that follow, human rights and related ideas are interpreted and reinterpreted across a variety of national, cultural and political boundaries,[8] and it is shown how deeply contentious they are: not only (for reasons discussed in chapter 2) and not even primarily in the courts, but also in the streets and on the internet, in books and bars, in lecture halls and on social media. Of course, one might say, views gathered in these venues are individual. For example, the above brief comments and attitudes of Zhang, Wang and Ye do not tell us much about the thoughts, expectations and aspirations of the 1.4 billion Chinese people as a whole. Taking stock of these as a whole would be a giant undertaking – and it would not be very helpful in any case, since all we would discover is that people in China, like elsewhere, disagree about big abstract ideas such as rights, wrongs and justice; and that what they say is not always coherent. Assessing what rights people hold as human rights, whether or how these are – or are not – protected, and how they are discussed and asserted and used in contentions between citizens and the state requires moral and legal judgment, according to the view adopted here. It cannot be limited to describing others' views, but needs to engage critically with the views and practices it describes, working through them towards a normative assessment.[9] To do so, it is particularly important to examine the views and attitudes of those who, like the three speakers above, experience human rights violations, those who are involved in addressing them, as well as those who perpetrate or justify violations – often, but not always, government officials.

The purpose of the following sections of this chapter is to give a sense of the most important disagreements and debates affecting human rights in China, understood as an interpretive social practice. It sets out what one might usefully call the justice and governance traditions of China: the conceptions and practices related to justice reflected in its political and institutional history, as well as in its vast philosophical and literary heritage. These traditions remain present in contemporary official and public discourse about rights. Subsequent chapters will address some aspects of the legal-political system, some basic substantive rights or groups of rights, and wider social practices related to rights assertion.[10] The picture that emerges is rich and colourful, as well as full of tensions. There are great differences not only in pre-PRC Chinese engagement with the concept of justice, but also within the history of the PRC, from the totalitarian years under Mao Zedong to the 'post-Mao reform' and what one might call the current 'post-reform' era. All of this history informs how justice-based claims and complaints about injustice are articulated and dealt with today. There are continuities, as well as tensions, ruptures and contradictions.

Three themes are particularly important. First, there is the tradition of bringing grievances and the closely related concept of *yuan*, 'wrong' or 'injustice'. It centres in the belief that the wrongs suffered by any individual person must be addressed and righted. Second, there is the concept of rights, part of a liberal conception of law and justice, which began to be articulated and debated in China from the nineteenth century onwards. By now, human rights have become part of the justice traditions of China. Lastly, there are what I will call human rights counterdiscourses: an assemblage of influential ideas and arguments, practices and institutions that propagate a vision of order in which human rights would have no place or, at best, a very diminished function, even though the language of human rights might still be used when convenient: a politically authoritarian order claimed to be more appropriate for China. Those who propagate these countervisions of order sometimes use morally relativist arguments; but far from upholding a distinctly traditional, Chinese conception of justice (as moral relativism might suggest), they suppress the more indigenous *yuan* discourse when convenient. These counterdiscourses explain, in part at least, why human rights in China remains so fiercely contested a practice. As they are propagated beyond China's territorial borders, they play a role in what some have discussed as a global revival of authoritarianism.[11]

THE *YUAN* TRADITION OF RIGHTING WRONGS

In the fourteenth century, the scholar and novelist Guan Hanqing wrote the story of *The Injustice to Dou'E*, an upright and virtuous young woman who had the misfortune of being falsely accused and, despite her protestations of innocence at her trial, executed for murder. Dou'E's wrong is eventually righted, but the justice she gets differs very significantly from what one might hope for in a modern and contemporary setting. Before she is led to her execution, she makes three prophesies – namely, that her body will shed no blood when she is executed; that there will be snow in midsummer; and that there will be a three-year drought following her execution. All her prophesies come true. Some years later, the father who had abandoned Dou'E as a child, and who is now a local magistrate, confronts her spirit and promises to redress the injustice that befell her in life. At that point, Dou'E's wronged spirit finally gets justice and peace, and vanishes from the earth.

Dou'E's story is one of the best-known in the Chinese canon, and it tells us a lot about what one might call ordinary conceptions of justice and injustice, or wrongs, *yuan*. There are at least three important points to be noted. The first is that Heaven is in charge of justice and will treat an injustice – especially such a great one – as a disturbance of the natural order. Second, wrongs trigger punishment; injustice will be avenged. This is what Ye Guozhu expresses in *Emergency Shelter* through the proverb 'no injustice without perpetrator, no debt without creditor'. Third, redressing injustice is an obligation in which everyone, including the victim, has a share. It is a moral burden that has to be discharged before anyone can return to their natural state. While injustice has not been avenged, the natural order is disturbed and the souls or ghosts of the wronged, *yuanhun*, are obliged to haunt the earth, where they make life miserable for those who have a responsibility to redress their wrongs. The obligation to redress injustice is especially potent with those in a position of power to provide redress, like Dou'E's magistrate father. Historically at least, *yuan* corresponded to mechanisms institutionalizing official or government reactions to wrongs.

The concept of *yuan* continues to be widely used in China. Many people who use it are, like Zhang Aixiang, Wang Guihua and Ye Guozhu, users of the so-called 'letters and visits' or petitioning system used in parallel with the courts as more modern institutions administering justice (as discussed further in chapter 2). Sometimes they refer to themselves as 'yuan people' (*yuanmin*). They have also been called 'Dou'E's brothers and sisters'.[12] Their grievances vary – many complain about having been forcibly evicted from their homes or their land for example; others have been caught up in the iniquities of the criminal justice system or they have relatives who were unjustly punished, like Dou'E. Like Dou'E, too, they go on a quest for a powerful, just-minded, morally pure official (*qingguan*) who will help them set things right. Some spend large parts of their lives engaged in these personal quests for justice. Many hardly ever get anywhere; but they keep looking for the right official to help them.

Even today, it is customary for petitioners to address officials as 'father-and-mother official' – a person in authority with a duty to offer a parental sort of care and concern.[13] Seeking redress for *yuan* wrongs occurs within a paternalistic and authoritarian political setting, where the seekers are supplicants, dependent on the impressionability of the official they have turned to, and supported only by Heaven (which might or might not take an interest). Uses of *yuan* also indicate, hardly surprisingly, that those wronged might 'snap' at some point, at which the wrongdoers are seen as enemies to be destroyed, like the evil they stand for. There is thus an element of enmity in the concept of *yuan*.[14] The wrong that has been suffered is chiefly addressed by punishing the wrongdoer. Just as in Dou'E's case, there may be no other justice for victims than punishment of those who wronged one and the clearing of one's name from false accusations. In that sense, one might think of a *yuan*-centred conception of justice as backward-looking.

The *yuan*-centred view corresponds to certain elements of the Confucian philosophical tradition, *rujia*. Redress of a wrong depends crucially on the figure of the good, morally striving and exemplary official. The good official (*qingguan*) is a person who safeguards the purity and equity of governance by being a well-taught and decent person, with a reliable sense of social and moral propriety, of what one ought to do (*li*), as well as the requisite character to act on this moral sense. Unlike the tradition of legalism or *fajia*, Confucianism does not set much store by the idea of written laws (*fa*), arguing, in one of the best-known passages of Confucius's *Analects*, that laws and punishments will make people 'avoid wrongdoing' but not allow them to develop a 'sense of honour and shame'.[15] Governance by virtue (*de*) and propriety (*li*) is preferable; but of course, virtuous governance depends on a good ruler and good officials, who through their own actions set a moral example, and use power only for righteous ends. The 'father-and-mother official' invoked here is also emblematic of a Confucian view of relational virtues: of the idea that everybody has particular moral obligations corresponding to their (inherently hierarchical) roles and relations with others – ruler and subject, parent and child, younger and elder sibling, student and teacher, and husband and wife.[16]

We can see the presence of *yuan* discourse in contemporary complaints, protest and resistance against (government) injustice reflected in what the three speakers say at the beginning of this chapter. If and when they use *yuan* discourse, Zhang, Wang and Ye take what one might call, following Ignatieff,[17] an ordinary virtue perspective on righting wrongs; and this perspective turns out to be somewhat vindictive. As we could see in the brief scene in *Emergency Shelter*, contemporary Chinese people tend effortlessly to combine the language of *yuan* with that of rights, by referring to people's grievances or wrongs (*yuanqing*) concurrently as rights violations. A closer look at the structure of (human) rights arguments nevertheless suggests that there is some tension between *yuan*-based and rights-based conceptions of justice.

THE RIGHTS TRADITION

There is some obvious similarity between the concept of *yuan* and that of (human) rights. Rights, like *yuan*, are typically used by individuals seeking redress or accountability for injustice. From a rights perspective, one might therefore think of *yuan* complaints as proto-rights because the assertion of wrongs through individual complaints or appeals to the authorities historically precedes the assertion of (moral or legal) rights, and has a somewhat similar function. *Yuan*, like rights, requires one to take the perspective of the individual who has been, or claims to have been, wronged.

However, there are also important differences between these two concepts. Rights are centred in ideas of individual liberty, interest and choice.[18] They most directly correspond to liberal legal-political orders, which emphasize a divide between the public and private and the need to limit public power over the individual – from a liberal perspective, coercion by the state can only be justified if it respects rights. Also, compared to the more backward-looking and punishment-seeking *yuan* complainant, those who seek, or who want to provide, redress to victims of human rights violations are more clearly forward-looking. Redress for rights violations can take the form of stopping an ongoing violation and of providing some form of damages or restitution, for example. Only secondarily are they about punishment or alternatives to punishment, for example, in transitional justice contexts.

There are many ideas resonating with that of rights as a particular conception of justice in China's long moral tradition; but the contemporary Chinese *words* for 'rights' and 'human rights' were only coined in the second half of the nineteenth century, when China was in the declining years of the Qing Dynasty. The most widely known version of what happened at this stage is that, as a result of losing in the Opium Wars and related clashes with aggressive Western colonial forces from the 1840s onwards, as well as the Sino–Japanese War of 1895, the Chinese socio-political elites became aware of weaknesses in their system and sought to react by selectively learning from Western systems in a conscious 'self-strengthening' effort to understand technologies and governance mechanisms of the west, without abandoning Chinese cultural essence. At the same time, a growing scholarly and wider cultural interest in the West, its ideas and its socio-political practices emerged.[19] As Weatherley has argued, the introduction of the concept was thus connected to a desire to strengthen the political system;[20] but once introduced, rights discourse took on a life of its own.[21] 'Human rights' as an explicitly referenced concept only then begins to inform some social practices in China, starting from academic, intellectual engagement and debate.[22]

All this contributed to a wave of important translations, including some seminal translations of liberal classics, in the course of which it became necessary to come up with a Chinese term that made sense of the idea of 'rights'. Candidates were 'reason' (*li*), 'power' (*quan*) and 'interest' (*li*).[23] Eventually the latter two were used, so that, today, we refer to 'rights' as *quanli*.[24] The term for 'human rights' is *renquan*. Discussions by liberal-Confucian scholars continue to examine the liberal ideas in light of traditional philosophy and concepts. Liang Qichao, for example, associates rights consciousness with the righteousness (*yi*) of the Chinese moral tradition.[25] As time passed, and as an indigenous Chinese liberal tradition emerged from this engagement with the West, these words took on their own history and associated interpretations. The notion of individual rights entered the 1908 Constitution drafted by Kang Youwei and others as a late consequence of the aborted 'Hundred Days' Reform movement'.[26] Had it been enacted, it would have become the first set of fundamental norms enshrining safeguards for individual liberties such as the freedom of expression and rights against unlawful (arbitrary) arrest, imprisonment and punishment in China's long history.[27] The effort was unfortunately aborted, and the last imperial dynasty collapsed a few years later. Yet, a seed had been planted and all subsequent constitutional documents in China have made some reference to the concept of rights.

Another source of the Chinese liberal tradition is Sun Zhongshan, or Sun Yat-sen. Not an explicit proponent of human rights as such, but acclaimed as a sort of intellectual father by contending political groups and parties that emerged in China in the early twentieth century, Sun Yat-sen was a modernizer who wished to introduce a form of separation of powers. He supported the central idea that it is possible – and imperatively important – to limit the power of the state through institutional mechanisms. His idea of *minquan*, loosely translated as 'people power',[28] has inspired both the Communist Party and its rival Nationalist (Kuomintang) Party, as well as Chinese dissidents up to the present day. Sun Yat-sen was also a political thinker who popularized the concept of the public, both in the sense of a sphere of public political participation, and in the sense of justice as a virtue of public institutions (*gongyi*). Contemporary human rights defenders, in particular the New Citizen Movement discussed in chapter 6, have sought to integrate Sun Yat-sen's vocabulary, arguments and even his calligraphy into their discourse and advocacy, knowing that, in doing so, they are tapping into indigenous resources of political reform advocacy.[29]

As discussed later on, human rights becomes a taboo topic during the early decades of the PRC, until post-1989;[30] but after a hiatus during the Mao era, it is 'readmitted' into tolerated discourse in the post-Mao era and, as discussed in the Introduction, receives a boost due to its recognition following the June Fourth movement. Human rights discourse is then championed by scholars such as Li Buyun;[31] but it is perhaps not until the 1990s that human rights becomes a powerful concept in contention between Chinese citizens and the Party-State. Initially, *weiquan* or 'rights defence' is an officially coined term and a Party-State-supported idea, albeit based on a very limited conception of rights defence.[32]

As it is woven into contemporary justice discourse and especially in its popular ordinary uses, the idea of rights adds important dimensions to the traditional, more authoritarian *yuan* settings. In these settings, the modes of interaction with the authorities, according to the analysis presented here, tend to 'flip' between supplicant submission of reasoned complaints (the ordinary, most common mode) and righteous resistance or even outright rebellion (in extraordinary cases). By contrast, rights discourse allows for ordered confrontation. Fresh ideas that the rights dimension introduces into this setting include, in addition to the aforementioned public–private divide, the related ideas of citizenship, equality and liberty. As the scholar Xiao Han has put it, 'Petitioners kneel. People with rights stand up'.[33] They stand up to confront the world of officials, those who hold power over them, at their own level. The image oversimplifies, but, in doing so, it does explain what may seem attractive about the notion of having rights and defending them. Even though the argument here has been that there are commonalities and some degree of functional equivalence between the idea of *yuan* wrongs and that of rights, the image also explains ways in which rights-based quests for justice can present a more transformative challenge to authoritarian systems than *yuan*-based ones.

The concept of rights is part of the reality of Chinese legal institutions today, while also being in tension with them. The Party-State has given rights recognition in its laws and regulations as well as its party propaganda. Rights could not be taken out of the analysis of any contemporary legal dispute; and they could not be simply eliminated from the normative language of State legislation either. In addition to official languages, laws and institutions, there is also a real and current popular practice of employing the concept of rights. The concept has become 'vernacularized',[34] and is now part of the vocabulary used to discuss questions of justice, law and power, as the short excerpt from the documentary by He Yang, quoted at the outset of this chapter, illustrates. And yet, as discussed further in chapter 2, which engages with liberal constitutionalists such as He Weifang and Zhang Qianfan, rights still sit uneasily with the current legal-political institutions.

Official rejections of the very idea of human rights have become more prominent especially in recent years, as counterdiscourse and counternorms to human rights norms and ideas have been actively promoted by the authorities. As Wang's experience at the hands of the authorities indicates, her complaints have not only fallen on deaf ears, but also led to her being abused; and Wang's friend Zhang points out that these abuses occur in the name of 'social stability maintenance'. Unfortunately, she is only one of many to have experienced this situation. Chinese authorities legislate in ways that unduly limit human rights. They engage systematically in rights-violating practices and persecute human rights defenders. To understand the authorities' viewpoint, it is necessary to study the rhetorical and justificatory strategies these authorities adopt when they argue against human rights. The next section turns to these counterdiscourses.

OFFICIAL COUNTERDISCOURSES

Human rights are contested, not only in the sense that there is disagreement about what constitutes a human rights violation, but also because powerful actors reject the very idea of human rights. After some four decades of an 'international human rights movement', beginning in the 1970s,[35] global contestation of human rights became more intense.[36] China is an important geopolitical force actively challenging human rights norms in these debates, even though – or perhaps because – human rights has become a significant strand in the domestic contestation of government power. Some arguments against human rights invoke authoritarian conceptions of sovereignty and national interest (or national security). Other arguments are morally relativistic, claiming that the alien, liberal human rights ideas are incompatible with traditional, indigenous and entrenched ideas of justice, and that at best human rights norms must be understood in a particularistic way. Yet other arguments reject the realization of human rights as unaffordable for the time being, or argue that priority must be given to improvements in socio-economic welfare (sometimes claimed to be identical with socio-economic rights).

The arguments and practices discussed briefly below (as well as in chapter 5, which addresses efficiency and growth-related arguments further) reflect these broader claims in China-specific ways, focusing particularly on discourses 'inside the system' (*tizhi nei*). They draw on the Confucian-Legalist discourse, the Maoist-Leninist discourse, arguments based on China's economic development and, more recently, power-based conceptions of law and Party-Statehood. These arguments are in some tension with one another; but incoherence does not preclude them from being used as needed to support the Party-State's fundamental aversion to the idea of rational constraints on its power.

Official readings of the moral tradition: Confucian 'harmony' and legalist order

Above, it was seen how China's Confucian tradition provides a conceptual repertoire for moral constraints on power-holders, as well as for (limited) criticism of the government, without calling for any of the liberal mechanisms of good governance associated with the concept of rights. The legalist tradition was juxtaposed with this as it took a

more favourable view of using law as a primary tool of political governance, while emphasizing the importance of law applying equally to all.
One can think of these two accounts of political morality as being
involved in a centuries-long dispute; but in fact, both schools have
influenced traditional legal thought and practice, in what Bodde and
Morris call a 'Legalist triumph but Confucianisation of the law'.[37] As
a result, the imperial tradition has always emphasized the dualism of
moral suasion on the one hand, and legal sanction on the other. It has
emphasized the idea of moral virtues and obligations of propriety (*li*)
owed to others within social relationships defined by status and hier-
archies, but also insisted on the central exercise of the power to punish
wrongdoing through laws (*fa*). In our time, these philosophical traditions have been exploited to come up with certain arguments used to
block and reject human rights ideas.

Take, first, the traditionally perfectionist conception of moral duty,
or righteousness (*yi*). Section 368 of the Great Qing Code famously
contained a provision prescribing punishment for doing 'what ought
not to be done' – whatever that is.[38] This reflects the view that there
is no moral value in protecting individual choice to do anything that
is morally wrong. By contrast, from a liberal perspective, not every
morally wrong action should be disallowed or attract legal punishment;
and in any case, an act can only be punished if it was known at the
time that it was punishable – a catchall phrase like that of Section
368 is not nearly specific enough.[39] If the liberal view protects choice,
then, from a Confucian perspective (and from any other perspective
of perfectionist morality), the argument that sometimes we have morally
sound reasons to leave the choice to do something wrong to the individual could appear odd and misguided. Instead, immorality must be
prevented through a continuous process of education and improvement
of the individual person, and where moral wrongs occur, the option
of punishment must be available. (The wrongs-centred view of *yuan*

complainants discussed earlier is similarly duty-focused.) Used by a powerful and ubiquitous government apparatus, this approach can be used to claim vast control over the individual's moral views, choices and actions. Once it is dissociated from the earnestness and sincerity of the good person (*junzi*), such control can be devastating.

Related to this there is, second, the perceived need for punishment administered by powerful rulers. In the Legalist perspective especially, rulers and their officials are custodians of legal rules to apply to all and everybody equally. From this perspective, it has been argued, the ruler is committed to rules that would, at least in principle, curb their arbitrary power, reflecting a fundamental rule of law idea.[40] However, the laws of legalism are in large measure laws of punishment. As Chang Wejen points out, drawing on Shang Yang, legalists have also suggested that 'people should be presumed wicked not innocent' and that the government should do what it could to 'use punishments to eliminate punishment (*yi xing qu xing*)'. Consequently,

> A person should be punished before his criminal scheme was carried out, and for that purpose everyone should be required to report on the schemes of others;…all persons with some connection with a culprit were to be given severe collective punishments; and…prohibitions should be numerous and punishments against minor offenses should be heavy, so that people would not dare to commit even petty crimes, let alone more serious ones.[41]

As discussed, for example in chapter 6, the persecution of those regarded as enemies of the Party-State seems rooted in similar attitudes, patterns and practices, and has seen a revival of fear-based governance techniques.

Third, there are Party-State claims derived from the Confucian tradition of 'valuing harmony' (*he wei gui*). As Confucianism places emphasis on moral suasion and leading by example, it regards uses of the law and its mechanisms to resolve disputes or address wrongs as an inherently inferior option. According to Confucianism, persuasion is preferable to punishment, in education as much as in administration of the law. As law is understood primarily as punitive law, its use should therefore be minimized, and litigation should be avoided.

> The Master said, 'In hearing litigations, I am like any other person. The point is getting people not to litigate in the first place.'[42]

The Party leadership has used this tradition of harmony to support their preference for restrictions of speech to prevent 'disharmonious' public discourse, and more widely the suppression of adversarial rights claims as inherently un-harmonious and, therefore, un-Chinese. In the era of President Hu Jintao and Premier Wen Jiabao (2002–12), 'harmonious society' was an almost ubiquitous formula used to indicate policy goals and to also justify repression, along with the (in historical perspective, more Legalist-sounding) trope of 'social stability'.[43] These concepts continue to be invoked. This is why Ms Wang, above, emphatically rejects being considered what, in bureaucratic terms, one would call an element of social instability, laying the blame for instability at the door of the authorities.

Importantly, some contemporary Confucians have roundly rejected the view that Confucian doctrines should be used to legitimize the Party-State, and sharply criticized attempts by the current Party-State to invoke the Confucian tradition as false and hypocritical. As one contemporary Confucian scholar puts it, China 'has all along had two schools of Confucianism: the Confucians who were oppressed, and the Confucians who oppressed others'.[44] Yu Yingshi distinguishes institutional Confucianism from critical Confucianism on this basis. The latter, he contends, would 'openly welcome' universal values including those of human rights. Thus the traditional moral (Confucian) perspective can be reconciled with a modern human rights-centred one.[45] Confucian conceptions of righteousness (*yi*) can support government criticism. When critical expression is suppressed in the name of institutional Confucianism, however, popular jargon will say it has been 'harmonized' away (*bei hexiediao*).[46]

The 'socialist' discourses

In *Emergency Shelter*, Ms Zhang and Ms Wang recall an attempt they once made to commit protest suicide.

> The two of us, we had everything ready. We were going to Tiananmen to jump off a building. But I wasn't going to die for nothing. Before I died I was going to remember Chairman Mao, say good-bye to Chairman Mao. Long Live Chairman Mao! I am remembering you.

Mao Zedong's revered status among many people who consider the current system unjust and who complain about human rights violations can seem strange, considering some of Mao's political ideas and his responsibility for terrible calamities, such as the famine of the Great Leap Forward and the devastation of the Great Cultural Revolution. But, it is also understandable, and it explains how fractured and problematic socialist arguments are in China today. The Mao these two women revere is a symbolic figure who represents a commitment to a more equitable society with a more clearly egalitarian ethos and less corruption amongst Party cadres. The historical record of the Mao Zedong era seems of little importance to this Mao mythology, which may also make strategic use of Mao's unassailable status in today's system – it is good to have Mao on your side when confronting his contemporary Party-State successors.

As a political writer and ruler, the real Mao's views changed multiple times in his lifetime;[47] but his work forms part of China's socialist legacy, as does Leninism and do some Marxist ideas. The core Marxist argument about law suggests that rights, like other 'liberal' ideas stemming from capitalism and the bourgeoisie, are a complex con – a product of false consciousness leading to mere illusions of liberty. However sincerely these beliefs may be held, perhaps by a majority of well-intentioned people in different walks of life in the capitalist society, they mask the reality of class struggle and exploitation. This idea was very important in the more radical episodes of the Mao era – in particular, during the Cultural Revolution.[48] Thus, radical scepticism about rights and law represents the most distinctive contribution to counterarguments weakening the idea of rights from the socialist tradition.

In China, during the Cultural Revolution (1966–76), some of the official discourse poured scorn on the very idea of law and its attendant notions of legal rights and equality before the law.

> Army, police, courts, and other branches of the state machinery are instruments for class oppression. To the enemy class, they are the instruments of suppression. Being a violent force, they are not at all benevolent. In sum, they have the single aim to deprive the reactionaries of the right of speech, which is to be granted only to the people. Dictatorship will be practiced with respect to the class enemies, whereas democracy will be practiced among the people.[49]

The idea that *everybody* would have legally protected rights is clearly wrong, albeit thankfully fictitious, from the perspective of this writer – it would be wrong for the class enemies to receive the law's protection and 'enjoy the democratic rights in the same way as the masses of the people', on a mistaken principle of 'impartiality toward all'.[50]

Powerful though these ideas once were, they had been to a great extent discredited by the end of the Cultural Revolution, after which China engaged in four decades of legal reconstruction. As of today,

China has, domestically, as well as through international treaty bodies and its role in a complex international and transnational community of nations, officially recognized human rights and committed to their protection. Reversing the attitude to law entirely would come at a great political cost. Even as the Party-State is changing and arguably becoming more anti-liberal, there is little evidence that it is attempting to revert to a Maoist rejection of law.

What is left from the first thirty years of the People's Republic are, first, political ideas, principles and precepts that, while not directly attacking or rejecting the idea of law and rights, are connected with basic distrust of law as an equalizing force protecting everybody. Some of these ideas remain codified in the PRC Constitution: in particular, 'People's democratic dictatorship' and 'Democratic centralism'. Others, such as the so-called 'mass line', Mao's 'theory of contradictions', and the principle of Party loyalty in various formulations are not enshrined in any constitutional or legal text, but are of tremendous importance to what officials of the system – and others who interact with the system – are expected to do. For example, 'People's democratic dictatorship' is still generally understood to mean that it is okay for the Party-State to act as a dictator towards those who are not part of 'the People'; and that it is up to the Party-State to determine who that is. Having fallen out of use for decades, the concept was prominently written into the 2015 National Security Law as a guiding principle.[51]

Second, the socialist legacies continue to have relevance to how the Party-State justifies its continued control over resources, such as land. In this context, the idea of controlling the means of production so as to protect the people from the iniquities of a capitalist system has become largely implausible, given the exploitative design of several markets, including that for corruption,[52] in the new 'Socialist Market Economy with Chinese Characteristics'.[53] But the claim that Party-State control over these resources is for the greater good survives in the developmental rhetoric used to justify some of the human rights violations discussed in chapter 5.

Party-Statehood and authoritarian and totalitarian re-conceptions of 'law'

Contemporary authoritarian conceptions of power, law and rights used in China bear some affinities to what would, in European terms, be the extreme right of the political spectrum. They also reflect authoritarianism's global comeback in the twenty-first century, with its heightened fears of terrorism and other threats to security. The new authoritarians draw heavily on concepts like 'sovereignty', 'enemies' and 'the nation'. They exploit a widely felt need for the state as a strong protector. They focus on, and at times glorify, the fact of power; and their understanding of law is derived from power, rather than from any requirement of rationally constraining power.

Zhang, Wang and Ye, the three petitioners introduced at the beginning of this chapter, and their fellow petitioners and supporters, have long known that law is on the whole ineffectual in constraining the power of the Party-State. Its failure to impose limitations starts in the minds of the system's officials – not all of them, of course, but some. Consistently, those who have studied the experience of petitioners and rights advocates have found that the reported attitudes of 'law enforcement', even of officials with legal backgrounds, reflect the authoritarian belief that law is no more than an expression of power, or of the will of the political power-holder, and that therefore it is dispensable and needs to be set aside in certain contexts. Thus, as lawyer and scholar Teng Biao recorded in an op-ed, a police officer told him during detention in a Beijing police station, using an oft-repeated phrase especially in contexts of detention and torture,

> Don't talk so much about the law with me. Do you know where we are? We are on Communist Party territory![54]

And in the words of a judge distressed at being unable to take an (in their own judgment) excellent criminal defence statement into account in the court verdict,

> You know that there is nothing I can do.[55]

The implication was that the judge, while greatly appreciating the efforts of the defence on behalf of their client in this criminal case, was unable to make an independent decision.

The question to what extent the mind-set captured by these anecdotal examples can be attributed to the public rules and principles, to the systematic design of the Party-State as an organization, is complex and difficult to assess. It is impossible to treat it in the depth required here, but a few points may be made. First, in their public pronouncements, the authorities are generally unlikely to produce straightforward avowals of the weakness or irrelevance of legal constraints on power. But, second, there are phrases and arguments that read like attempts to obfuscate, or like pointed refusals to clarify and recognize the subjection of the Party to the law. Take, for example, the claim that

> Party Leadership and Socialist Rule of Law are identical. Socialist Rule of Law must maintain Party leadership and Party leadership must rely on Rule of Law.[56]

Or take a speech by General Party Secretary and President Xi Jinping entitled 'The question of whether the Party or the law is greater is a false question'.[57] Phrases of this kind begin to make sense when one takes their obscurity to be intended, and sees them in the context, for example, of intensive elite engagement with the philosophers of twentieth-century authoritarianism and totalitarianism, such as Carl Schmitt.[58]

Schmitt argues that 'the political' can only be understood through a fundamental and axiomatic friend–enemy distinction. The enemy, according to this definition, is he whom one has the right to kill ('right' in the sense of a morality transcending ordinary constraints or right and wrong). Laws must generally be followed, but they are controlled by the sovereign who is also 'he who controls the state of exception' – of uses of power no longer constrained by ordinary law. Separation of power, constitutional rights guarantees limiting the exercise of power and majority voting are enfeebling notions, on such an account, to be rejected in favour of strong sovereignty. Indeed, the very idea of norms and reasons *determining* legal decisions, from a Schmittian viewpoint, would betray the power of the sovereign. It would weaken and hollow out the sovereign power to decide what the law is, as well as to decide on exceptions from ordinary law's application, as would evidently, the acceptance of any 'universal' moral principles such as those underpinning human rights.[59]

Carl Schmitt has received a significant reception amongst Chinese legal-political scholars such as Chen Duanhong, Jiang Shigong, Liu Xiaofeng and Wang Shaoguang; and even some scholars who do not much discuss Schmitt 'tacitly reflect' his theories.[60] In some ways, the connection is obvious: Schmitt's theory can help explain and justify the Party-State with its new re-emphasis on Party leadership. It defends the identification of the Party with the People, and the principle that Party leadership must not be challenged on democratic or rule of law grounds.

In sum, in contrast to the Mao era, the Party-State authorities today no longer reject law. However, by putting an explicitly anti-liberal version of 'law' and 'legal governance' or 'rule by law' centre-stage, they claim to be the natural custodians of the law, and use this so far as it suits their own purposes. This will not only lead to a complete denial of the possibility of rights held just by virtue of being human; more widely it can lead to arguments against rational constraints on public power.[61] In rejecting universal values, the Party-State view now also differs from that of the imperial system, which fully and emphatically recognized the existence of stringent moral constraints and duties, and which accommodated the demands of 'righteousness' and other moral duties, even though it did not propose human rights protection or separation of powers as distinctly liberal solutions to the challenges of ensuring moral government.

CONCLUSION

As the above discussion has shown, there are many ways in which rights discourse connects to China's indigenous practices and ideas – through the idea of wrongs (*yuan*), as much as through the idea of rights that was imported into elite and, later, general public discussion from the late nineteenth century onwards. But equally, there are widely used and influential counterarguments, drawing on a number of different traditions and discourses, to feed into arguments used by the Party-State when it rejects human rights (or rule-of-law-based) arguments. As seen, for example, in chapter 3 on the liberty of the person and chapter 4 on freedom of expression, justificatory strategies used by Party-State actors who violate human rights derive from these counterdiscourses – in particular, the account of strong Party-Statehood with its characteristic equation of law and power. It is therefore important to understand the role of these justifications in coordinating and institutionalizing Party-State practices.

2 Institutional Avenues of Human Rights Advocacy

At least by some measures, China is a consistent and egregious violator of human rights. Reports by Amnesty International, Human Rights Watch and other organizations,[1] the assessments by the Committee Against Torture and other UN bodies, Freedom House's reports on free speech,[2] as well as some foreign governments' periodical reports and statements on China's overall human rights record[3] all indicate serious and sustained failures to protect human rights. To be sure, the Chinese government,[4] as well as the domestic debate on human rights in China by established and approved think-tanks and research institutions tend to take a more sanguine view.[5] But then, the systematic suppression of criticism of human rights violations within the establishment discourse is also one of the major human rights concerns.[6] What, then, to expect from the domestic institutions that should give effect to human rights? Not too much, according to some political scientists who have argued that ratification of human rights treaties 'have their strongest effects in countries that are neither stable democracies nor stable autocracies',[7] or in others words, countries already undergoing democratic transition.

This chapter, which turns from discourses (discussed in chapter 1) to institutions, suggests nevertheless that a nuanced assessment is required. Drawing on cases, as well as rules and principles (and not attempting any comparative ranking of China), it argues that institutional changes introduced in the *Reform and Opening* era have enabled the rise of human rights advocacy, even though the institutions remain ultimately largely intransigent to such advocacy. It thus aims to show why the legal institutions are important, but also offers some structural explanations for why it is so difficult to defend and protect human rights in China using the avenues they provide. The chapter also discusses why and how human rights abuse survivors and human rights defenders are likely to try extra-institutional means to defend their rights when thwarted in their efforts to use the institutions provided by the Party-State.

Accordingly, the chapter first considers the place of human rights in 'the system' (*tizhi*) – the legal-political framework and institutions. It is argued that control by the Party disrupts the ability of legal institutions to protect rights. As a consequence, some of those who think they have been wronged will use alternative avenues to complain. These alternative avenues include the so-called 'letters and visits' system, as well as conventional and new media and various forms of street action, and are discussed next. As complainants move outside and further away from the system that (in their view) fails them, they become more likely to turn against the system. Complaints that could, in a different institutional setting, be merely about specific violations of their rights can thus become wider, political grievances and causes. The case of Qi Yuling, the 'Sun Zhigang Incident', and the experience of lawyers and petitioners including Liu Zhengyou and Cao Shunli will serve to illustrate different parts of this argument.

THE PLACE OF HUMAN RIGHTS IN THE NORMATIVE FRAMEWORK

The Chinese system of governance is organized on Leninist principles, the most important of which is the duality of Party and State institutions. With some over-simplification, scholars have described the Party as a principal acting through the State as its agent.[8] The Party's centrality[9] rests on the axiomatic assumption that the Party represents the People as their vanguard. This means that according to official dogma, the Party cannot be in conflict with the People because it has no interests separate from those of the People.[10] This dogma explains in part why the Party's relationship with the State and its laws is left in many ways unclear, and why the Party is conspicuously absent from much of the written law.

A wide array of written norms affects the place of human rights in Chinese law. In the discussion below, 'legislation' as defined in the 2000 Legislation Law,[11] includes laws made by the National People's Congress, the highest State authority according to the written Constitution, as well as administrative regulations produced by central and local administrative authorities and local People's Congresses. These laws and regulations are an important source of written rules the judiciary draws on; but they are not the only ones. There are also 'interpretations' by the Supreme People's Court and Supreme People's Procuracy – texts which are supposed to be merely explanatory of the laws – and further 'normative documents' issued by various authorities including Party organizations.

All these norms differ widely in their impact on human rights: there are norms that protect or purport to protect human rights, norms constituting systemic rights infringement and norms effecting dilution or confusion of human rights principles. The resulting possibilities of confusion and inconsistency have long been recognized. As seen below, it took some individual complainants, lawyers and officials of the system to raise these issues and seek to resolve them through cases.

Rights-protective norms

When Qi Yuling realized that a former classmate had stolen her college entrance exam scores to get access to higher education and good jobs using her name, she turned to the law for protection. Her case was going to become one of the most momentous decisions in China's post-Mao legal history because it relied on giving effect to a rights-protective constitutional norm. It helps to illustrate the complex status of such norms, which have been created to impose obligations on China as a country – through international human rights treaties – as well as to create constitutional and statutory law obligations that require the state authorities to respect and protect human rights as a matter of domestic Chinese law.[12]

At the international level,[13] China has signed and ratified the International Covenant on Economic, Social and Cultural Rights (ICESCR),[14] but not yet ratified that on Civil and Political Rights (ICCPR).[15] Since the 1980s, China has also been a more active member of the International Labour Organization (ILO) and has accepted some of the labour rights standards of the ILO.[16] In addition, China is a party to the Convention on the Elimination of All Forms of Discrimination against Women (CEDAW),[17] the Convention on the Elimination of All Forms of Racial Discrimination (CERD),[18] the Convention against Torture and Other Cruel, Inhuman or Degrading Treatment or Punishment (CAT),[19] the Convention on the Rights of the Child (CRC)[20] and the Convention on the Rights of Persons with Disabilities (CRPD).[21] It has not acceded to the Convention on the Protection of the Rights of All Migrant Workers and Members of Their Families (CPRM)[22] and the Convention for the Protection of All Persons from Enforced Disappearance (CPPED).[23]

At the level of the national Constitution, which was adopted in 1982 as the PRC's fourth Constitution,[24] there is a catalogue of rights encompassing important civil and political rights, such as freedom of speech, freedom of religion, freedom of assembly and association, liberty of the person and inviolability of the home, in addition to social and economic rights, including the right to education and the right to health services. In addition to this list, in 2004, the National People's Congress (nominally the highest authority in the constitutional system) amended the Constitution to state that 'the State respects and safeguards human rights'.[25]

But, there are as yet no effective institutional mechanisms for safe-guarding the standards and principles these international and consti-tutional norms purport to commit to. At the international level, China has opted out of all the individual complaints procedures that might allow a person whose rights have been infringed to bring a complaint before UN institutions. At the domestic level, Chinese courts are virtu-ally unable to use international human rights norms in deciding cases. The country is nominally 'monist' in the sense that public international law automatically becomes part of the domestic system once a treaty is ratified. But, as Ahl has pointed out, '[c]ourts in general have applied treaty provisions on the basis of statutory reference provisions or judicial interpretations.' While in non-human rights matters, it is 'quite pos-sible that local courts would prefer the application of a treaty norm to the application of a national statute, provided that the application of the international treaty is promoting local economic interest', it seems there are no human rights cases satisfying either condition.[26]

So far as constitutional human rights norms are concerned, the Supreme People's Court (SPC) has in some of its judicial interpreta-tions explicitly instructed the lower courts not to apply constitutional provisions directly. Only in one known case, in 2001, did it seem about to change its mind: and this was when it decided Qi Yuling's case. Her case turned, at least as the SPC saw it in a sparsely worded reply to a lower-order court request for instruction, on giving effect to her con-stitutional right to education. According to the SPC, her constitutional right had been infringed by public authorities, as well as (!) by Qi's classmate, so Qi could claim damages. The SPC decision might have established a principle of judicial protection of constitutional rights; and SPC Vice President Huang Songyou euphorically compared it to the American *Marbury vs Madison* decision.[27] But seven years later, the decision was officially revoked and Huang was sent to prison for economic corruption.[28] As of today, there is nothing approaching robust judicial protection of constitutional or international human rights norms and principles, although the Chinese judiciary does on occasion *mention* rights-protecting norms of international law or constitutional status.[29]

Just because the Constitution is not judicially enforced does not mean that there is *no* codified human rights protection in China, however. As discussed in the following chapters, numerous important human rights have been codified through national-level laws and administrative regulations. For example, the Criminal Procedure Law (CPL) provides for the right of access to counsel and the right to refuse self-incrimination for those charged with a crime. It also prohibits the use of torture to extract confessions. Through various further legislative reforms, some progress has been made, for example, to reduce reliance on 'confessions' which may have been extracted through torture.[30] There is a system of welfare support that, at least on paper, requires the provision of public services required to protect fundamental socio-economic rights. For example, as discussed in chapter 5, China as of today not only stipulates nine compulsory years of schooling, but also that these nine years are tuition-free. It has a complex legislative framework for the protection of certain labour rights (albeit not of the right to strike), and it has laws protecting against certain kinds of invidious discrimination, unlawful dispossession and exploitation. As with constitutionally protected rights, these statutory rights, too, must be justiciable, however; and as discussed below, their enforcement can remain difficult or even impossible.

Rights-violating norms

In the early 2000s, liberal constitutionalists were still expectant; and they were not only hoping for the opening up of judicial avenues of constitutional rights enforcement. Only two years after the *Qi Yuling* decision, the 2003 'Sun Zhigang Incident' became a widely noted example of their active efforts to explore other avenues, when, following the death of a young man held in custody under unconstitutional rules, legal advocates sought the removal of these rules by the National

People's Congress (NPC). In doing so, they tackled the problem of rights-violating norms, or 'bad laws' (*efa*).

Rights-violating norms include some we have already encountered, such as the principle of 'People's democratic dictatorship' as one of four 'cardinal principles' enshrined in the PRC Constitution.[31] The difficulty with understanding these norms, however, is that they do not *explicitly* say anything about human rights. We have to draw on how the authorities explain, for example, the principle of 'People's democratic dictatorship' to get a sense of why this constitutes a problem: it denies equal status as human rights bearers to those regarded as 'enemies of the people'.

Below the level of the Constitution, there are certain laws and regulations that purport to authorize systematically rights-violating practices. For example, Article 73 of the Criminal Procedure Law, in its revised 2012 form, allows for a measure called 'residential surveillance in a designated location'. A person held under this rule is not only *de facto* detained but can also be denied access to counsel. In effect, this means that they will be completely isolated and at serious risk of torture. These problems are further compounded by the fact that, even though the CPL allows for evidence obtained through torture to be excluded, those rules are extremely hard to rely on in practice as research has shown.[32] The CPL 'allows' the authorities to deny someone access to counsel if they meet the criteria of Article 73; and, so far as it does, this violates human rights. The CPL does not allow torture. On the contrary, it prohibits it. However, so far as it sanctions situations in which torture can be applied with near impunity, one might say that, in fact, the CPL *enables* torture through these rules.[33]

As noted, local legislative and government authorities also have the power to make rules; and this creates the possibility of normative confusion. The Legislation Law assigns the status of binding state law to 'statutes' (*falü*), 'regulations' (*fagui*) and 'rules' (*guizhang*).[34] In Articles 62 and 67, the Constitution describes the National People's Congress

(NPC) and National People's Congress Standing Committee (NPCSC) as institutions responsible for supervising the enforcement of the Constitution. In 2000, the Legislation Law created a mechanism whereby it was possible to challenge the constitutionality of certain low-tier kinds of legal norms.

The challenge that followed Sun Zhigang's violent and untimely death is the most widely known example. Sun had been held under the State Council Regulation on Custody and Repatriation, an administrative detention system used specially for those rural–urban migrants who were found without the required documents showing they had a right to be in the city. Abuses to the system included ransom-taking from, as well as violence in custody against, these *sans-papiers*. Sun's death was not an isolated incident, but his case was widely reported in the news media; and in its wake some scholars wrote an open letter to the NPCSC. They argued that the system violated the Chinese Constitution and that the NPCSC ought to declare this regulation invalid. In the wake of an unprecedented level of media reporting and discussion, the State Council repealed the regulation in 2003.[35]

The human rights scholar Teng Biao, one of the promoters of change in the wake of Sun Zhigang's death, described the case as one that 'brought the Constitution alive (*jihuo xianfa*)',[36] even though, according to his own account, some abuses persisted in the system.[37] The underlying mechanism of 'unconstitutionality review' is far from effective; it is non-transparent and non-adversarial, and even after reforms it does not give ordinary citizens more than a right to 'suggest' review (Article 99),[38] a suggestion that may or may not be taken up.[39] There are not many known cases in which citizens achieved similar success with this mechanism. Plenty of rights-violating and unconstitutional norms continue to be applied in China, and as discussed in chapter 6, Teng Biao and others involved in this case later suffered persecution. Moreover, in practice, local authorities sometimes give precedence to lower-order norms not even mentioned in the Legislation Law, such as 'notifications', 'provisions', 'commands', 'letters', 'opinions', 'views', and so on, over 'statutes' or 'regulations'. Yet, the repeal of the regulation in 2003 had shown that at least in principle, constitutional human rights norms had greater legal force than rights-violating rules produced by authorities subject to the Constitution.

Rights-undermining and violation-enabling norms

Sun Zhigang had been victimized because of the unconstitutional and rights-violating Custody and Repatriation system; but indirectly, he was also the victim of the so-called Household Registration system, which turned him into a second-class citizen in Guangzhou. His case thus also raised the problem of rights-undermining and violation-enabling norms.

A perusal of the Constitution shows that the basic rights it mentions are in some ways undermined by the basic (negative and positive) constitutional duties of Articles 50–56.[40] For example, Article 50 stipulates that citizens 'may not damage the interests of the State, of society or of the collective'. There is no available guidance on how far the restrictions of, say, the interests of the State or of the collective go. Since courts of law do not, as noted, consider themselves authorized to engage in constitutional interpretation, we cannot draw on judicial practice to interpret the meaning of these limitations. At face value, they seem far-reaching, as they suggest that individual rights may *never* outweigh considerations of state interest. So, rights claims could be completely undermined by (claimed) state or collective interest, a problem discussed further in chapter 5 in the context of land-grabs and housing demolitions. Examples for problematic positive duties are Article 53, requiring citizens to 'observe labour discipline', and Article 54, requiring them to 'safeguard the honour of the motherland', leaving it an open question how such duties are compatible with the exercise of labour rights or rights of free speech.

The fragility of rights thus constitutionally undermined or threatened is well illustrated by the situation of migrant workers like Sun Zhigang, the majority of whom are rural migrants. The system known as the 'household registration system' (*huji zhidu*) makes vulnerable outsiders of China's large internal rural–urban migrant community. Even though migrants like Sun can no longer be held under the old regulation, the fact that they have an outside – usually rural – household registration creates perfect conditions for their exploitation in ways violating labour and other fundamental rights. The household registration system has remained in place ever since it was introduced in the late 1950s by a State Council regulation. While it no longer effectively curtails the right of freedom of movement,[41] it has given rise to significant social discrimination, some of which is supported by further legal rules. For example, migrant workers without a Beijing household registration will not have access to free healthcare in Beijing, and their children will have difficulties accessing a state school. Also, a Beijing resident has better chances of studying at a Beijing higher education institution than someone from outside Beijing, even though there are certain rules granting advantages to ethnic minority children.

Beyond laws and regulations, a particularly problematic large body of undermining and enabling norms consists of the norms produced by the Party. For example, there is a rule requiring all Party members who are subject to a 'discipline and inspection' procedure to 'appear in a prescribed place at a prescribed time to answer questions'. This simple rule, innocuous though it reads at first glance, is not part of what is sometimes called 'the formal legal system', in the sense that no authority of the State has produced it. However, it is a very powerful and important rule upon which a whole system of secret detention of Party members known as 'two-prescribed' or *shuanggui* detention has been built. *Shuanggui* detention has given rise to horrendous human rights violations, including systematic torture.[42] Thus the rules on *shuanggui* are great enablers of human rights violations, even though they do not have the effect of law. The state at times acts ignorant of the existence of the procedure and does not, for example, make any reference to statements obtained in *shuanggui* when it tries and convicts Party members in the criminal process.[43] Other times it treats the process as based on rules voluntarily agreed to by Party members, or claims, without further particulars, that it is based on 'national law and internal party regulations'.[44] The existence of *shuanggui* rules is testimony to the Party's power, and to the fact that all state agencies operate in the Party's shadows, or as agents of the Party-principal.[45]

The coexistence of rights-protective, rights-violating, rights-undermining and violation-enabling norms in the legal system begs the question of why the system has been designed this way. Why write rights into the Constitution, laws and regulations in one set of provisions and then write them out of it again in another? And how is it possible that constitutional norms, acknowledged to be the highest-ranking within the domestic legal system, are left unenforceable not only against binding laws and regulations, but also against the norms of the Party?

Przeworski has argued that the constitutions of communist countries tended to be instances of 'ruling against rules', rather like a manual for a car, but not the car one would actually be driving.[46] The Polish Constitution of 1952, on this account, merely coordinated activities of law avoidance and was thus an inherently accident-prone project. But as communist constitutions were revised or newly drafted, they became more explicit about the role of the Party. There might be parallels with the evolution of constitutional law in China. Chinese scholars and advocates committed to the idea of (global) constitutionalism as a liberal value[47] have tended to focus on the rights-protective constitutional norms as the morally, politically and legally better justified and more coherent ones.[48] But those who aim to justify the current power-holder, the Party, have argued that there are 'unwritten constitutional rules' giving clearer authority to the Party than the written Constitution does, and called for the position of the Party to be made more explicit.[49]

It can become necessary to take a position in this debate, not only for academics, but for all who are touched by this system's iniquities, who have complaints, who are seeking redress for injustice. The argument of 'you promised!' has potency even when the promisee knows full well that the promise will not be kept, or, indeed, that the promisor is under orders not to keep it.[50] From the perspective of a person seeking justice in the Chinese system, what is primarily important is that the Constitution holds out the promise of respecting legal rules, protecting rights and upholding justice.[51] In their quest for justice through the institutions of the Party-State, citizens invoke these safeguards, even though they know how difficult it is to obtain effective institutional protection of their rights. As they try to make use of the system to defend their rights, the seemingly deliberate ambiguity of the rules of the system just surveyed shapes their options, as does the design of the institutions of the justice system, and the importance of wrongs and rights in legal culture. These options are briefly discussed in the following section of this chapter.

INSTITUTIONAL AVENUES: THE JUDICIARY

In a courtroom in Luzhou, in 2009, lawyers Liu Wei and Tang Jitian, defending a Falun Gong practitioner, were instructed by the presiding judge that they:

> were not allowed to engage in an analysis of the nature of the crime, and not allowed to analyse the application of the law to that case...I think that's really strange: If they can't analyse the nature of the crime or the application of the law to the case, what are lawyers supposed to say [in defence of their client]? These are the key issues in a criminal case![52]

Lawyer Liu at the time thought that the judge was receiving nonverbal prompts from an unidentified person in the audience. Refusing to be shut down by the Presiding Judge, she and Tang eventually handed their written statements to the Court and left.[53]

This story is unique in its particulars, not least because Falun Gong is a politically (very) 'sensitive' topic and Liu and Tang are unusual lawyers, who risked – and got – disbarment for their action. But Liu's narrative gives a sense of how the judicial process is controlled more widely. This wider problem, reflected in conversations with many dozens of advocates over a number of years, is apparent also from a study of the rules and mechanisms that govern courts and judges.

The point of adjudication is to exchange reasoned arguments on the basis of evidence,[54] and to determine the correct answer to a legal question: is the defendant guilty? Can I keep my home or can the state take and demolish it? Do the authorities owe you damages for unlawfully detaining you? The well-functioning of this process depends on impartiality and fairness in deciding disputes. Of course, there is no perfect protection against judicial bias and other disturbances of the judicial process; but tried and tested mechanisms include, for example, security of tenure and adequate salaries for the judges. Fairness generally also requires a public judicial process. Public scrutiny can help expose or prevent procedural irregularity, such as apparent bias; and a public record of past decisions benefits those who want to understand what the law on any particular point requires.[55]

Some of the constitutional provisions for the judiciary in China broadly reflect the principles of adjudication just mentioned. The judicial process is 'to take facts as basis and law as standard' in deciding legal cases, and the courts are to adjudicate cases 'independently'.[56] As of today, the laws regulating the courts and selection of judges provide, moreover, that judges must have some professional legal qualifications. Historically, this has been a problem. Established in fits and starts since the decline of the last imperial dynasty, the judicial institutions drew not only on continental European (Swiss and German) law but also on the system of the Soviet Union, and there used to be discussion as to whether being 'expert' was as important as being 'red'.[57]

At the time of writing, the judiciary consists of some 200,000 appointed professional judges.[58] They operate at the four levels of the administration (Supreme, High, Intermediate and Basic Level People's Court). China also has a legal profession currently consisting of some 300,000 licensed lawyers,[59] and a similar number of People's Procurators (an institution with functions modelled on the Soviet *prokuratura*). The vast majority have formal legal training and there was no indication that the Presiding Judge in Luzhou, for example, had lacked professional knowledge.

Notwithstanding the principles just cited, the judiciary's institutional design does not support independence from other authorities of the Party-State. The judiciary is supposed to be independent – but is also supervised and subject to a complex system of 'quality control'. Judges are required to apply the law to facts – but they must also be loyal to the Party, according to their professional oath. They draw a salary from the State – but low salaries and a practice of paying bonuses and imposing financial penalties for judicial wrongdoing or mistakes make them economically vulnerable to inducements. Thus, in fact, they operate, as the scholar Li Ling has explained, under a principle of 'judicial dependence'.[60] Judicial dependence manifests in two ways: as a disciplinary regime whose stated purpose it is to address judicial misconduct (such as bending the law or taking bribes),[61] and as a political regime maintained to ensure that major or sensitive cases are handled in accordance with the perceived political exigency.

In a criminal process, the lack of judicial independence weakens protections at the pre-trial stage in investigating an alleged crime, in preparing cases for public indictment, and at trial. In ordinary cases, lawyers, if present, may not be actively prevented from speaking up in defence of the client; but in many cases, there is no legal counsel or legal counsel is ineffective.[62] A pervasive further problem that contributes to explaining criminal conviction rates of over 99%,[63] is that of coerced confessions and the fact that torture remains widespread in the criminal process. A saying summing up the relationship between the institutions in criminal cases goes 'the police prepares the food, the procuracy serves it and the court eats it', meaning that the court does not get much choice on how to decide the case before it.

It is against this background that we must understand cases like the Luzhou one above. The rules in operation were partly hidden. Following rules for 'major cases', the Presiding Judge was holding the trial but not adjudicating the case (a practice known as *shen er bu pan*). While no specific rule would have supported the Judge's alleged attempts to suppress the two defence lawyers' interventions, law firms are, as of 2017, required to prevent their staff from 'denial of the state-determined nature of an evil sect organization or other conduct seriously disrupting court order [sic]',[64] a rule clearly referring to Falun Gong cases.

When citizens try to sue the authorities, they are the complainants, and the power imbalance between them and the authorities accordingly has different consequences. In these cases, lack of judicial independence can mean that judges and courts do not want to adjudicate cases brought against the government at all, and refuse to put them on file. This is a frequent problem in housing demolition cases or complaints against unlawful detention, for example. If a case has been accepted and goes to trial, courts may be reluctant to find in the complainant's favour even where the law would require them to do so, as in the case of Liu Zhengyou, discussed just below. They may on the other hand also be concerned about the 'social stability' implications of a decision – for example, if they hold a trial or make a decision perceived as unfair by the complainant, this can trigger further complaints, which in turn might affect how courts or individual judges are appraised by their superiors.[65] As discussed in chapter 6, there can be small-scale demonstrations outside court buildings and unruly, even raucous scenes during court hearings when the case is one that has attracted the attention of the socially aggrieved and *déracinés*. Complainants may decide to use the petitioning system, discussed in the following section, or to put pressure on the courts by complaining via social or the official media.[66] They may also resort to more serious collective tactics, especially in mass grievance cases such as land-grabs.

All this can make 'mediated' outcomes desirable as a means of avoiding trouble for the courts, who may try to pressurize complainants to accept a settlement following *tiaojie* mediation.[67] It explains why 'taking the facts as basis and the law as standard' is not always an available option in handling cases, especially those which, like human rights cases, involve a confrontation between citizens and the Party-State (and not even taking into account the problems with legislative inconsistency discussed in the previous sections).

From the above, it has become clear that there is an entrenched principle of judicial supervision that serves purposes of control of the courts for political as well as disciplinary reasons. Just as the Party asserts that there can never be any conflict between the interests of the People and the Party, so too, does it insist that the socialist rule of law and Party leadership are identical. The authoritarian nature of this view makes it appear more compatible with the so-called 'letters and visits' system at first blush: but as argued in the following, this system presents challenges of its own.

INSTITUTIONAL AVENUES: 'LETTERS AND VISITS' AND THE MEDIA

Liu Zhengyou, a villager on the outskirts of Zigong City in Sichuan, was one of those complainants who could not get their case – a land-grab case dating back to the 1990s – into court. The villagers affected by the taking, ostensibly for the purpose of building an industrial park, sought to lodge a case in court in 2000. But over a period of several years, the courts refused to 'file' the case. As a result, Liu and fellow villagers went to petition the Supreme People's Court about the fact that the Intermediate Court had not accepted their case. They became *fangmin*, petitioners, or users of the 'letters and visits' system.

As its name says, this system allows people to write 'letters' and pay 'visits' to the offices designated to deal with petitioners. A right to 'criticize and make suggestions regarding any State organ or functionary' and 'to make to relevant State organs complaints or charges against, or exposures of, any State organ or functionary for violation of law or dereliction of duty' is safeguarded in the Constitution's Article 41, which also prohibits 'fabrication or distortion of facts for purposes of libel or false incrimination'. Some have related this to the right to petition.[68] The 2005 Letters and Visits Regulation issued by the State Council,[69] as well as numerous local regulations and further 'normative documents', outline the further institutional features of the system. In principle, offices receiving visitors who come to seek help or complain are established by all Party-State authorities, including notably the State Council, the national level ministries and the Supreme People's Court. Petitioners have many different kinds of complaints. For example, some protest wrongful accusations, persecution or punishment. Others seek a resolution of socio-economic grievances. Like the petitioners encountered at the beginning of chapter 1, they typically use the more traditional language of submitting wrongs (*shenyuan*) concurrently with that of defending (human) rights (*weiquan*).

In December 2001, partly because they were helped by academics running a 'legal clinic' in one of Beijing's major universities, Liu and others managed to get an interview with the Supreme People's Court Letters and Visits Office. There, they were given an unnumbered 'official letter' (*gonghan*) addressed to the Sichuan Provincial High Court, instructing it 'to receive [Liu Zhengyou] and take care of him conscientiously, and to handle the matter in accordance with law'. However, back at the Intermediate Court in Zigong, they were laughed at, and an official told them that their letter was worthless, 'as long as there's no approval from the leadership'.[70] As of this writing, Liu Zhengyou has still not given up petitioning, even though he has been targeted in numerous ways, including by being sent to prison (following a conviction which, according to him, was trumped up).[71]

In their quest for justice, Liu Zhengyou and his fellow villagers tried not only the courts and the petitioning system. They were also desperate to catch the attention of the official Party-State-controlled media, and were overjoyed when in June 2003, China Central Television decided to make their case the subject of a 30-minute report. They felt certain that this would lead to a thorough investigation into local officials' misconduct by officials of the Party-State and, eventually, to justice. But the villagers' joy quickly turned to dismay and anger. Following the report, an official investigation team was sent to Zigong; but local officials prevented the rights defenders from meeting the team.[72]

The Zigong case is a classic example of how the petitioning system and the media have been used by complainants. Both channels can offer opportunities to express grievances, and it is possible that a simple act of pointing out a mistake may lead to rectification. But the case also shows that seeking redress is precarious. The system can be viewed as an alternative to the adjudication system, as Carl Minzner has characterized it,[73] but it is not a functional alternative. As the work of the scholar Yu Jianrong and others has shown, petitioning too often leads nowhere, for example because petitioners spend months or years without even getting an opportunity to speak to someone in the petitioning office. If they do get an interview, the person they speak to may lack the power to help them, as in the Zigong case. Even a well-functioning petitioning system could disrupt adjudication, as scholars have pointed out, *inter alia*, because they undermine the finality of court decisions.[74]

In addition, the fact of petitioning creates distorting incentives for officials, as the authorities have sought to reduce petitioning as a source of perceived 'social instability'.[75] Any occurrences of petitioning, especially petitioning activities deemed 'irregular',[76] will affect the appraisal of officials, whether or not the petitions were well founded.[77] This means that officials, on the one hand, have an inducement to accommodate those who complain loudest outside of the system. On the other hand, they have incentives to stop petitioning by all means, fair and crooked, and thus to become complicit in the repression of petitioning activities. Such repression could take the form of being forcibly escorted back to one's home-town, but also of incarceration in 'black jails'.[78] In extreme cases, repression could include psychiatric incarceration of petitioners deemed to suffer from 'paranoia' because, from a government perspective, they kept litigating unreasonably.[79] It would be easy to conclude from narratives like this that the problem lies with local-level iniquities and infractions of law, not with the centre: for, after all, the central state has no hand in a faraway illegal land-grab, and (some of) its laws do prescribe that (at least some of) the rights of evictees be protected. But this analysis would overlook the degree to which the institutional design of the judicial and 'letters and visits' systems is centrally driven, and the degree to which central authorities will support local illegality and cover-ups.

The connection between local persecution and central-level decision-making was further driven home by the example of petitioner Cao Shunli, a law graduate, who became a petitioner after exposing corruption in the government department she worked in, and being dismissed. Cao got involved in efforts to collect 'human rights condition questionnaires', thousands of individual petitioners' cases which she thought should be taken into account in the process of formulating the State Council National Human Rights Action Plan.[80] She also initiated efforts to use the human rights reporting mechanisms of the UN to include civil society complaints about China's human rights situation, and participated, *inter alia*, in a two-month sit-in action in front of the Ministry of Foreign Affairs in 2013. As a result of her activism, she suffered numerous detentions and physical abuse in various settings. On 14 September 2013, she was 'disappeared' in Shanghai, to prevent her from boarding a plane to Geneva where she would have taken part in human rights NGO activities. After being placed under criminal detention, on suspicion of a public order offence, her already damaged health deteriorated badly. Denied medical treatment and the use of medication she had brought with her, according to her lawyer, she was 'released on parole' and transferred to a hospital only after falling into a coma. Repeated earlier requests for medical parole had been denied. Cao died on 14 March 2014.[81]

At the Universal Periodic Review she had tried so hard to contribute to, a civil society organization announced it would use half a minute of its allotted speaking time to remember Cao Shunli in silence; but the PRC representatives would have none of it: they insisted that 'speaking' time must be used to make 'general comments', not to be silent. The bizarre squabble among diplomats that ensued[82] reflected the pressures and tensions within the system that had led to Cao Shunli's death. The officials seemed obsessed with maintaining appearances, as though insisting on speaking could drown out the silence left by Cao's death.

ADVOCACY AS RESISTANCE

The experience of the few individuals and their cases discussed in this chapter has served to illustrate how difficult human rights advocacy is. We may take a moment to reiterate what happened to these individuals: Teng Biao, the advocate in the Sun Zhigang case, was persecuted (in ways not fully outlined here but partly discussed later on in the book); the Falun Gong practitioner tried in Luzhou was convicted; lawyers Liu Wei and Tang Jitian were disbarred; Liu Zhengyou, as of now, has spent many years petitioning and facing retaliation without any substantial result; and Cao Shunli died after denial of treatment in custody. Even SPC Justice Huang Songyou, who had so enthusiastically welcomed the Qi Yuling decision in 2001, was thwarted, if his expectation had been that of an eventual liberal transformation of the judicial system, since the decision was officially revoked. Each of their unique individual stories and cases occurred within a system whose structural flaws were exposed by these (and many other such) cases and stories.

Longer-term petitioners express themselves aware of this nexus, no less than legal professionals. The woman depicted on the book cover, who has been a petitioner in a demolition case from the Northeast for eighteen years, for example, displays the following words on her 'petition garment' (*zhuangyi*):

> Petitioning is impossible and there's no recourse to the law; they don't acknowledge the injustice while I'm still alive and won't address it even after I'm dead.

The scroll she wears over her face reads, simply, 'power is corrupting the law'. According to the photographer,

> She does not believe that she can win, 'because, when the courts themselves have bent the law, how could they admit their own wrongdoing?'[83]

The experience of these individuals not only shows that human rights advocacy as an attempt to assert human rights claims through the institutions is unlikely to be successful. Reflecting on his experience of over ten years, a lawyer said:

> As long as there is no judicial independence, whatever you do in the courtroom in those cases of repression really just amounts to helping them act out a piece of theatre. They don't care. You have to take the action from inside the courtroom to outside, and let the Great Public Jury [the Court of Public Opinion] decide. That's what they fear now: all the constraints [they impose] are in this area.[84]

Lawyers faced with institutional intransigence have quite literally 'taken the action to outside'. For example, lawyers being prevented from seeing their clients or accessing the files in their cases have used the technique of standing outside court buildings, holding a sign that reads, 'CRIMINAL DEFENCE LAWYERS DEMAND ACCESS TO FILES', and posting such images online.[85] The move from avenues and mechanisms designed and controlled by the system to spaces less well controlled by the authorities captured in this example can also be a means of communicating their (the lawyers') grievance to a wider public. In a system that does not tolerate such public protest, however, advocacy of this kind is treated as tending to subversion; it becomes resistance. Thus, in communicating a sense of injustice about the existing system, lawyers, petitioners and members of the public entering the discussion are expressing systemic grievances that translate into a call for a different system. A human rights lawyer commented in 2011,

> The fact that the petitioners are now getting more organized is the result of years, perhaps even decades of going back and forth [petitioning in their particular cases]. The petitioners have been raised up to being what they are through oppression. They now know that they cannot possibly resolve their own case. So if they cannot each resolve their own problem, they want to resolve the system.[86]

The move from inside to outside the courts, or from inside to outside 'the system', is of course particularly problematic in a system that censors speech, in particular, political expression, especially if performed by individuals and groups that are already targets of 'stability maintenance' programmes. During the first two decades of the twenty-first century, those who protested got better at evading censorship through use of the internet and social media – without the emergence of the social media, indeed, coordinated protest and action would not have been possible. But concurrently, the Party-State got better at using the same social media platforms as a tools of surveillance and control of protesters' activities.[87] In some cases, rights advocacy was itself treated as a disturbance of order, or even as subversive of the system, even if and when it relied on the mechanisms provided by the Party-State.

CONCLUSION

The normative frameworks and institutional structures briefly surveyed here offer a number of explanations for why those who try to defend their human rights in China may be disappointed not just by the outcome of a case, but also by the systems and avenues used. Yet, the discussion here also supports the conclusion that institutional failure does not defeat the purpose of human rights law altogether. Despite these failures, human rights as a political and moral idea has been important in shaping how people think about justice and injustice, law and power, and how they translate their grievances into political expectations and demands.

On this basis, we should revert to Simmons' model suggesting a categorization of countries into those which are already consistently complying, those which are in transition towards better compliance, and those that are impervious to human rights norms.[88] Only in transitional systems, it was suggested, does treaty ratification and attempts to be part of the international human rights law order create significant momentum for change.[89] It was found here that as complainants turn away from the system, they are likely also to turn against the system, opposing it on political grounds. This dynamic turns human rights defence into an activity that implicitly also challenges the fundamental structure of the political system. Even if human rights defenders act with the intention of creating better institutional structures, the Party-State sees them as politically subversive, and it does so increasingly, as it abandons the liberal reform trajectory which dominated the immediate post-Mao era. As discussed in greater detail in chapter 6, their activism becomes a direct cause of their persecution. Yet, their persecution can, in turn, spur wider calls for political change.

3 | Liberty and Life ——————————

In March 2014 four lawyers, Jiang Tianyong, Tang Jitian, Wang Cheng and Zhang Junjie, set out in search of their clients, thought to be held in the 'Qinglongshan Legal Education Base' of Jiansanjiang, Heilongjiang Province in the northeast of China.[1] The clients had been taken away by the police because they were members of the spiritual group Falun Gong. Their lawyers feared that they might be tortured. Joined by some other supporters, and wearing the heavy cotton-padded coats and hats used by soldiers in the bitter winters of the Northeast, the lawyers gathered outside a gate where they thought their clients might be detained, and held up signs appealing for access to their clients. When they posted pictures of themselves online, the police placed them under 'administrative punishment detention' for 'disturbing public order'. They were held in a police detention centre for five to fifteen days, and there they were severely beaten. One of them, Tang Jitian, later spoke to the BBC about his experience.[2] Unfortunately, torture at the hands of the police some three years earlier had already left him seriously ill, and the beatings in Jiansanjiang had now worsened his condition.

Following this, some twenty-odd of the lawyers' colleagues and friends travelled to Jiansanjiang to protest the detentions in a peaceful demonstration, including a small-scale hunger-strike outside the local police bureau. These friends, too, held up signs, took more pictures, and also posted them via social media, where the news now spread fast. In response, the police blocked further supporters from joining these protesters and, without giving any reasons, or indicating what procedure they were following, detained some of the supporters who had already arrived.[3]

Released from administrative punishment detention after a few days, the four originally detained lawyers were forcibly escorted to the nearest airport. One, Jiang Tianyong, was immediately placed under an informal form of house arrest known as 'soft restraint' upon returning to his home in Beijing.[4] The story neither began nor ended there – for example, two of the initially detained lawyers had been subjected to long-term surveillance and frequent informal detention; some of their clients had already suffered a history of police abuse; and the 'Jiansanjiang Incident' is connected to the '7-09 Crackdown' on lawyers, which occurred in 2015.[5]

But this snapshot is enough to illustrate, first, the seriousness and pervasiveness of external restrictions placed on individuals, and the connection of such restrictions with mental and physical torture. Incarceration puts one in the hands of one's captors and at their mercy. Losing one's personal liberty threatens the sovereignty over one's mind, as well as her body.[6] Second, the Jiansanjiang Incident also illustrates the particularly fluid interaction between different mechanisms to curtail people's freedom[7] and invade the security and integrity of the person in China.[8] Some are highly formalized, others seem informal and even casual. Some may be governed by rules that we, on the outside of the departments concerned with public security, national security and the Party-controlled mechanisms of detention, may never get to see.

The Party-State has recognized the rights to liberty, security and integrity of the person and the right to life in principle. And, in some respects, it has complied with public international law obligations and expectations of reform of the death penalty. Yet as this chapter argues, the Party-State seems unable to abandon the mechanisms for arbitrary curtailments of personal liberty and the power to kill people as a rightfully available form of punishment. Moreover, in both of these contexts, it has not overcome the problem of torture. Thus it finds it difficult to accept and respect even those limitations it has clearly imposed on itself, let alone further-reaching requirements that can be found in international human rights law. As a result, these rights make for one of the most important spectacles of contention between citizens and the Party-State.

RESTRICTIONS OF PERSONAL LIBERTY

As Fu Hualing has pointed out, internment in a so-called Re-education Through Labour (RTL) camp could be quite an informal process during the Mao era. In part, this was because, under a system of planned economy and (since the late 1950s) 'household registration',[9] individuals had little choice of where to work and live in the first place, and thus effectively no freedom of movement. Working conditions and living spaces under the old system of the *danwei* work unit were physically restrictive anyway.[10] Even until the early 2000s, the practice of locking residents up in universities and factory dormitories at night remained quite common.[11] Today, it seems that these practices are less common; but restrictions and control methods have become technologically far more sophisticated; and even today, some are exercised in casual and informal ways.

Those targeted by the police (Public Security), its domestic security forces, State Security and Party-State entities such as the 'Discipline and Inspection' commissions have developed a complex vocabulary to capture the manifold ways of restricting the liberty of the person and the liberty of movement. A look at this vocabulary shows the complexity of interlinking systems. Target persons speak not only of being formally called in for questioning (*chuanhuan*), detained (*juliu*) as part of the criminal process or of one of several administrative detention mechanisms regulated by law, or of being arrested (*daibu*) in the criminal process. They also talk of being 'soft-restrained' (*ruanjin*), 'placed under guard' (*bei shanggang*), 'travelled' (*bei lüyou*, in the passive voice), 'retrieved' (*jiefang*) (as a petitioner), 'black-hooded' (*bei hei toutao*), 'abducted' (*bei bangjia*) or 'disappeared' (*bei shizong/qiangzhi shizong*), and being treated as mentally ill (*bei jingshenbing*) on a fake diagnosis such as 'petitioning paranoia'.[12] Communist Party members may experience being placed under *shuanggui* detention (or, in the case of officials who are not Party members, *shuangzhi/liangzhi/lianggui*), measures briefly discussed below. The places of detention can be regular police detention centres, prisons and facilities to hold those detained under various state-operated administrative detention systems. They may also be (called) 'black (i.e., unofficial) prisons (*hei jianyu*)',[13] 'study classes' (*xuexiban*) or even – like the place where the Jiansanjiang detainees were held – 'legal education centres' (*fazhi jiaoyu zhongxin*). Sometimes the place of detention is a hostel or holiday resort. The great fluidity of restrictions of liberty is heightened by the fact that it is not always possible to determine which one is being used in any given case.

The PRC Constitution safeguards the right to liberty of the person in Article 37, which reads:

> Freedom of the person of citizens of the People's Republic of China is inviolable.
>
> No citizens may be arrested (*daibu*), except with the approval or by decision of a People's Procuratorate or by decision of a People's Court, and arrests must be made by a public security organ.
>
> Unlawful (*feifa*) detention (*jujin*) or deprivation (*boduo*) or restriction (*xianzhi*) of citizens' freedom of the person by other means is prohibited, and unlawful search (*feifa soucha*) of the person of citizens is prohibited.[14]

There are also statutory (NPC) laws protecting the liberty of the person. For example, the Criminal law contains the punishable offence of false imprisonment.[15] The Criminal Procedure Law, prison law and numerous further laws and regulations regulate detention under a number of detention systems. Liberal scholars have long argued that restrictions of the general right to liberty of the person must themselves be lawful. As seen in the Sun Zhigang case, they were persuasive and, on occasion, successful in arguing so: it followed from Article 37 in conjunction with sections 8 and 9 of the Legislation Law that the administrative regulation that allowed Sun's detention was unlawful (unconstitutional) since these provisions require that the deprivation of liberty be based on NPC law and premised on a judicial or procuratorial decision.[16]

In making this argument, Chinese liberals draw on the structure of the right to liberty of the person inherent to all major international treaties dealing with this liberty. For example, Article 9 (1) of the ICCPR requires that no one be subjected to arbitrary arrest or detention and that no one be deprived of their liberty 'except on such grounds and in accordance with such procedures as are established by law.'[17] Reflecting this structure – and the importance of the concepts of arbitrariness and lawfulness of limitations of liberty and integrity of the person – Fu Hualing has employed the terms 'legal', 'extra-legal' and 'extra-extra-legal detention'.[18] This categorization reminds us that there have been attempts to put detention on a legal basis, and that practical consequences attach to being detained under one or another form.

Formal and informal deprivations of liberty

In the formal criminal justice process, the authorities rely heavily on the incarceration of suspects; but in contrast to the Mao era,[19] detention is regulated under the Criminal Procedure Law (CPL). The most common basic form of detention used in this context is criminal investigation detention, *xingshi juliu*. Both the 1996 and the 2012 Criminal Procedure Law provide that criminal detention can last for up to 37 days, at the end of which period there must be a decision to recommend indictment followed by the People's Procuracy's decision on indictment. But, there are various ways of extending criminal investigation detention in accordance with legal rules – for instance, by sending a case back 'for further investigation' – and investigation detention may be followed by detention awaiting trial after the indictment. Detention under these measures usually means being held in a police detention centre (*kanshousuo*) whose operation is subject to rules safeguarding some procedural rights. After a person has been detained, the family will be notified. One has no right to be visited by family; but after a prescribed period of time, the detainee can see his appointed lawyers. There are also procedures for making complaints. The CPL also contains a mechanism for being released on bail (or 'released pending trial').[20]

Then there are a number of forms of administrative detention that could be called 'extra-legal' or 'extra-judicial' in the sense that their imposition is based on administrative regulations that fall short of the requirements of Article 37 of the Constitution in conjunction with Articles 8 and 9 of the 2000 Legislation Law. The violation of these provisions was the basis of the unconstitutionality review in the Sun Zhigang Incident.[21] The oldest of these extra-judicial systems, the so-called 'Re-education Through Labour' or RTL system, was abolished in 2014.[22] Targeted groups used to involve persons designated as petty criminals, persons who, like petitioners, are deemed socially harmful, and prostitutes. It was the largest-scale system of detention in which a person could effectively be locked up, for a period of three years, just on the say-so of the police.[23] There had been long-standing criticisms of the system that drew on the Sun Zhigang Incident, but these were not successful in triggering the procedure of unconstitutionality review.[24] When the abolition of RTL was announced, new concerns arose regarding systems that might be introduced to replace RTL.[25]

Other forms of extra-legal detention – leading to spells of custody based on legal norms purporting to empower the authorities, but not based on a 'judicial decision' and therefore not satisfying the constitutional requirements set out above – include drug rehabilitation, shelter for education (used for those designated as prostitutes), shelter for education and formation (used for juveniles), administrative punishment detention and judicial detention.[26] As they are imposed by administrative decision, detainees can theoretically bring legal complaints against the authorities that imposed them as a concrete administrative act.[27]

Virtually outside the scope of any laws or regulations is a wide range of further practices and systems. These do not have a basis in State law and generally do not even purport to have one. At one end of a range of these kinds of detention measures is 'soft restraint' (*ruanjin*), a kind of flexible house arrest. For the target person, 'soft restraint' often begins with discovering *guobao* police outside their front door, informing them they will not be allowed to go out. But levels of restraint typically vary from one day to another. On some days, at certain times, the police might allow a person to go outside for a bit, on foot or in a police car, or to receive visitors at home. If they are allowed out, target persons (and their family) will usually be followed or at least put under electronic surveillance. In some cases, the *guobao* police move into the same building or compound, or indeed (rarely) into the target person's own flat, to monitor and control more effectively – physically as well as mentally. The experience of 'soft restraint' was brilliantly documented through the use of secretly taken video footage by Hu Jia and Zeng Jinyan, dissidents subjected to this measure on and off from 2004 onwards.[28]

At the other end of the spectrum are enforced disappearances, defined under international law as 'the arrest, detention, abduction or any other form of deprivation of liberty by agents of the State or by persons or groups of persons acting with the authorization, support or acquiescence of the State, followed by a refusal to acknowledge the deprivation of liberty or by concealment of the fate or whereabouts of the disappeared person, which place such a person outside the protection of the law.'[29] Such deprivations of liberty take place in a variety of settings. One entrenched, systematic and rules-based, albeit 'extra-extra-legal' setting is that of *shuanggui*, the practice of requiring Party members to appear at a prescribed time in a prescribed place to 'answer questions'. The practice is a crucial tool the Party uses to investigate its members. Doing so allows it to project a claim of nearly limitless power, reflected in Party Charter requirements to 'conscientiously observe the Party discipline, abide by the laws and regulations of the state in an exemplary way, rigorously guard secrets of the Party and State, execute the Party's decisions, and accept any job and actively fulfil any task assigned them by the Party.'[30] It also allows the powerful Party Discipline and Inspection Committee or the Party leadership to stay in control over who is designated as an internal enemy, and to screen Party members from unwanted scrutiny by the State crime investigation or prosecution authorities, as long as they have the protection of powerful superiors. *Shuanggui* is governed by written rules at least some of which are publicly available. But these rules are not rules of State law.[31] By many accounts, *shuanggui* involves torture.[32]

As Falun Gong practitioners, the lawyers' clients in the Jiansanjiang case were held under a system called, apparently without intended irony, 'Legal Education Base'. 'Legal Education Bases' and 'Centres' are not mentioned by any NPC law, administrative regulation or even any other publicly available official document. No term of imprisonment is prescribed; inmates are held until they renounce their faith (through 'conversion' or *zhuanhua*) in a written statement. Their irregularity makes these centres a form of 'black (or irregular) prison', a term most frequently used for the places of usually short-term irregular detention where petitioners are held before being taken back to their hometowns.[33] (Euphemistic official terms for such places include 'study class' and 'legal study class'.[34]) Those held in such extra-extra-legal settings have no safeguards and no recourse to any legal process to protest their incarceration, which, as the lawyers in Jiansanjiang pointed out, constituted the crime of false imprisonment (Article 238 CL) and made the 'Legal Education Base' a 'classic euphemism for what is in fact a base for the perpetration of crimes'.[35] These crimes are thought to include routine torture.[36] Requests for criminal investigation are rarely successful in such cases.[37]

The lawyers' own detentions and treatment in detention took multiple forms. Jiang, Tang, Wang and Zhang were given administrative punishment detention, a measure that has a basis in the Administrative Punishment Law and is limited to 15 days. However, the lawyers later claimed that their detention had been carried out in 'kidnap style'. They had been tortured by 'shackling of the hands in the back and suspension [by the hands], combined with beatings, repeatedly and over a lengthy period of time'.[38]

None of these occurrences are unprecedented or even – for the communities of the persecuted – particularly unusual. If there was anything unique about the Jiansanjiang Incident, it was perhaps that there were such strenuous and dedicated efforts to expose the chain reaction of detention–advocacy–and further detention and abuse. This resulted in an open letter protesting their colleagues' detention and mistreatment,[39] as well as a collective complaint reporting the officials responsible for the false imprisonment[40] and numerous follow-up actions, including an administrative complaint against the measures to restrict access to the hunger-striking lawyers.[41] It was these actions that transformed a chain of familiar-seeming, retaliatory and repressive measures into an incident of advocacy for the right of personal liberty.

It was also these actions that, in July 2015, led to the forced disappearance of some of the lawyers and others working with them on the Jiansanjiang Incident in the so-called '7-09' crackdown on human rights lawyers.[42] They were placed under 'residential surveillance in a designated location', a new measure introduced through a Criminal Procedure Law revision effective since 2013. It means that State security, terrorism and major corruption suspects can be detained in holding places, not their own residence, and the authorities may refuse them access to legal counsel. Thus, in a Carl-Schmittian move, the CPL revision created zones of exception from the operation of the ordinary law;[43] and as discussed in chapter 6, this provided ample further opportunities for inhumane treatment and torture.[44]

TORTURE

In conversations with Chinese human rights defenders, torture has always loomed large. Today, there is also an increasing number of publicly available video-recorded statements by torture survivors: statements by or about young men caught up in the criminal justice process out of sheer bad luck,[45] by evictees tortured because they protested,[46] by officials taken into *shuanggui* Party detention,[47] by regular detainees under one of the sprawling and interacting detention systems[48] and by rights defenders in various settings including enforced disappearance.[49] Treatments that interlocutors have spoken of and/or experienced have included stress positions and sleep deprivation, beatings to the head with fists or with filled plastic mineral water bottles, suspension from walls by handcuffs, beatings with batons leading to bone fractures, electric shocks to sensitive areas of the body such as the inside of the mouth and the genitals, prodding with cigarette stubs and toothpicks, cold room treatment, not being allowed to go to the bathroom, to use toilet paper, to wash or to blink, denial of medical treatment following torture, death threats or threats of violence to the victim or their loved ones, and the threat that 'next time we will make your family watch this'.[50]

According to the most widely recognized and influential definition of the Convention Against Torture (CAT), torture means 'any act by which severe pain or suffering, whether physical or mental, is intentionally inflicted on a person for such purposes as obtaining from him or a third person information or a confession, punishing him for an act he or a third person has committed or is suspected of having committed, or intimidating or coercing him or a third person, or for any reason based on discrimination of any kind, when such pain or suffering is inflicted by or at the instigation of or with the consent or acquiescence of a public official or other person acting in an official capacity. It does not include pain or suffering arising only from, inherent in or incidental to lawful sanctions.'[51]

China has signed and ratified CAT and signed the ICCPR. China is also, in general terms, bound by the UN Body of Principles for the Protection of all Persons under any Form of Detention or Imprisonment. Domestic Chinese law has outlawed coercive interrogation to obtain statements (*xing xun bi gong*) and criminalized torture (although its domestic definition is narrower than public international law ones), as well as other forms of violence and false imprisonment.[52] While, in contrast with the right to liberty of the person, the Constitution does not contain a comparably explicit right to life or to integrity of the person, the Criminal Procedure Law also contains rules reflecting the ban on torture, including rules to exclude evidence obtained through torture in the criminal process, which were added only in 2012. Yet torture remains common; as the Committee Against Torture accurately stated in its 9 December 2015 report, it is still 'deeply entrenched in the criminal justice system'.[53] A wealth of further academic literature,[54] NGO reports,[55] in addition to videographic materials such as those mentioned, essentially support this conclusion.

An attempt to understand the continued widespread use of torture should start from its different purposes. There is the purpose of 'education' or 'brainwashing', for example, when torture is inflicted on members of Falun Gong[56] or on human rights lawyers who refuse to desist from their advocacy activities. In these contexts, a primary goal of torture is often to get the victim to renounce fundamental personal convictions or articles of faith. In such cases, torture also serves intimidation purposes – in an often-used phrase, by 'killing a chicken to scare the monkeys (*sha ji gei hou kan*)'. As shown by many previous researchers, the psychological process involved is complex – it may involve merely getting professions of compliance or submission, but can also involve the breaking of a victim's spirit through pain, numbing, humiliation, shame, guilt and fear.

There is also the criminal justice process, where the most widely understood, primary goal of using torture is to obtain a 'confession' that will allow the authorities to prosecute and convict.[57] Of course, this purpose is rarely isolated from others in practice. As McConville reminds us, 'police practices involving brutality and torture are...often part of the wider repressive (social disciplinary) role of the police.'[58] In these criminal justice contexts, torture victims may be innocent of the wrongdoing they are accused of. A typical case of wrongful conviction is that of a brutal rape in Leping, Jiangxi Autonomous Region, which led to wrongful convictions as a result of brutal torture. Even when another person, already on death row, confessed to the crime, the authorities were reluctant to admit error, as they feared being held responsible. As Jiang notes, 'the use of torture by the police to extort "confessions" is on the one hand shocking; on the other...it becomes virtually impossible for the institutions of the system to correct this grievous mistake "from within."'[59]

Legal and technical reforms introduced to reduce torture have so far had limited effect. While the introduction of the 'exclusionary rule', demanding that evidence obtained though torture not be used in the criminal process, has led to some hopeful cases, reports suggest that this mechanism has remained relatively ineffective so far.[60] Advocates attribute the persistence of torture to a combination of hard-to-change attitudes and institutional factors. As lawyer Chen Youxi points out, the victim-suspect who suffers torture in the criminal justice process is marginalized and distrusted, officials collude to protect each other, and there is a lack of transparency that is achieved *inter alia* through media control,[61] as well as through continued obstruction of detained suspects' access to counsel.

Judging from conversations with victims and the wider literature on this phenomenon in China and beyond, many of those involved appear to *understand* that the use of torture is unlikely genuinely to change minds, or to extract truthful statements, yet this changes neither their practice, nor their overall attitude towards the practice. Victims will do anything to stop the torture. Torture can never be regarded as a likely means of identifying the guilty; and at some level, this seems to be understood by the torturers.

> The police said to me, 'There is no confession that we cannot obtain.'[62]

In fact, producing false confessions that lead to wrongful convictions leads to complaints about the criminal justice process, as for example in the Leping case, in which the victims used the petitioning system, made accusations of criminal responsibility against alleged perpetrators, and sought to obtain retrials for their loved ones.[63] Yet those who practise or condone torture in their professional roles accept it as a necessity. Even some criminal defence lawyers seem inclined to accept the practice. For example, a lawyer spoke of the practice in terms of 'wrongful' and 'right' beatings, clearly assuming that beating the guilty was fine.[64]

From the perspective taken here, the most central problem is that, in the authoritarian system, torture is 'needed' to obtain a statement whose truth has been predetermined and merely needs to be affirmed by the victim. That need for affirmation is widely accepted even though it is understood that 'mistakes' will occur. Notwithstanding differences of aims and goals of torture, the bureaucratic context within which it takes place tends to be intensely preoccupied with the production of a document, a statement by the torture victim, usually combined with expressions of repentance and/or promises to desist. And, once such a statement has been produced, it becomes important to conceal the circumstances of its production.

This is why torture, as practised in China, is not only euphemistic and pseudo-clinical in the argot used to describe torture methods. It does not only increasingly prefer 'white' or 'clean' torture methods, as in any system where torture is criminalized yet systematically used.[65]

A further, distinctive feature seems to be the tone of educational superiority adopted. Practices are connected to a claim of 'rectifying thought' and of ensuring submission to the rightful authority of the Party-State. This may, to some extent, explain the bureaucratic obsession with producing documents titled 'statement admitting guilt', 'statement of repentance', 'self-criticism', and so on.

Some details of victims' experience testify to the at times bizarre earnestness with which the educational goal of 'thought reformation' (*sixiang gaizao*) was pursued. Interrogators would insist, for example, that the target person write such statements themselves, and in some cases, that they rewrite them over and over until they were finally acceptable. One lawyer commented on his own experience:

> Not only did they want to make you say that black was white. You also had to explain why black was white.

One interlocutor reported that, in his view, some of his interrogators sought confirmation that 'thought reformation' was genuine:

> I wanted to leave. So of course I did not want to raise the fact that I had been tortured with [the interrogators, who came in after torture had been carried out]. I had to make them believe that my thought had changed. There was this one person who asked, 'What you wrote there, was that your real thinking or did you write it under pressure?' Of course I replied, 'It was my real thinking.' These people did not necessarily know what exactly had been done to me. [And even if they had known,] they will not necessarily think of many of those things as torture.[66]

In other contexts, according to torture survivors, the executioners of torture insisted they were merely 'doing their job'.

All of these reported attitudes – of torturers and interrogators – point to the warped psychology of torturing: the assumption that torture is 'necessary;' the euphemizing of torture; the apparent need to pretend that statements made are genuine and 'free'; and the perceived need for these statements to confirm that lie. The statements produced are in fact 'required' to affirm the authority of the Party-State, and the correctness of its exercise of power, by creating a pretence of acceptance, which the system cannot generate in any other way.

The story of another detainee, a lawyer and political prisoner, may help to illustrate this last point. He described how, facing a threat of severe physical torture, he had decided to give in and write the required statements. But, in his statement,

> I wrote, 'Under such-and-such bad influences, I mistakenly believed that the Communist Party must also respect the law and is also constrained by law, that it must also accept citizens' supervision.[67] I now recognise my mistake.' This in fact is contrary to what the authorities officially claim to be the case. But they accepted it![68]

He saw this as a tiny victory over 'them', a small act of resistance, because it exposed his jailors' lawless and authoritarian mind-set. The fact that they seemed satisfied coheres with other instances in which police officers and their helpers claimed to be 'on Party territory.'[69] It supports Waldron's argument that torture is repugnant to the very idea of law in any legal system.[70] It also points to the conclusion that torture serves the goal of affirming the principle of authoritarian Party-Statehood, or the authoritarian denial of, in J.S. Mill's words, individual 'sovereignty over body and mind'.

THE RIGHT TO LIFE AND THE DEATH PENALTY

Several of the human rights defenders involved in the Jiansanjiang Incident had worked on the death penalty – primarily by defending death row clients. Some had been involved in advocacy on the already mentioned 'Leping' case. One of them had at one point worked as a prosecutor and been responsible, *inter alia*, for supervising executions. In that earlier role, he had vainly sought to prevent another case of wrongful conviction as a result of severe torture of the defendant.[71] Lawyers with experience in death penalty cases were not all agreed that the death penalty was *per se* a violation of the right to life. But judging from these conversations, they all thought that the death penalty as practised in China today represented a terrible, systematic violation of human rights. The discussion here will therefore need to address not only the wrongness of the death penalty as such but also what makes its practice unacceptable.

The sources and mainstream doctrines of international human rights law, which provide a starting point for an assessment, do not completely rule out the death penalty – or at least the relevant UN bodies have not done so. Article 6 of the ICCPR, which protects the right to life, states that 'in countries which have not abolished the death penalty, sentence of death may be imposed only for the most serious crimes in accordance with the law in force at the time of the commission of the crime and not contrary to the provisions of the present Covenant.'[72] The Human Rights Committee has elaborated 'that all measures of abolition should be considered as progress in the enjoyment of the right to life within the meaning of article 40, and should as such be reported to the Committee' and that the 'death penalty should be a quite exceptional measure.'[73]

China prescribes the death penalty for some 46 crimes, following an August 2015 revision of its criminal law, which reduced the number of crimes carrying the death penalty, in accordance with a long-term trend.[74] In practice, it is thought that the vast majority of executions occur after conviction of a violent crime, in particular, homicide. However, when the death penalty is imposed for other crimes, for example for corruption crimes, this tends to be widely reported and discussed in the domestic media.[75] The law stipulates shooting and lethal injection as the two permitted methods of execution.[76]

From the perspective of the official Government position, as well as what might be regarded as the academic mainstream, several arguments are used to defend the continued use of the death penalty in China. There is, first, an appeal to a longstanding cultural preference for retribution. The Chinese tradition, according to these arguments, is one of 'repaying a life with a life' (*sha ren chang ming*) – and there is strong popular support – indeed, even demand – for the death penalty.[77]

These arguments are of limited force. As Bakken has pointed out, the claim that Chinese culture is historically committed to the death penalty is empirically tenuous: China is the first country known to have officially abolished it for a period of seventeen years during the Tang Dynasty, and it has a long tradition of emphasizing leniency in criminal justice.[78] As for popular support, one needs to understand that, prior to abolition, there was majority support for retention in numerous other countries, including, for example, France. Current support for the death penalty in China is at ca. 58%, according to survey evidence; there is marked opposition to the imposition of the death penalty for nonviolent crimes.[79] Survey evidence also suggests that educated elites are, on the whole, more supportive of the death penalty even if it leads to executions of the innocent than the less educated, a finding that calls into question the oft-repeated claim that it is the masses of ordinary people in China who most want to retain the death penalty, because it is a practice deeply entrenched in Chinese culture.[80] Bakken points out that socio-political elites and, in particular, the legal establishment, have tended to show stronger pre-abolition support for the death penalty in other countries as well, and that it makes sense for those classes most likely to be affected by its iniquities to be opposed to the death penalty.[81] Most importantly, of course, cultural difference does not constitute an argument for moral relativism.[82] The arguments advanced by Bentham and Beccaria *inter alia* remain forceful, and they have influenced the Chinese debate about the death penalty, at least within scholarship.[83]

The Government generally claims that China has conformed to international law requirements by framing official discourse as a matter of gradual abolition, including the reduction of crimes carrying the death penalty, ruling out the death penalty for minors and the mentally impaired. Its official death penalty policy is dubbed 'killing fewer, killing cautiously' (*shao sha shen sha*). The Party-State claims to have implemented this policy not only by gradually reducing the number of crimes carrying the death penalty. It has also used a punishment option called 'death penalty with two years' reprieve'. It means that nominally, a decision on execution is deferred, and in practice it often results in commutation of the death penalty to life imprisonment.[84] Also, the power to conduct 'death penalty review' was in 2007 resumed by the Supreme People's Court. In China's two-instance system, this means that a further opportunity for challenges and scrutiny is provided. This was done in the declared expectation that it would lead to a reduction of uses of the death penalty and fewer executions of the innocent.[85] Sure enough, in September 2016, academics reportedly claimed that the number of executions had decreased from over ten thousand a year to 'a few thousand', representing a percentage decrease of some 60%.[86]

However, there are many problems with this statement as well. For a start, the number of death penalty sentences and executions is an officially designated absolute state secret (*juemi*), its disclosure triggering criminal liability.[87] Thus, the Government's or the establishment's occasional claims of having reduced the number of executions by a particular percentage cannot be verified because no accurate absolute figures are available; and, indeed, it is not even possible to ascertain if proper records are being kept. Whatever support there may be for the death penalty as such, the secrecy around its use does not have majority support. In the abovementioned survey, unsurprisingly, 'most people correctly state that they do not know the number of executions' and some 64% 'agreed that the government should publish the number of yearly executions'.[88]

Numbers would fail to capture the terrors and iniquities of the criminal process in death penalty cases. The aforementioned central flaws of the criminal justice process – including, in particular, torture – are replicated and compounded in these cases. The 'Leping' case is an example. The majority of death penalty cases involved serious violent crimes such as homicide, which means that officials of the criminal justice system are put under great pressure, under the maxim that 'capital cases must be solved' (ming'an bi po).[89] Reforms have not effectively addressed any of these issues. The NGO China Against Death Penalty pointed to numerous specific procedural flaws in the death penalty review process. It does not involve a hearing, the judges concerned often opt to question the death row convict via video-conferencing, and criminal defence lawyers have little or no opportunity to present their evidence and arguments effectively.[90] In the well-documented case of Fan Qihang, for example, criminal defence lawyers obtained videographic evidence of the defendant's torture – his oral statement and pictures of the deep scars torture had left on his wrists – and sent it to the Supreme People's Court; but they did not hear back. After some two or three weeks, they went public with the information and organized an open-letter campaign. The UN Special Rapporteur on Arbitrary and Summary Executions also sent a letter to the Chinese government.[91] None of these efforts had any effect, and Fan was executed within a few weeks of the initiation of the 'death penalty review' process.[92]

In the survey quoted earlier, 58.9% agreed and only 16.7% disagreed with the statement the current judicial system cannot make sure that the death penalty is applied fairly to different social classes or geographical regions.'[93] This response indicates a wide sense that the marginalized and vulnerable communities (ruoshi qunti) in Chinese society are disproportionately affected by the death penalty (as is also the case in other societies). This circumstance is somewhat related to the practice of settling for minor punishments in cases where the defendant or their family are able to pay compensation to the victim or their family, or where influence is used in other ways to achieve a settlement. While the procedure of 'criminal reconciliation' is not in fact available, similar methods are used in these cases.[94] They can trigger considerable public discussion. As Rosenzweig has pointed out, public opinion can affect these cases in diametrically opposed ways, depending on how the perpetrator is perceived. Although the Supreme People's Court has practised a policy of heeding 'popular opinion' in death penalty sentences, public opinion in favour of leniency is, however, at times ignored. For example, when a harassed street vendor killed two *chengguan* [municipal management officers], there were public pleas on his behalf. Yet his defence that two officials had violently attacked him was suppressed at his trial hearing, according to his defence lawyer, Teng Biao. Consequently, he was executed.[95]

A final aspect, one which Government official defences of the death penalty and officially tolerated debate about death penalty reform rarely address, is the widely understood practice of using executed prisoners' organs for organ transplant purposes. While the apparent practice was to ask death row prisoners to 'consent', it is evident that such 'consent' would have no ethical value.[96] In 2014, the Government announced that it would end this practice, implicitly acknowledging its existence until then.[97] However, a year later it introduced regulations allowing Chinese citizens to register for organ donation, and it is thought that this meant Chinese death row prisoners would be 'simply reclassified' as citizens for the purposes of organ transplants.[98] In the context of organ transplants, it has been claimed for a long time that the authorities murder members of certain target groups, in particular Falun Gong,[99] in order to obtain their organs, and that such extrajudicial killings are carried out in systematic – genocidal – fashion. Those advancing this view have been struggling to compile compelling and conclusive evidence. They mainly point to the unexplained origins of organs for an assumed high number of transplants.[100] However, as the then Special Rapporteur on Torture has pointed out, the Government has not helped to dispel the fear that such reports might be true either.[101]

Summing up his experience with the death penalty, Teng Biao, the scholar and criminal defence lawyer for the executed street vendor Xia Junfeng and director of the group 'China Against the Death Penalty' commented: '[t]otalitarian and post-totalitarian politics need the death penalty, the way they need enemies'.[102]

CONCLUSION

For a long time, during the Reform and Opening Era, there was confidence that both arbitrary detention and torture were issues to be gradually eradicated. The aforementioned efforts to reduce the use of the death penalty appeared to complement this trend. The discussion in this chapter casts doubt on axiomatic expectations of improvement of reform, however. First, the system finds it difficult to accept and respect the limitations it has clearly imposed upon itself. Partly due to the criminality of some of these abuses discussed here in terms of the domestic legal system, many rights violations occur in conditions of 'black box' obscurity, inscrutability and uncertainty; and maintaining intransigence itself leads to further rights violations, as the 'Jiansanjiang Incident' illustrated. Yet the authorities claim to be operating under the rule of law, and new forms of limitations of liberty, such as 'residential surveillance in a designated location,' also known as 'non-residential residential surveillance',[103] indicate that the system is becoming 'smarter', especially in restricting personal liberty and creating settings in which torture is likely to occur.

Second, the discussion of detention systems, torture and the death penalty reminds us of the connection between the freedom of the mind and the freedom of the person – that one is easily diminished when you do not have the other. As seen here, the connection between these freedoms is negatively reflected in some of the practices discussed. Often, albeit not always, people who are locked up – whose freedom of the person is restricted by the Party-State – are told that this is for their own good, to educate and form their minds so as to make them better persons. In this, the practices of detention, torture and the death penalty affirm a connection between such rights' violations and the authoritarian principle of Party-Statehood.

4 | Expression and Thought ————

Visitors to urban China today will find it a vibrant, colourful, cacophonous and in many ways diverse place, very different from the Mao era with its uniformity and its tightly controlled public expression through newspapers, placards and loudspeakers blaring out propaganda messages. Public expression today includes the self-expression of consumers and commercial advertising; art galleries, cinemas and performances; newspapers and magazines and a large variety of news websites servicing different ages and interests; bookshops offering a wide choice of works including international literature in Chinese translation; and university campuses that offer an impressive range of academic activities, events and exchange programmes, prompting a foreign academic visitor to say that Chinese university campuses are 'freer' than US ones.[1] One will see propaganda slogans, to be sure; but these usually compete for attention with adverts and other commercial displays. There is so much expression: it is so widely available, it has so many different authors, and it so easily transcends – or blurs – the boundary from private to public. Via social media, for instance, it is possible to post to a potentially unlimited internet audience through the Chinese version of Twitter, *Weibo*, as well as to chat-groups including up to several hundred participants, via *Weixin*, Telegram, Whatsapp, and so on. In a way, expression is also remarkably cheap – it is within almost everybody's reach or, as the legal sociologist Yu Jianrong put it, nowadays 'everybody has a microphone'[2] because nearly everyone has access to a mobile phone and can use social media to express themselves publicly.[3] In all these respects, the difference compared to the Mao era could hardly be greater.

Given this apparent wealth of public, diverse and sophisticated expression, why is it that Freedom House and other organizations consistently give China bad – and, as of 2016, worsening – marks on the freedom of the press and the internet?[4] What is amiss in China's expression landscape is far less easily noticeable than it used to be, because repression has become smarter. Understanding how, when and why expression is curbed requires a study not only of the institutions and principles, but also of the mechanisms and technologies of censorship, communication control, and communicative practices of the Party-State.[5] What emerges from the – necessarily broad-stroke – discussion here is that crucial changes, both in terms of freer exercise and of tighter control of expression, have occurred at the level of technology, and that the past few years have in many ways been retrogressive. As the challenges posed by expression became gradually more acute in the post-Mao reform era, they led to a rejection of what the authorities now termed 'so-called "universal values" '; and a return to stronger but, compared to the Mao era, emptier endorsements of what is described as a principle of Party-State tutelage below ensued. As the authorities realized they could no longer control expression, they reverted to more intensely 'guiding' thought – or at least they tried to.

To make this argument, the discussion in the following begins by juxtaposing the constitutional and international law guarantees of freedom of expression and its cognate rights of association, assembly, freedom of religion and conscience, with the principle of Party-Statehood, and practices of censorship, criminalization and bureaucratic-technical control. It then moves on to the topic of freedom of thought and its curtailment through classic propaganda, public opinion guidance, and what is referred to as 'thought work' in bureaucratic jargon.

THE LIMITS OF THE RIGHT
OF FREE EXPRESSION

When, in 2008, drafters of an online appeal known as Charter '08 called for better protection of freedom of expression, they consciously drew on a century-old liberal Chinese tradition of asserting this and other fundamental rights, even though 'institutional Confucian' doctrine could be read to reject freedom of expression.[6] In 1908, Kang Youwei's draft Constitution had promised that 'the subject shall be granted freedom to express himself through the spoken and written word and in publications, and to assemble and associate, within the limits of the law'.[7]

A hundred years have passed since the writing of China's first constitution. 2008 also marks the sixtieth anniversary of the promulgation of the Universal Declaration of Human Rights,[8] the thirtieth anniversary of the appearance of the Democracy Wall in Beijing, and the tenth of China's signing of the International Covenant on Civil and Political Rights.[9] We are approaching the twentieth anniversary of the 1989 Tiananmen massacre of pro-democracy student protesters.[10]

The Charter calls, *inter alia*, for 'freedom of speech, freedom of the press, and academic freedom', a Press Law, the abolition of the crime of incitement to subvert state power, and more widely, the practice of 'treating words as crimes'; and it states that to achieve a better protection of human rights, profound constitutional reform is necessary.[11]

Guarantees of the rights of freedom of thought and free expression can, of course, already be found in the current Constitution, which states that 'Citizens of the People's Republic of China enjoy freedom of speech, of the press, of assembly, of association, of procession and of demonstration.'[12] In providing these guarantees, the current Constitution seems to conform to the standards set by international law – in particular, Articles 18 and 19 of the Universal Declaration of

Human Rights (UDHR), Articles 18 and 19 of the International Covenant on Civil and Political Rights (ICCPR), which China signed but has not ratified. It was problems at several levels that prompted Charter 08's call for constitutional reform.

The first problem is at the level of constitutional text. As noted in chapter 2, the Constitution also provides that, *inter alia*, citizens 'in exercising their freedoms and rights, may not infringe upon the interests of the State, of society or of the collective, or upon the lawful freedoms and rights of other citizens.' It confers a duty – especially problematic for expression rights – on citizens 'to safeguard the security, honour and interests of the motherland' and not to commit 'acts detrimental to the security, honour and interests of the motherland'.[13] Public international law does not accommodate such sweeping duties restricting the exercise of speech rights. While the ICCPR does provide that, under Article 19(3), countries may impose certain restrictions or limitations on freedom of expression if such restrictions are provided by law and are necessary for the purpose of respecting the 'rights or reputations of others' or protecting national security, public order, public health or morals, not all restrictions are compatible with these standards.[14] As the UN Human Rights Council clarified in 2009, restrictions of 'discussion of government policies and political debate', of 'peaceful demonstrations or political activities, including for peace or democracy' and of 'expression of opinion and dissent' are inconsistent with Article 19(3) of the ICCPR.[15] Political dissenters cannot be stripped of their right to express themselves; and even less can they be categorized as enemies – whereas the constitutional principle of People's Democratic Dictatorship, discussed in chapter 2, clashes with the notion, so central to freedom of speech, that freedom of speech must include the right to criticize political power-holders.

Another problem is structural; it can only be understood when looking beyond the Constitution to statutory laws and further regulations, as well as to the kinds of 'normative documents' mentioned in chapter 2.[16] Personal liberty rights, it was noted, can only be limited on the basis of a law, as the 2000 Litigation Law confirmed, and at least some of the laws dealing with detention seem to accept this implicit limitation: they provide criteria for detention, set limits on deprivations of liberty, define and thereby restrict the conditions under which the State may kill, and prohibit and criminalize torture. The language of some of these laws is clearly devoted to liberal goals, such as ensuring access to counsel and the right not to self-incriminate. There is also some implicit recognition of the need to minimize invasiveness, especially in criminal justice contexts. It was observed that these laws are systematically ignored and undermined by the Party-State authorities, resulting in a multitude of unlawful detention practices, systematic uses of torture and numerous grave concerns regarding the application of the death penalty. Yet, the existence of these laws at least gives lawyers a basis to argue from when defending the rights of their clients.

By contrast, the freedom of expression and cognate rights and freedoms – the freedom of speech, of thought, of conscience and religion, of art and academic endeavour and so on – are barely reflected at all in the language of laws and regulations ranking below the Constitution. One might, for instance, expect some iteration of the principle of freedom of speech and the press in a Press Law. But, there is no Press Law (yet).[17] There are only numerous laws and regulations, some of them contained in the Criminal Law, touching on the freedom of the media and of expression more widely.[18] Since the Constitution itself is thought not to be justiciable,[19] this means that lawyers have little to go on when defending these rights. They tend to invoke just the Constitution's Articles 35 and/or 36[20] and to make reference to international law instruments.[21] In doing so, they know that they are invoking excellent principles, but also that, no matter how eloquent they or their clients are, they are almost certain to be ignored.

Lastly, there is the problem of all the many counter-norms that guide actual government practices restrictive of expression. These go much further than the principles and rules in the PRC Constitution that are in tension with free speech. Official news, Party documents, and – to a lesser degree – laws and regulations contain numerous affirmations of norms and beliefs that assume a general mandate of the Party-State to ensure 'correct' political thinking. It assumes implicitly that expression can be curbed accordingly, without acknowledging any inherent limitations of this right – indeed, as discussed later on in this chapter, the rhetoric on the Party's opinion-guidance mandate has been stepped up in recent years. The Party-State casts itself as the custodian of public expression, as well as political thought, and operates on a principle of authoritarian tutelage.

CENSORSHIP AND CRIMES OF EXPRESSION

While much censorship takes the form of control through prior restraint and technologies of blocking and deleting online content, the best clues on what is legally proscribed content comes from the *ex post* rules of censorship, in particular, from criminal law. Criminal law rules by which the system restricts the freedom of thought, conscience and expression include public order crimes such as 'creating a disturbance',[22] state secrets crimes,[23] the crimes of subversion and inciting subversion,[24] the crime of defamation[25] and of obscenity.[26] Chinese criminal law also targets religion through the 'crime' of 'abusing an evil cult to undermine implementation of the law',[27] as well as assembly and association, for example, through the crime of 'illegal assembly'.[28] Like in other jurisdictions, the authorities also make use of defamation law, which can trigger criminal, as well as civil liability in China, to go after critics of individual officials;[29] and despite some encouraging case law, there is no in-principle recognition of a doctrine allowing for wider criticism of 'public figures'.[30] All of the aforementioned rules are broadly worded; and it is difficult to discern a coherent approach in their application through the criminal process.

To give an example, take the prosecution of Liu Xiaobo, detained in 2008 for his contribution to Charter 08, the aforementioned manifesto calling for reform of the Chinese Constitution and for an end to one-party rule. Charter 08 was initially signed by some 350 Chinese intellectuals, lawyers and other citizens. But, while many of them suffered other reprisals, only Liu Xiaobo was convicted and sent to prison for this. Numerous commentators pointed out that, if there was a reason for selecting Liu Xiaobo, it could not have been his actual contribution to the Charter, as he was not one of the main drafters, but merely one among hundreds of core supporters.[31] Indeed, hundreds of these signed a public 'Statement of shared responsibility' (which the authorities tried to suppress).[32] If there was anything that could explain singling out Liu Xiaobo in preference to the Charter's main drafters, it was his relative fame as a public intellectual and writer with a notorious past as a dissident prominently involved in the June Fourth protest. Perhaps this status made him a convenient tool to signal the Charter's subversive nature from the perspective of the Party-State.[33] So, Liu Xiaobo was convicted of the crime of inciting subversion.[34] As his case was deemed to be serious, he was sentenced to fixed-term imprisonment of eleven years. Tragically, Liu was not to survive prison. He died on 13 July 2017 of a cancer of the liver that had been left untreated for too long, having been denied permission to leave China with his wife. His wife Liu Xia is forcibly disappeared as of this writing.[35]

The selection of Liu Xiaobo was typical of contemporary practices with regard to speech crimes. According to the human rights advocate and scholar Teng Biao, the authorities lack the capacity to pursue criminal liability for subversion crimes with consistency.[36] The rules themselves are not constructed to delineate zones of transgression, but rather, as Teng puts it, to provide a basis for arbitrary 'enforcement'. Seen that way, singling out Liu Xiaobo allowed the authorities to signal effectively that any other supporter might be similarly targeted if the authorities deemed it useful. Teng Biao argues, further, that the Party-State's wording of the 'subversion' provision is even more sweeping than in the Mao and immediate post-Mao era, when the crime of choice was that of counterrevolution, just because the definition of subversion has essentially been stripped of definite, specific political content. It now punishes 'whoever incites others, by spreading rumours or slanders or any other means, to subvert the State power or overthrow the socialist system.' While it remains committed to maintaining its own authority, it would be hard to claim that the Party-State today was still clearly committed to coherent socialist principles.[37]

During the 1990s and early 2000s, an era dominated by tropes of reform and transition, the extreme openness and opacity of the statute, combined with the closedness of the legal process, allowed the Party-State to use 'subversion' crimes as a flexible tool. It allowed the authorities to claim that they complied with rule of law maxims, while seeking to minimize the visibility of its human rights violations, thereby reducing the political costs of using it. For example, the trial of Liu Xiaobo was conducted after he had unlawfully been held incommunicado for a considerable length of time, in a half-closed fashion, ignoring or suppressing[38] the substantive arguments of the defence – which, of course, emphasized that Article 105 itself, or at least its use in this particular instance, represented a violation of the freedom of speech.[39] The verdict stated blandly that the speech for whose exercise Liu was punished was 'outside the domain of free speech', without specifying any reasons for this assessment. Only outside this legal process were some two or three law professors wheeled out to provide justifications in the news media. Pointing to the criminalization of hate speech and 'holocaust denial' in Europe, and to now-repudiated criminal prosecutions of perceived enemies in wartime in the US, they argued that after all, all countries restricted speech *to some degree*, without engaging with the centrality of political criticism at all. They also claimed, without any attempt to address the public criticisms of the legal process, that Liu's trial had been fair and lawful.[40]

Ultimately, the curious weakness of these defences of the conviction was related not only to the fragility of China's criminal process, but also to the emptiness of the crime Li was convicted of, which was in turn related to the near-randomness of political doctrines of the day. Teng Biao commented, with some bitterness, in 2011, shortly before he was to face accusations of 'inciting subversion' himself:

> [W]hether it is 'Three Represents'[41] or 'Harmonious Society'[42] or 'Scientific Development',[43] none of these slogans can command genuine respect. In fact, not only do the people show zero enthusiasm for the slogans of the government, but even government and party officials have stopped believing in these rigid dogmata…The Communist Party has…become a for-profit group lacking in self-confidence; it is an organization for mutual benefit endowed with special powers; and it no longer has anything to do with ideological attitudes.[44]

Between 2010 and 2013, dissidents of the 'Jasmine' protests, 'New Citizen Movement' and 'Southern Street Movement', such as Xu Zhiyong, Guo Feixiong and Tang Jingling, continued citizen protest initiatives. To a degree of greater sophistication than the initiators of the 'Charter 08' campaign, their independent and oppositional public discussion of rights-based complaints and demands made use of online and social media platforms. They, too, were prosecuted and convicted.[45]

The use of social media by these activists prompted the authorities to amend criminal law rules to punish the posting of rumours if it received 500 or more reposts or 5,000 or more viewings.[46] Yet attempts to prosecute on these grounds could backfire, as in the case of the criminal detention on suspicion of rumour-spreading of a sixteen-year-old boy named Yang Hui, who had posted messages expressing his suspicion of police involvement in the cover-up of a local crime.[47] His case triggered a storm of largely hostile public commentary, and the boy was released after a few days – a rare victory for human rights lawyers.[48] Perhaps even more importantly, when we consider the possible effects of online expression, it is virtually inconceivable that every 'netizen' who might be held liable for 'spreading online rumours' in this way would in fact be held so liable. If the selection of Liu Xiaobo out of hundreds of initial contributors and signatories seemed random, a person posting content similar to that posted by Yang Hui must be working at a far lower risk, at least so far as the risk of encountering the criminal justice system was concerned.

In the two cases, one protagonist was punished and awarded the Nobel Peace Prize, while the other went free: one became a world-renowned symbol of the struggle for free speech in China, while the other sank back into near oblivion (and perhaps some level of normalcy). Yet their experiences reveal important similarities. The experience of the Liu Xiaobo and Yang Hui cases suggests that the practice of free speech – the assertion of the right to free speech, implicitly[49] or, in the case of Charter 08, explicitly – has normative significance because it reminds the Party-State of obligations that it has, and that it has recognized, albeit only in fragmentary, incomplete and incoherent ways. Collectively, through their exercise of speech rights, Liu Xiaobo, Yang Hui and many other Chinese citizens engaging in comparable forms of expression put pressure on a Party-State unwilling to be reminded of its promises. They expose, albeit at great cost to themselves, the arbitrariness of the enforcement of speech crime liability. They thereby also invite the public to think critically of extant rules and principles of censorship and speech criminalization.

In sum, the legal rules of censorship and their implementation are significant tools of Party-State censorship. But they are barely operable rules. The criminalization of expression is constantly challenged by the availability of forceful and straightforward legal arguments to deny censorship legitimacy. Further rules and norms that aim at 'regulation' of expression do not help much to clarify what content is meant to be off-bounds, either. 'Regulation' would suggest the use of public rules expressing standards of rightness that could be rationally understood, and that could ensure coherence and predictability in the way the rules are enforced. The control system in place does not satisfy this standard. If there is a logic to this system, it is the logic, in Perry Link's famous image, of 'the anaconda in the chandelier'[50] – a logic of latent violence and intimidation. Even though this system evidently results in shutting down some critics, such as Liu Xiaobo, and although we have hard-to-quantify knowledge of its intimidating effects leading to self-censorship, a system trying to rely on such fragmented and weakly enforced rules would have to consider its efforts as partly failed. It is therefore not surprising that the Party-State relies on other tools of control, in addition to only selectively applied legal punishments for ill-defined rule infractions. It is a principle of more selective and 'smarter' control of speech that most clearly distinguishes the current from the Mao era, and it is to smart control that we turn in the following section.

'SMART' TECHNOLOGIES OF EXPRESSION VS 'SMART' CONTROL TECHNOLOGIES

The technical conditions of expression and its repression have changed in dramatic ways. This could hardly have been foreseen when, in the early 1980s, the Party-State renewed its promise of free speech in the 1982 Constitution. At that time, the print media was the main forum of political communication. It was firmly controlled by the authorities, as well as non-commercial. Today, by contrast, the media, print media included, operates at least in part on commercial principles. Large media companies with numerous outlets, such as the power Southern Metropolitan group, produce newspapers, magazines and so on, that need to sell; and this need to sell has, of course, translated into efforts to produce copies of interest to readers.

It is impossible to understand the Sun Zhigang Incident, mentioned in chapters 2 and 3, for example, without the public's attention triggered by investigative journalism from reporters at *Beijing Evening News* and *Southern Weekend*. The fact that, in the wake of Reform and Opening, these media companies operated in a commercial way did not mean a complete liberation from control, however: *Ex post* censorship rules such as the criminalization of 'inciting subversion' apply to media companies; and, even today, censorship can take the crude and cumbersome form of cutting pages out of books, as exemplified by the systematic removal of a page with an entry on 'Taiwan' from copies of the Merriam-Webster English dictionary sold in China.[51] There is also (and more importantly) a wide network of prior restraint rules and practices,[52] implemented in part by ownership structures, administrative control and financial constraints and temptations. An example of the economic dynamics this creates is what has been dubbed 'red envelope journalism', i.e. 'reporting' in exchange for money.[53] This practice can make dedicated journalists vulnerable by exposing them to the risk of false accusations of extortion. Scholars such as Bandurski and Hala, Saether and Svensson have explained how print producers of media content found ways of getting around the institutionalized controls.[54] One form of circumvention, for example, consists of reporting on what happens in regions outside the control of one's supervising government authority – Beijing newspapers can report on issues possibly implicating Guangdong government officials and vice versa without risking direct interference.[55]

Changes in communication technology have been no less radical than commercialization. Introduced in China in the 1990s, internet use became more widespread throughout the 2000s. Mobile phones were introduced around the same time. When smart phones became available, the availability of communication technology exploded, with the introduction of Chinese microblog (*weibo*) fora and of social media applications, such as WeChat, adding to the variety of communication channels, leading to an almost complete permeation of Chinese society by such communication technologies as of early 2016. It is against this background that scholars have written about China's 'embryonic' or 'emerging' public sphere.[56]

So far as the exercise of expression rights is concerned, the cases of Liu Xiaobo and Yang Hui already illustrate the most salient effect of these changes: the theoretically unlimited multiplication of authors, and – with important qualifications explained later – the possibility of communicating to a theoretically unlimited audience. This has led to the emergence of 'citizen journalism', as a form of non-professional (and possibly not paid for) reporting by persons who do something else for a living. Due to the rules and practices of prior restraint, a considerable contribution to this field of journalism comes from professional journalists who are unable to disseminate their riskier pieces via the media that employ them, and may decide to forego payment.[57] The government every now and then creates rules ordaining, for example, registration requirements for users and providers of related services, or prohibiting online news reporting (thus going after the providers rather than the consumers of such reporting).[58] Yet it is doubtful how effective these measures have been so far. Despite restrictions, social media use at this point continues to flourish, and *zi meiti* or 'self-media' received a further boost through the introduction of online mechanisms whereby audiences can award compensation to posters.[59]

Communication via the internet and mobile networks thus also changed the conditions of censorship and wide control of public expression and private communication. In important respects, technology-based control has virtually replaced rule-based regulation and censorship.[60] While the institutions and technologies are far too vast and complex for a comprehensive account here, some examples illustrate this apparent trend. First, there is the institution of the Great Firewall of China (GFW) and the technology of targeted deletion of online content.[61] Rather than *prohibiting* certain online content, the Great Firewall *blocks* access to foreign websites in a way that makes is harder, if not impossible, for Chinese users to access them. It also barely bothers to tell would-be viewers of such off-bounds content why they cannot access it. Examples include the blocking of English-language newspapers following critical reports about the Chinese government or individual officials and their families,[62] as well as Google and its affiliated websites, blocked after Google decided not to continue collaborating with the authorities in censoring searchable content. In both contexts, foreign actors have to make choices affected by censorship.[63]

Whereas some sites are subject to a blanket ban, in other cases, content deemed impermissible is *deleted* after being posted – sometimes so fast that it renders the difference between *ex post* censorship and prior restraint empirically difficult, other times only after users have been able to repost the item in question. A standard notice given, for example, on a micro-blog post by Professor Yu Yingshi titled 'The Communists are not Confucians' (or, in the Chinese original, 'Mainland invoking Confucianism is Confucianism's Kiss of Death') states, baldly:

> This content has been reported multiple times by users. The related content cannot be viewed.[64]

Thus there is no engagement with the lawfulness or otherwise of the content expressed at all, beyond a hint that the anonymous complainers *may* have had good reason to complain. The content is merely rendered inaccessible.

Second, in order to avoid disruption of their work, business operations or research, email communications and so on, those who know how and (in the case of commercial options) can afford it, may choose to use circumvention technology, including, most importantly, the so-called virtual private networks or VPNs,[65] which channel users outside the Chinese internet to access via another country. Once they have 'scaled the Great Firewall' (*fanqiang*), they can also make use of social media tools such as Facebook and Twitter, which remain banned inside the GFW. Again, as in the case of internet blocks, VPNs are designed to circumvent. The authorities have not indicated clearly if VPNs are illegal,[66] and as of June 2016, there is a non-binding draft UN

Resolution that 'condemns unequivocally measures to intentionally prevent or disrupt access to or dissemination of information online in violation of international human rights law and calls on all States to refrain from and cease such measures.'[67] While there are many stories of repressive reactions to internet postings, there is little indication that the authorities seek to impose legal sanctions or retaliate against infracting any web access prohibitions as such. Indeed, on occasion, senior Chinese officials in the sprawling censorship apparatus have publicly used VPN tools themselves.[68] Nevertheless, 'VPN crackdowns' have become more common in the Xi Jinping era; they have consisted of technologically disrupting or destroying the viability of the software provided and updated as a commercial service.[69]

In sum, if we try to measure it according to the wealth of technological measures being implemented to block or otherwise restrict internet use for free communication, and the resources apparently devoted to this goal, the Party-State's control of the internet is impressive. The Party-State asserts its mandate to control; and it engages in control activity that can at times seem almost frenzied. Yet, it is hard to assess the effects of all this control activity on what is its apparent ultimate target: people's minds. This may in part be due to the fact that the Party-State rarely claims to have a specific legal basis for its pervasive attempts to limit expression; that it has not even, so far, created comprehensive statutory (NPC) laws that might begin to tell us what the basis for restrictions in major areas such as the print media might be, or that might indicate the boundaries of its power to curb expression. The authorities have also failed to engage in substance with the human-rights-based argument, made prominently by the UN Human Rights Council of which China is a member, to the effect that intentional prevention and disruption of internet access can violate the human rights standards China has committed to by signing the ICCPR.[70]

It is perhaps not clear, then, how these technological successes relate to curbing *freedom*, or indeed if freedom or lack of freedom can be measured at all, although organizations like Freedom House do provide certain measures and give China extremely bad ratings.[71] Even though there is empirically no doubt that the blocks 'work' in a technical sense, the society affected by them still seems to have expectations of a right to free speech that is characteristic of liberal-democratic societies. Even as they face blocks and risks of 'legal' sanction, many keep exercising their free speech rights, offline and especially online. The occasional flare-up of public opinion in favour of a free speech campaigner, illustrated by the Yang Hui case, suggests that irritation with restrictions is latent.[72] Neither criminalization and regulation, nor technology-based control appear to have inculcated genuine social acceptance of these curbs. Perhaps this is why the Party-State is now reverting to targeting 'hearts and minds'; why it has begun to focus more on an attempt to limit the freedom of thought.

'PUBLIC OPINION GUIDANCE', 'THOUGHT WORK' AND 'SOCIAL CREDIT' GOVERNANCE

'The Party's media must bear the Party's surname',[73] General Secretary Xi Jinping declared in February 2016 during a visit to the three major Party-State media outlets: People's Daily, Xinhua News Agency and China Central Television. Bearing the Party's surname – belonging to the Party Family – meant, he elaborated, holding firm to the principle of Party Spirit (*dangxing*) and propagating the Party's theories, line, principles and policies in such a way that 'the People's masses will spontaneously put them into action'.[74] His instruction to the media re-affirmed a Marxist-Maoist idea of inculcating correct political views, and eradicating incorrect views as a way of changing society – this is the principle of 'thought reform' (*sixiang gaizao*)[75] that has long been part of the official approach to the media. It reaffirmed this approach, as well as 'Party Spirit', meaning 'loving the Party, defending the Party and acting for the Party'. Together, these messages signalled that the leadership meant to put a stop to believing in the kind of Party-independent media work that had enabled the rise of investigative journalism and more diversified commentary.[76]

The previous two sections argued that the rules of *ex post* censorship, practices of prior restraint and control and limitation of online content could not succeed fully in diminishing an expectation of freedom. These rules and practices were not fully effective in diminishing the consciousness of a right to free speech, a right asserted through exercise, even when such exercise was constantly curbed and in peril. It is against this background that we should try to understand the resurgence of 'public opinion guidance' and 'thought work', as well as the emergence of 'social credit' governance and similar tools and systems in the Xi Jinping era.

As Bandurski has shown, a Party mandate to 'supervise', 'guide' and 'channel' public opinion was articulated already at earlier stages of the post-Mao reform era.[77] The use of the Party-State-controlled mass media to generate messages steering public opinion and dispelling sources of discontent has also been a traditional tool of the authorities. In the post-Mao era, it included reporting mass grievances such as labour disputes sympathetically, identifying with workers and encouraging the use of the law, while at the same time 'omit[ting] problems associated with implementation of the law', and overall supporting the view that the system was working.[78] The doctrines and techniques for guiding opinion needed to be refined with the rise of the internet from the late 1990s. Rather than merely deleting content or punishing dissidents, the Party-State makes use of messages that appear to be coming from disparate sources, yet are produced at the behest of the authorities. The best-known symbol of this type of 'public opinion guidance' is the role of the so-called fifty-center (*wumaodang*), that is, a person hired to participate in online discussions. Their name derives from the fifty cents they were once thought to be paid per online intervention. In 2012, the artist-activist Ai Weiwei published an anonymous interview with a fifty-center, who told him:

Usually after an event has happened, or even before the news has come out, we'll receive an email telling us what the event is, then instructions on which direction to guide the netizens' thoughts, to blur their focus,[79] or to fan their enthusiasm for certain ideas... This requires a lot of skill. You can't write in a very official manner, you must conceal your identity, write articles in many different styles, sometimes even have a dialogue with yourself, argue, debate. In sum, you want to create illusions to attract the attention and comments of netizens.[80]

'Guidance' efforts have been strengthened and given a more clearly anti-liberal direction under Xi Jinping.[81] In 2013, addressing universities, the Party issued an official document renouncing 'so-called universal values' including 'western democracy and human rights', and announcing an ideological re-orientation.[82] In 2014, Xi Jinping delivered a speech on the role of the arts, claiming that they must serve the Party and criticizing 'some artists' for 'ridiculing what is noble, distorting the classics, subverting history and smearing the masses and heroes', as well as failing to 'tell right from wrong, distinguishing between good and evil', and 'present ugliness as beauty and exaggerating society's dark side'.[83] His 2016 speech on 'bearing the Party surname' was reissued a year later, in an apparent attempt to canonize its message.

Campaigns inspired by this rhetoric have featured clearly contrasting accounts of heroes – such as Party members working for the greater good – and enemies – such as 'foreign enemy forces' and internal enemies of the state, including human rights defenders and seditionists in border regions.[84] For example, a slick propaganda video titled 'Who Am I?' depicts a number of ordinary people – street cleaners, doctors, teachers, fishermen – in situations of model selflessness and dedication to their work, and says:

Who am I? Maybe you have never thought about it. I am the one who leaves last. I am the one who comes into work first. I am the one who thinks least of myself. I am the one who insists on following the rules to the end. I am the quickest to act. I am the one most concerned about others. I am the Chinese Communist Party, and I will be with you from the beginning to the end.[85]

The message here seems to draw directly on the self-image of the Communist Party created by the Communist Party Charter, which requires members to be selfless and exemplary.[86] If, like a commercial or competitive political campaign ad, it were competing with other such messages, it might seem innocuous. Considering the Party's paramount status and vast powers, the line 'I will be with you from beginning to end' can read rather Orwellian.[87]

Another video titled *Color Revolution* displays a number of external and internal enemies. It depicts scenes from various US-led wars around the globe and miserable refugees arriving in Europe, as well as Chinese human rights defenders, who were later swept up in the '7-09 Crackdown',[88] holding a small demonstration demanding access to their clients. The video-clip depicts a real occurrence, but the banner the activists had unfurled is twisted, their message illegible.[89] It is not the message the Party wants to show. What they want viewers to see is evidence of unruliness, disorder and threats to stability. The Party, in this video, is cast not so much as a selflessly caring everyday presence. Rather, it appears as the one force that can protect people's comfortable everyday lives from the enemies lurking without and within. Romanticizing political power, it also reassures viewers that the Party will keep them safe:

China now is peaceful and stable. Most people live a simple life, but they are happy. Yet even with increasingly powerful armament in the motherland, the clouds of domestic troubles and foreign dangers have never disappeared from China's skies...[they] present a constant danger to security on China's borders and harm the national interest. The

Tibetan, Xinjiang, Hong Kong, and Taiwan independence movements, as well as dissident leaders, diehard lawyers and other agents of western forces: they are destroying China's domestic stability and harmony with all possible means. Behind all these incidents, we can often see the shadows of the stars and stripes. In fact, year after year, the western forces, led by the US, under the banner of democracy, freedom and rule of law, create social contradictions in targeted countries with the intention to overthrow governments. Their slogans are loud, their lies are beautiful; but they will not become facts.[90]

Can these attempts to propagate the Party's image, and to streamline and unify public media messages succeed? On the one hand, it seems doubtful that those working in the media and 'self-media' will be so easily swayed. Some, indeed, made this clear very promptly. For example, following Xi Jinping's February 2016 media tour, one senior editor decided to quit the Southern Metropolitan news group because, as he put it on his resignation form, there was 'no way I can take your surname'.[91] His lone act of recalcitrance reminded the authorities of their failure to achieve comprehensive subordination. On the other hand, less critical-minded recipients of their messages might be more easily persuaded, or at least decide not to oppose the message to avoid being viewed as an 'enemy' themselves.

Slick or old-fashioned in style, official or fake-'popular' in origin, these 'opinion-guidance' activities are clearly based on the assumption that it is possible to steer the public's thinking.[92] In that, they bear remarkable similarities to the attitudes and approaches that character- ize PR and marketing activities in commercial contexts anywhere in the world. As in these contexts, and in some contrast to the more earnestly Marxist propaganda messages of the Mao era, they also have an air of 'post-truth' about them. The spreading of such messages is facilitated by social media technologies, also available in freer and more pluralistic systems, in which the use of algorithms supposedly ensures that recipients of such messages are targeted in maximally effective ways, according to observable preferences and previously expressed views.[93]

The special challenges to freedom of thought and expression associated with the centrality and comprehensive control of the Party are further illustrated by the Party-State's plans, as of 2016, to create what is described as a system of Social Credit Governance.[94] Functioning rather like a credit score check writ large, it would assemble vast amounts of information about each Chinese citizen in one database and compute one single score to assess their trustworthiness or 'social credit'. On the basis of their social credit score, the individual citizen might be eligible for being issued with a passport or not; they might or might not have a high enough score to get a loan, or to place their child in a good school, for example.[95] If introduced successfully, the Social Credit scheme would be able to merge existing systems of electronic surveillance of 'social stability maintenance' targets, such as dissidents and human rights defenders, with the system for keeping files (*dang'an*) on ordinary citizens, and become a surveillance state's unchecked dream tool to control the entire population. The regulation does not clearly specify what conduct would be considered as 'trust-breaking'. But the system could become a basis for punishing government criticism by deductions from the social credit score, and thus a dystopian prospect for freedom of thought and expression, as the population targeted by such total monitoring would be under constant pressure to self-censure.[96]

Another crucial difference is in the characteristic equivalence (from the perspective of the system) of persuasion, coercion and intimidation as means of 'guiding thought', a feature discussed in the previous chapter in the context of torture. 'Thought work' (*sixiang gongzuo*) captures a wide range of measures taken to work on someone's mind and get them to reform and rectify their 'thought'. Such measures might begin with calling their home to talk to them. However, they can also include detention and torture which, as discussed in chapter 3, are quite often associated with the idea of 'education'. The violence with which the Party-State can coerce citizens, if not to think 'correctly', then at least to profess that they do, is an important element in the control system considered in this chapter.

And yet, if thought, or at least reason, is inherently free,[97] it presents a constant challenge to the system, which needs to keep engendering fear to stop citizens from thinking for themselves. For instance, consider one of the torture victims quoted earlier, commenting on his experience of forced disappearance and torture:

> Not only did they want to make you say *that* black was white. You also had to explain *why* black was white.[98]

On the one hand, this account of 'thought reform' supported by torture could be described as 'post-truth' in the grimmest possible sense; and in some ways, the effects of such 'thought reform' can be further enhanced by the 'algorithms of fear'[99] – the spreading of fear through accounts in the new media. Yet, in narrating his experience, this interlocutor also exercised and affirmed a right of critical analysis and exposure that showed his resilience in the face of attempts to control them. A similar spirit – informed, sceptical, at times even rebellious – seems to drive much of the politically critical commentary we continue to be able to hear and read, despite the authorities' best efforts to 'guide thought'.

CONCLUSION

Rawls famously argued that a non-liberal system could be still decent without having freedom of speech, requiring only 'a sufficient measure of liberty of conscience to ensure freedom of religion and thought.'[100] The empirical evidence discussed in this chapter supports a sceptical assessment of this contention, primarily because the nexus between freedom of expression and freedom of thought and conscience, as well as religion, is too close for one to obtain without the other. China, at any rate, does not confirm the possibility of a decent system without freedom of speech. Its authoritarian system is not only unable to control expression without targeting thought. It is also relying on a principle of moral-political tutelage to support the idea of 'thought guidance' and inculcate 'correct' thought. In that, the limitations the system imposes on speech reflect an approach entirely different from any available justifications for limitations of freedom of speech, which must not attempt to control thought.[101] As chapter 6 explores further, the suppression of principled challenges to government decisions is also closely connected to the suppression of rights advocacy more widely.

5 Inequality and Socio-economic Rights

'China has lifted millions out of poverty'. This is the most common challenge to criticism of the Chinese government's human rights record typically heard in casual conversation. The government also tends to argue that it has improved the socio-economic rights situation, through policies that have raised the GDP and incomes, and by adding to the provision of public goods and services. For example, in its June 2016 report on the implementation of its Human Rights Action Plan, the State Council lists how many million people have been 'lifted out of poverty' – some 65 million over a period of five years, according to the State Council,[1] as their incomes have been raised.[2] Sometimes the Party-State goes on to argue that socio-economic rights must be improved before civil and political rights can be addressed. If people lack the basic means of living, how could they even begin to worry about their right of free speech, this argument goes. Often, the most centrally referred to right is that of subsistence or of life, *shengcunquan*, a right not directly mentioned as such in the Constitution, but frequently referred to in official documents from the very first 1991 White Book on Human Rights onwards,[3] and reminiscent of the 'right to adequate living standards' of the ICESCR.

This chapter critically addresses the Party-State's developmental perspective. It argues that while there have been important post-Mao prosperity rises, anti-discrimination and socio-economic rights are in tension with the goals of development, as the Party-State defines them, when 'development' is the result of these rights' violation. To make this argument, it is necessary to acknowledge at the outset that socio-economic rights and anti-discrimination rights – their basis and the question how best to give effect to them – remain contested not only in China. Contestation is partly about how, if at all, differences between and differential treatment of people are morally and legally relevant. There is also debate about the extent to which human needs, such as that of subsistence,[4] translate into legitimate entitlements to receive support from society or from the state. Some of the critics of socio-economic rights argue that *enabling* people to do things or obtain public services is primarily an issue of resource allocation, not of rights, and thus subject to policy decisions.[5] As seen in the following, the Party-State view of socio-economic rights shares with this assessment a simplistic tendency to equate progress in socio-economic rights with aggregate welfare increases. This approach is problematic, and this chapter's engagement with the developmental Party-State treatment of socio-economic rights can help us understand why. Most importantly, no adequate system of socio-economic rights can be established without adequate mechanisms institutionalizing these rights and providing accountability for the violation of these rights and of the rights required to defend socio-economic rights. Seeking to prioritize one class of rights over another in a general and abstract way is pointless, because at least at the ground level of citizen-state contestation, they interdepend to a large extent.[6] Also, as Shue and others have pointed out, all rights engender negative and positive obligations, and have resource allocation implications, for the State;[7] and in promoting poverty reduction and prosperity, States must respect individual rights, including socio-economic and non-discrimination rights, which limit the burdens that may be imposed on the individual for the sake of 'growth'.

The concerns that socio-economic inequality, unequal treatment and human needs give rise to are addressed by intersecting rules and principles of international human rights law, including not only socio-economic, but also anti-discrimination rights. The most important international human rights treaty covering the rights discussed here is the International Covenant on Economic, Social and Cultural Rights (ICESCR).[8] It safeguards, *inter alia*, the right to work and labour rights such as the right to strike and to join (form) labour unions,[9] the right to social security, the right to an adequate standard of living, the right to health and the right to education. Important rights understood to flow from these safeguards include the right to housing, the right to food and the right to water.[10] The ICESCR obligates signatory states to 'take steps, individually and through international assistance and co-operation, especially economic and technical, to the maximum of its available resources, with a view to achieving progressively the full realization of the rights' and to guarantee the exercise of such rights without discrimination.[11] Some of the aforementioned rights are also protected by other treaties, including the ICCPR.[12] In addition to these specific economic and social rights, there is another group of human rights protected by international treaties, such as the CERD,[13] protecting the right not to be discriminated against on racial grounds.

Domestic-level norms protecting some of these rights can be found in the Constitution, which addresses the right to work and rest, social security, healthcare and education, as well as non-discrimination, and in further laws and regulations.[14] The Constitution mentions a right to freedom of association,[15] but does not mention the right to form or join trade unions. It is also silent on housing. Freedom of movement as the right of citizens to move around in the country internally (relevant to the household registration system discussed below) was initially safeguarded, but taken out of the Constitution in subsequent drafts, as was the right to strike.[16] At the level of statutory law and further regulations, numerous norms have been introduced to protect certain rights. For example, as discussed with regard to housing rights, laws and regulations reflect a broadly liberal approach to what makes takings lawful. Yet, as the example of education rights shows, laws and regulations can also institutionalize inequality. Moreover, looking beyond the institutionalization of socio-economic rights to accountability mechanisms, the particular way in which these rights implicate issues of resource allocation, and tend towards producing mass grievances, affects their defence in the shadows of authoritarianism.

Exemplary issues discussed in the following – land and housing rights in the context of urbanization, the problem of *hukou* discrimination against peasants and urban peasant migrants, and human rights issues arising in the wake of environmental degradation –illustrate how 'development' can propitiate rights violations, and how 'development'-based arguments are used specifically to undermine socio-economic and anti-discrimination rights. The examples of forced eviction (or in the Chinese phrase, *chaiqian*, 'demolition and relocation') and land-grabs show the developmental-welfarist argument of the Party-State at full play, as it is in these contexts that the authorities tend to demand individual 'sacrifice' for the greater good. The example of access to education shows how China's legislated rural–urban divide has aggravated education discrimination against children registered as 'rural'; it calls for a discussion of the often tacitly accepted connection between development and the plight of exploited second-class citizens. Environmental degradation illustrates the importance of access to justice mechanisms in contexts where the Party-State is in principle intent on addressing the problem – the aggregate welfare decrease – that gives rise to individual complaints. Viewed together, these examples show that the absence of accountability for violations is as much a problem with regard to socio-economic as with regard to other human rights. They also suggest that mass grievances like these are bound to trigger calls for political accountability where no functioning legal accountability mechanisms are available.

THE IMPACT OF URBANIZATION ON LAND AND HOUSING RIGHTS

Urbanization has been an important part of China's economic success. It is virtually unimaginable that economic progress could have been achieved without the expansion of the cities and a movement, over several decades, of people from the countryside into the cities.[17] Urbanization and infrastructure projects have not only led to a change in the kind of work available – for instance, the creation of millions of factory jobs in the urban centres of Eastern and Southern China has been a 'pull' factor for rural–urban migration. They have also been an immediate generator of economic growth, measured as GDP that is as the market value of all final goods and services produced.[18] Moreover, growth, including notably growth through property development, has generated revenue and enabled the local Party-State to provide public services – for example, through the sale or granting of land use rights for a fee.

Urbanization has also led to large-scale changes in land use and to millions of people being evicted from their homes and land. To understand the enormous scope of this process, the bifurcated land tenure system is key. It prescribes different forms of ownership for rural (including suburban) and urban land. The latter is state-owned, whereas the former is owned by collectives. There is no private ownership of land, but there are private usufruct or use rights created in the 1980s in the course of the Reform and Opening policies under Deng Xiaoping. These use rights, limited to specified terms of time, as well as to types of permissible land use, can be held by private individuals (urban land use rights) or by rural households.

Urban property 'development' generally rests on property developers' acquisition of urban land use rights from the government as the owner of the urban land.[19] Before such an acquisition can take place, there is a process whereby the urban government 'resumes' possession of the urban land it already owns or expropriates collective owners of rural land, and evicts any current occupants to make 'cleared' land available for construction. In the course of this process, the State usually also expropriates the owners of any buildings on the land,[20] which are demolished. It has been argued that some 120 million people were affected by rural expropriations as of 2012.[21] For the urban takings, no estimate or official figure is available. It is these processes, their legal regulation and the practices that have arisen in this context that have led to human rights violations. These include, but are not limited to, housing rights violations.[22] No figures or even estimates are available on how many people have been affected by human rights violations in this context.

The fact of a taking as such is not necessarily a violation of housing or other rights. There is no absolute right to property or to continue occupying a land or building. There are, however, domestic legal rules governing takings. Generally, according to Chinese law, which reflects rules and principles of public international law, the State can take land only if it would serve a 'public interest' purpose, if there is compensation, and if procedural requirements are fulfilled. In reality, takings can be flawed in all three respects. The most pervasive issue is the 'public interest purpose' justification, which does not effectively limit takings. As property developer Ren Zhiqiang observed in 2010:

> There is no such thing as demolition and relocation that is not in the public interest. As long as it is [for the purpose of] urban construction, it is in the public interest.[23]

This comment well reflects a widely held attitude. Virtually every property development project serves (or is expected to serve) economic growth and is thus deemed 'in the public interest'.[24] In the case of Liu Zhengyou, encountered in chapter 2, villagers were told an industrial park would be built, and that they would be given employment, as well as 'urban resident' status. In fact, the developers built residential buildings that were far too expensive to be affordable; and they paid little compensation, roughly only one seventieth of the price the land fetched when the urban government 'granted' it to the property developers. Deprived of their livelihood for their own and generations to come, the villagers were left with barely sufficient money for a few years, after which they faced the prospect of being unemployed. Urban developers and officials, on the other hand, reaped the benefits of market transactions and official 'achievement', and the villagers' complaints about suspected corruption went unaddressed.[25]

Evictees like Mr Liu have virtually no chance to argue against a taking. This is not just because there is no body of court decisions finding a taking illegal or stopping an eviction on the grounds that it is not in the public interest.[26] It is also because of the many coercive (in addition to remunerative)[27] techniques developers and local government use to incentivize acceptance and deter potential complainants. In the run-up to taking over the land and demolishing buildings on it, the authorities are required to seek an 'agreement' about the proposed compensation and/or resettlement plan with residents (occupants), so as to avoid having to seek a forced demolition permit.[28] Where problems are envisaged, a climate of violence and fear tends to be created in the context of these processes. What propaganda terms harmonious demolition and relocation thus means that residents are put under pressure, threatened, intimidated and, in some cases, assaulted to secure 'agreements' and compliance.[29] If these tactics are not successful, the authorities can generally obtain forced demolition orders, but the process of the ensuing compulsory eviction can be violent and deeply flawed as well. In the film *Emergency Shelter*, for example, the inner city evictee rights defender Ni Yulan describes vividly how her own resistance led to her being tortured so badly that she became wheelchair-bound, and she and her husband talk about the feeling that their neighbourhood had been 'invaded' as though by foreign soldiers.[30]

As a result, the process of land-grabs and evictions can violate not only the right to housing and rights against forced evictions, and the right to an adequate standard of living more widely – for example, when residents are forced off the land they used to rely on for farming or other uses, and left with inadequate means of securing a sustainable livelihood for themselves and their families. The violence accompanying such processes, and the persecution of those trying to defend housing rights, can constitute further rights violations, including of expression rights, personal liberty, the right not to be tortured and even the right to life – for instance, when suspicious deaths occur in the context of forced demolitions. These issues are compounded by the problems with access to justice outlined in chapter 2, and by social unrest as a consequence of takings.[31]

The Party-State relies on a developmental perspective to justify its takings practice. The basic structure of this argument is utilitarian – it claims that the beneficial consequences of property development outweigh its effects on individuals, seen as 'cost'. Takings issues (whether they concern the taking of land or homes) are thus regarded as issues of *merely* economic interest, defined in terms reducible to monetary compensation. Once this premise is accepted, it is easy to accuse those who are critical, protest or resist of being greedy – rather than joyfully accepting their role in the grand, national development project, they selfishly demand more for themselves. According to Peng Chun's critical analysis of the Party-State's view,

> [D]ispossession by the state is neither a sacrifice nor a transaction but an honourable duty that reaffirms and reinforces the fundamental and long-term harmony between individual interest and the common good.[32]

Thus, when, in December 2009, the evictee Tang Fuzhen committed suicide by self-immolation in protest against the forced demolition of her home, triggering wide public debate about the underlying issues,[33] an official concerned with her case reacted by publicly accusing her of putting her own interest above the public interest, insisting that he had nothing to feel sorry about. The scholar Yu Jianrong commented that:

> Social bifurcation has already provided a mental construct of 'us' and 'them'; and this classification of individuals results in a lack of sympathy that strips 'them' of their humanity.[34]

This discourse diminishes the role that rights – including property rights understood in a broad, constitutional law sense, housing rights and non-discrimination rights and the wider right of access to justice – play in conceptualizing and addressing such cases. It obscures these rights' deep connection with the value of the individual's right to have some control over what happens to them as a person, not just a wealth-holder.[35]

In sum, despite the plausibility of the growth-through-urbanization narrative, urbanization has some far-reaching and invasive adverse consequences. The state-controlled, state-driven process of property development affects not only rural citizens but also the vulnerable original urban residents facing eviction to make way for construction projects; and it leaves these groups very little say on the 'how', even less the 'if' of this process. Because it uses pressure, threats and violence that remain hidden and suppressed, it is hard to assess the scope of rights violations that occur. It is clear, however, that rights violations do occur, that they affect a plurality of socio-economic and other human rights, and that access to justice in response to such rights violations does not function properly for many in these communities.

Members of rural communities face other kinds of challenge when they go to the cities for work. One of them is discussed in the following section.

EDUCATION RIGHTS OF RURAL AND MIGRANT WORKER CHILDREN

Since the 1980s, rural–urban migration has been on an unprecedented scale. According to Ren, the 'floating population' (*liudong renkou*) – people living in a place outside the household registration or, in technical terms, the internal migratory population (both inter- and intra-provincial) – stood officially at 221 million in 2010. Armstrong states that, as of 2012, it had reached 250 million. Within that population, those without household registration – effectively illegal aliens within their own nation, as discussed in the following – exceed 160 million.[36] The majority of migrants are rural–urban migrants who have come to the city to find work that pays better than what is available in the countryside, where they are registered.[37] In 2013, the Government announced that some 250 million more residents would move to the cities in the next dozen years.[38] Economically, the background for this is, in part, the persistent wealth difference and better opportunities in urban centres. However, as the Government announcement made clear, rural–urban migration is also part of the official plan for ensuring continued economic growth.

Legally, the bifurcation of rural and urban citizens is rooted in the *hukou* or 'household registration' system. This system was created in the late 1950s, when China practised a planned economy, to impose restrictions on the freedom of movement within the country. It required citizens to register and prohibited them from moving around without registration changes, which were difficult to obtain. Moreover, people were, for example, not able to get the coupons necessary for access to food in places other than those where they were registered. The system thus established control over migration. With the Reform and Opening era, this situation changed radically. Freed from planned economy restrictions, and incentivized to move to factories as internal migrant workers, tens of millions of people left their rural places of residence and moved to the cities. But since the household registration system was never abolished, these internal migrants are treated in some ways like illegal immigrants, and in others as second-class citizens in the urban centres. The ensuing bifurcation between rural and urban has been consolidated by the land tenure system.[39]

The rural migrant *sans-papiers* is no longer subject to a special administrative detention system following the system's abolition in 2003.[40] However, they remain subject to the so-called Statutes on Household Registration, which were passed by the Standing Committee of the National People's Congress in 1958,[41] a law that continues in force, greatly modified by further laws, which has resulted in a requirement to obtain a change of household registration if they are not in the city merely temporarily. The problem today is not so much that persons from the countryside cannot migrate, but that they take their rural status with them when they do so, remaining tied to their communities of origin even into the second generation, and exposed to the stigma of being outsiders without full legal status. Urban centres have tended to create decentralized rules of 'immigration' control:[42] since they generally set high barriers to household registration, most migrants are unable to change their household registration while residing in the cities. The further implication is that they have no or only limited access to vital public services, including healthcare and education for their children (who are generally given the household registration of their parents).

According to the work of Goodburn and others on access to education for migrant children, the vast majority of them are unable to provide the documentation required to allow them access to urban state schools.[43] These schools are generally reluctant to allow them access anyway. As a result, they have to go to privately established schools for migrants, most of which are inferior to the state schools in a number of ways, with an overwhelming majority of children reporting dissatisfaction with their school.[44] The teaching and facilities tend to be poor and inadequate. The teachers are paid less and are less qualified than at state schools. There are reported problems with, *inter alia*, violence at school.[45] In addition, the authorities have shown themselves intolerant of these schools. Not all of them (not even a majority of them) have obtained official licences to operate. Waves of closures of these schools as illegal operations have been reported, and on occasion, migrant children's school buildings have been demolished as 'illegal structures'.[46] In November 2016, the government announced restrictions for privately run schools that would undoubtedly disadvantage migrant worker children even further.[47] According to bureaucratic logic, the children's right of access to education in such cases is satisfied by access provided in the place of their household registration, even though this would mean separation from their parents.

The approach taken by the authorities has engendered a further social ill, referred to as 'left-behind children' – children who stay in the villages of their parents' origin, usually with elder relatives, but sometimes all by themselves, when their parents migrate to the cities to work.[48] In the countryside, children can generally access education; but the quality of such education varies greatly and can be very poor. As a consequence of administrative and fiscal devolution policies under Deng Xiaoping, educational and other public services are locally funded, so that, in poor areas, there may be very little money to spend on education and teachers may be badly paid.[49] As of 2010, there were some 222.6 million rural children, according to the official census.[50] According to official figures, the number of 'left-behind' children is around 20 million as of July 2016, whereas other estimates put the number at around 60 million as of April 2016.[51] The psychological burdens alone suffered by these children can be terrible, as cases of suicide by left-behind rural children indicate.[52]

A related, wider issue is that, just like their working parents, children classed as 'rural' migrants encounter social stigma, generally associated with the idea of being of 'low quality'. According to the mainstream discourse about 'population quality' (*renkou suzhi*), large parts of the current population are at an inferior cultural, educational and moral level.[53] The segregation of rural people is inherently related to their household registration status, tying them to the countryside, their origin or – in the case of second-generation rural migrants – that of their parents, rather as *ius sanguinis* does with regard to citizenship in some countries. As a dependent factor, it is not as concrete as 'race' but, in the experience of those discriminated against, it may nevertheless be hard to change. The categorization of peasants as people of lower quality is manifest in official and semi-official studies and projects on 'raising the quality of the rural population' (*tigao nongmin suzhi*),[54] as well as in organized programmes to teach migrants from the country-side how to be 'civilized urban people'.[55] With official discourse so clearly biased, wider social discrimination is not surprising.

While a rural hukou can translate into significant difficulties with equal access to education, there are also citizens who have no household registration at all, because they were born as 'excess' children – that is, children in excess of the limitations of the population control policies, which are supposedly in accordance with assessments of the number of births likely to serve the goal of general welfare.[56] Their situation is akin to statelessness – they are treated as though they did not exist for the purpose of access to public services. They can also not be issued with a personal citizens' ID card or passport. This has given rise to a practice of demanding a 'social upbringing fee' (*shehui fuyangfei*) for a household registration for these excess children.[57] The level of the fee again depends on which household registration is acquired in this way, with rural fees considerably lower than urban ones. The practices that have arisen out of the existence of these 'black' or unregistered children thus enable us, ironically, to put a monetary figure on the extent of rural–urban discrimination.

In December 2015, the Government took some steps to address the issue of persons without registration, who numbered around 13 million according to official media reports. A State Council Regulation that came into effect in January 2016 provides that those born as excess children can apply to be registered at their mother's or their father's place of household registration, and that it is prohibited to establish criteria that must be fulfilled for registration.[58] However, as critics have pointed out, it is not clear how this regulation will be implemented, considering the existence of other regulations and documents (see chapter 2) that continue to demand the payment of fees.[59] The new Regulation is silent on the legal status of already extant rules to this effect. It also seems to have no direct bearing on the many local rules imposing fines for violating the population control rules by giving birth to an excess child, which could, in practice, discourage parents from applying.[60]

In sum, household registration-based discrimination continues to affect tens of millions of people and their children. It is a form of discrimination that is created by Party-State rules and aggravated by discriminatory social attitudes. The Party-State every now and then introduces reform initiatives to improve the system for household registration changes and offers rural migrants better opportunities to become citizens with equal rights in the cities where they live, or to de-couple social services from registration. But local administrations unwilling to be burdened with the cost of treating migrants as equals find ways to resist this pressure. The Party-State justifies the regulatory framework that forms the basis of this discrimination by the need to stay in control of the 'floating population', a justification suggesting that the authorities see some continued utility in the strictures affecting 'rural migrant workers'.

Despite its great social importance, there is relatively little indication that efforts to address the discrimination issues arising from household registration can be effectively addressed as a rights advocacy issue. With regard to some forms of discrimination, beginning with employment discrimination against bearers of Hepatitis B (a common infection in China), advocates have achieved remarkable success, as discussed in chapter 6. At least in the 2000s, advocacy against such discrimination was a growth sector. By contrast, other forms of discrimination, such as that based on household registration (discrimination against 'peasants' and 'peasant migrants'), persisted without mitigation through effective advocacy for another decade. A rights advocate asked to explain this in 2011 commented that it was hard to address household registration and gender discrimination issues through rights advocacy, precisely *because* their scope was enormous, and therefore, addressing them could be seen to cause 'social instability', and thus lead to repression.[61] In 2017, however, a rights defender detailed their new advocacy group's successful efforts to obtain household registration for 'excess children' by bringing complaints against local government authorities. Yet, by February 2017, the advocacy group in question had already been forced to close down, for reasons addressed in chapter 6.[62]

There were also some attempts to challenge education discrimination against migrant worker children, undertaken by parents themselves. Equal education rights became an important part of the agenda of the New Citizen Movement initiated in 2012. The Movement's initiators drew on years of working with migrant worker parents who sought to protect their children from the closure of privately run schools, and/ or get them admitted to public schools. But, as discussed further in chapter 6, the authorities showed no tolerance when called out on this type of mass discrimination.

THE HUMAN RIGHTS EFFECTS OF ENVIRONMENTAL DEGRADATION

As a result of urbanization, mass migration, changes in land use, changes in consumption habits and changes in industrial and agricultural production methods, pollution has become a very serious concern in China. This also has an impact on human rights,[63] although, of the public international law norms China has signed up to, no treaty body explicitly acknowledges a right to a healthy environment, as, for instance, the African Charter on Human and People's Rights does.[64] However, it has become increasingly clear that in many ways how we treat the environment directly affects our own enjoyment of human rights, as the UN Special Rapporteur on Human Rights and the Environment has stated.[65] Most immediately, in ICESCR terms, one might think of the right to health and the right to an adequate standard of living. Pollution is known to cause numerous health problems, from respiratory diseases due to air pollution, to poisoning with toxic substances such as lead and chemicals released in the context of waste disposal. In many instances, it is possible to identify some causal links. For example, as the Council on Foreign Relations notes, life expectancy north of the Huai River is 5.5 years lower than in the south due to air pollution; and overall, air pollution is thought to contribute to an estimated 1.2 million premature deaths in China annually.[66] Yet it is important to note, in this context, that different kinds of pollution affect people differently. Here, I juxtapose the emergence of so-called cancer villages as a result of soil pollution in certain parts of the countryside with the problems of air pollution in urban centres such as Beijing.

According to a study published in May 2013, of the 1.86 trillion *mu* (Chinese acres) of farming land in China, 1.3 trillion are deemed to have 'medium' or 'low' productivity, and '70% of farmland is polluted due to overuse of fertilizer and pesticides or industrial effluent pollution and similar reasons, affecting the nation's food safety.'[67] It was seen earlier that, as a result of the land tenure system, the rural population is tied to their places of supposed origin through the interlocking mechanisms of collective land ownership and household registration. As a result, rural residents can find themselves locked into collective land ownership in areas where natural resources are so polluted that they represent health hazards. They have no, or only inadequate, access to safe food and water satisfying minimum standards.

Pollution affects communities whose members are tied to polluted land and water resources via the collective ownership system in especially harsh ways in the case of 'cancer villages'[68] and lead poisoning affecting certain areas.[69] Such pollution reaches far into rural areas where there is not necessarily much industry.[70] Scholars have argued that, partly as a result of the development of 'model cities' showcasing positive and healthy development, pollution has been outsourced to these rural areas. As described in the previous section, it is possible for rural residents to leave their villages; but, if they do so, they face discrimination and exclusion from access to social services. As a result, the older and younger generations often stay behind, and it follows that they – children included – would be especially likely to be affected by the 'cancer village' phenomenon. It is, therefore, a case of intersecting discrimination against children (particular age groups) belonging to the wider community of 'peasants'. Because of the local nature of the issue, conflicts over pollution of this kind resemble rural land disputes, as is well illustrated by the struggle of the villagers of Qiugang captured in a documentary.[71] Rightly, accounts of these struggles focus on the local community that sees itself trapped in an unequal conflict. Consequently, like in land takings cases, the test of effective advocacy would be successful court cases. The existing record on environmental pollution litigation is mixed, with scholars indicating that there is a tendency for punitive litigation and going after small-time perpetrators.[72]

Air pollution, in contrast, is a phenomenon that is, in principle, impossible to confine or contain geographically, and that naturally tends to be especially concentrated in the urban centres, where it affects anyone who lives there. As Zhang Jiake, whose documentary *Smog Journeys* focuses on how two families from different social strata are affected by smog, observes,

> …no one gets to be different when it comes to smog. No matter what jobs we do, it is still a problem we all face.'[73]

The Party-State's attitudes to pollution are in some ways similar to its attitudes to land use. There is a general recognition of responsibility manifest, *inter alia*, in a legislative framework for environmental protection that includes requirements for environmental impact assessment, the regulation of pollution and the imposition of civil and criminal liability for polluters. This indicates that the authorities are willing to make pollution control their own business. Arguably, at least in some cases, pollution is a by-product of growth,[74] much as coercive changes of land use are. But in contrast to the logic of land-grabs and forced evictions, the creation of pollution has no *direct* beneficial effects. Yet the creation of 'cancer villages' indicates that, in this context too, the authorities are willing to tolerate the sacrifice of the well-being of a few, to displace the harms of pollution to communities that are already comparatively marginalized. Following this cruel logic, it makes sense for the Party-State to aim at channelling such protest by ignoring it as long as possible, and strategically repressing it where it threatens the perceived social stability.

Air pollution presents even greater challenges, because in this context, nearly everyone's well-bring is sacrificed to the aims pursued by allowing such pollution to continue – be it industrial production, or the use of cars producing air pollutants. Being so vast and indiscriminate in nature, air pollution would naturally call for some nationwide initiative or organization to address it. Due to the nature of the problem, any such initiative would, therefore, inherently be on a large scale. Given widely acknowledged problems with demonstrating causation of harm through air pollution in any jurisdiction, moreover, advocacy for better protection of the public's health through the reduction of air pollution would almost certainly have to involve wider political as well as legal initiatives.[75] An example of how big the problem of air pollution was, and how widespread the public's concern was, was provided when, in 2015, Chai Jing, a young TV presenter faced with the illness of her infant child due to air pollution, made a documentary film about air pollution, which she called *Under the Dome*.[76] The film, *inter alia*, documented how factories flouted emissions standards, and how badly the Chinese population's health was affected by air pollution. It was watched several hundred million times within days; but then, without official explanation or comment, it was removed from the Chinese internet.[77]

CONCLUSION

The discussion here suggests that the 'lifting out of poverty' argument considered at the beginning of this chapter is facile in a number of ways. For one thing, it seems to claim agency for the Party-State, or simply to obfuscate the question of who the agents of change have been – perhaps in conformity with the thesis that the People and the Party are identical. For another, it is wrong to imply (as is sometimes done) that 'lifting out of poverty' is equivalent with defending socio-economic rights. The socio-economic rights issues arising from urbanization – the problem of land and housing rights, discrimination with regard to education rights and rights violations in the context of environmental degradation – have served as examples.

While it cannot be denied that overall economic development has raised wealth and welfare in the aggregate, it has also produced adverse consequences for rights, showing that those who suffer a violation of their economic and social rights are likely also to encounter further rights violations. The suggestion, so frequently made by the Party-State, that individuals bear a duty of sacrifice towards the Nation, or indeed that subordinating their interests to those of the Nation is glorious and not even a sacrifice, suffers from the flaws of utilitarian theories with which it has a clear connection: it ignores the individuality of socio-economic right bearers and sees them only as contributors to a social aggregate.

As the UN Special Rapporteur on Extreme Poverty and Human Rights has observed, the Chinese government's argument, as outlined above, is common to many state parties to international conventions:

[T]he most telling evidence of the extent to which economic and social rights remain unacknowledged as human rights is the frequency with which debates about them slide imperceptibly and almost naturally into broad discussions of development. States challenged to explain how they respect economic and social rights will describe general development or social welfare initiatives as though they are necessarily synonymous with such rights.[78]

China's example shows that, while welfare increases are generally welcome, they do not necessarily translate into improvements in the socio-economic rights situation, or help address issues of discrimination and wider inequality; they fail to take seriously the position of the individual and her claims to justice.[79] On a credible account of socio-economic and anti-discrimination rights, this argument fails: even if some violations of socio-economic rights might raise aggregate welfare (an empirically difficult claim), they are nevertheless not permitted, *qua* violations. And even where individuals can be required to accept dispossession, inequality in public services, or pollution, they must not be deprived of the right to criticize and challenge public power.

Protest against violations of socio-economic rights sometimes challenges the inadequacy of framing the issue narrowly as a matter of making sacrifices to the greater good. For example, when protesting socio-economic injustices, people not infrequently refer to the concept of the right to subsistence.[80] Complainants also demand equality; and frequently, because of the connection between socio-economic rights, material goods and gains, they complain about official corruption when asserting their socio-economic rights. Rejecting the suggestion that these conflicts have been exclusively about economic interest, a lawyer said:

> These issues do not merely concern interest, they do not merely have to do with money. They directly concern the right to speak (*huayuquan*).[81]

And, a comment made by a scholar would seem to resonate with the experience of mass grievances more widely, be they caused by landgrabs, education inequality or environmental degradation:

> We are all members of one society whose fates are intimately connected; we must change our attitude, we must care. If today you don't care about this case, then perhaps tragedy will strike you tomorrow.[82]

There is thus some evidence that the 'sacrifice' theory that subordinates individual socio-economic rights to larger goals is resented and resisted. The examples used here also illustrate the interconnectedness of rights, as it is impossible to create efficient accountability without also protecting central civil and political rights. The exercise of these is central to all human rights advocacy efforts. Yet, as the next chapter discusses, human rights defenders are facing worsening limitations.[83]

6 Rights Defenders

Human rights defenders and advocates are vital to the promotion of human rights.[1] The discussion in previous chapters has already drawn attention to their roles. In addition to the three petitioners encountered in chapter 1, and the many anonymous interlocutors whose contributions this book draws on, crucial actors in rights defence and rights advocacy encountered earlier included the lawyers and other 'rights defenders' (*weiquan renshi*) of Jiansanjiang, the three doctors of law who made an unconstitutionality review request after Sun Zhigang's death, the boy critic Yang Hui who wrote a few microblog posts, the writer Liu Xiaobo who contributed to Charter 08, the evictees Liu Zhengyou and Ni Yulan and the many land and housing rights defenders they stand for, the nameless education rights activists demonstrating against education inequality, and Chai Jing, the news presenter who risked so much by producing *Under the Dome*, a plea for air pollution to be addressed. Their roles reflect the great importance of human agency in quests for justice.

The roles of advocates and complainants in responses to injustice have always been recognized in China, even though the role of the traditional complainant was thought of in somewhat different ways. The difficulty of getting redress is reflected in popular phrases and images, for example, the Kafkaesque image of seeking doors that are not there, will not open, or cannot be passed through (*shang fang wu men*) or the phrase *han yuan wu gao* – crying injustice, but having nowhere to complain to.[2] Traditional accounts of legal advocates tended to be sceptical, if not disparaging,[3] and as noted in chapter 1, lawyers along with other professionals seen as 'revisionist' were persecuted in the Mao era.

The emergence, from the late 1970s onwards,[4] of a global web of civil society actors in the wake of the major public international law treaties occurred just as China was opening up and beginning to revitalize the legal system. As these organizations and institutions grew, they themselves became the focus of international attention through some human rights instruments, such as the 1990 UN Basic Principles on the Role of Lawyers and the 1998 UN Declaration on Human Rights Defenders.[5] The 1990s, when many of the transnational organizations first became active in China, were also a time of political recalibration in China, following the 1989 suppression of the democracy movement. The authorities increasingly allowed more transnational organizations to open offices and interact with Chinese organizations and individuals. It became possible for different domestic actors including, for example, lawyers working in criminal defence and other areas, investigative journalists, and advocacy groups, non-governmental organizations and charities to engage in rights defence aimed at witnessing, documenting and exposing violations, bringing complaints before the courts, seeking systemic improvement through better laws and more transparent, better scrutinized government actions,[6] and so on.[7] China seemed to choose a familiar path of transition towards a political-legal system modelled on the liberal constitutionalism that is required for a better protection of human rights.

But almost as soon as it opened up, the system also intensified its efforts to control and close down some of the options for change through incremental improvement. The Party-State has always remained wary and latently repressive towards civil society and the 'embryonic' public sphere, as already seen in previous chapters: the 'anaconda in the chandelier' image introduced in chapter 4 held throughout this period.[8] Drawing on the successes achieved in areas such as anti-discrimination and women's rights defence, as well as the adverse experience of examples of NGOs and individuals prominent in human rights defence, it is argued here that the restrictions of human rights advocacy have become more comprehensive and sophisticated in the Xi era. Repression has got worse, and rights defenders are increasingly portrayed as enemies of the state; and the more they are treated as enemies, the more their existence and vitality represents a challenge to the Party-State system.[9] This chapter considers the deeper implications of this challenge, focusing successively on rights defenders with professionally defined roles (in particular, lawyers),[10] civil society organizations, and coordinated political action growing out of human rights advocacy efforts.

THE EMERGENCE OF CIVIL SOCIETY ADVOCATES

Professional actors: lawyers, journalists and others

Recreated at the end of the Cultural Revolution, the legal profession was given an increasingly prominent and vital role in the revitalization of the legal system; and, over some forty years of post-Mao development, it grew from a few hundred still left over in the late 1970s to some 300,000 registered lawyers in 2017.[11] Out of this total number, a very tiny fraction, some 300–500 (up from a dozen or so ten years earlier) describe themselves as 'human rights lawyers'. A much larger number is concerned with human rights (including rights in the criminal process, access to justice, and so on) in their daily work, even though they might not opt to describe themselves as human rights defenders.

There are no fixed criteria for what makes a lawyer a 'human rights' or 'rights defence' or 'rights lawyer', because all lawyers' core professional duty is to defend rights. Legal professionals who see themselves as part of 'the system' may one day find themselves on its outside, for example, because they have taken on a case deemed 'sensitive' or chosen to support a human rights lawyer colleague. As legal professionals, of course, they all engage with 'the system' one way or another. Thus, the distinction between rights lawyers and other lawyers is, as rights lawyers emphasize, an open one. What tends to set rights lawyers apart from their professional colleagues is their focus on the rights of their clients in a system which, as seen in previous chapters, discourages rights-centred approaches, for example by refusing to decide certain legal disputes, blocking courts from adjudicating on the basis of constitutional or international human rights provisions, and pressurizing litigants into 'mediating' or 'reconciling' in ways that can serve to cover up rights violations. Rights lawyers take on the cases deemed 'sensitive', and, when encountering limitations of their right to practise, many of them are willing to 'take the action outside the courtroom'[12] in the manner described in chapter 2. In other words, they are lawyers who insist on the free exercise of their right to engage in legal and political rights advocacy, and who refuse to collaborate with the system or to be co-opted by it in ways that would compromise their professional role.

In the 1990s and 2000s, lawyers were often able to use the legal process for advocacy purposes, even though they were unable to obtain fair trials, let alone just outcomes, for their clients or themselves to avoid unjust and human rights violating convictions (usually for a variety of public order or national security crimes). This allowed them to expose the wrongs of the system, even though they did so at the price of persecution. When they found that the courts and other legal institutions of 'the system' were closed against them, they took their advocacy to more genuinely public spaces. Thus a typical image of Chinese lawyers' rights advocacy became the picture of lawyers holding up signs demanding access to their clients or the release of their colleagues.[13]

As Halliday and Liu have pointed out, lawyers have been important 'agents of transformation' in different historical and geographical contexts;[14] but rights lawyers are not the only group whose profession has an affinity with human rights defence in China. Journalists are professionally differently situated, but their work and role reflects similar fault lines. Their work – especially the work of the hard-hitting kind of investigative journalism[15] – is of great importance to human rights advocacy. It is also connected to that of a growing army of 'citizen journalists' who report on human rights issues in independent fashion, posting their reports and commentary via social media platforms. The dividing lines between professional and citizen journalists are somewhat blurred. Professional journalists, unable to post certain stories via official media channels may – foregoing the fee the article would otherwise have earned them – decide to publish work screened out in this manner via social media,[16] while other citizens from all walks of life may become prolific bloggers and online commentators. While rights defenders thus operate in different roles and professions, their core role of standing up for victims of human rights violations unites them.

Party-State control of professions prone to rights advocacy takes pervasive, as well as invasive forms. For lawyers, the main actors imposing bureaucratic control are the Justice Ministry and its subordinate bureaux, the All China Lawyers Association (ACLA) and its subordinate organizations, as well as – as an entity with numerous committees and branches exercising influence and control – the Party. Any lawyer and any law firm must individually obtain licences to practice, and be subject to annual assessments by these governing bodies. The assessments are complemented by a complex system of disciplinary measures implemented jointly by the lawyers' associations and judicial bureaux. According to current law, lawyers can be deemed to be 'incompetent' (bu chengzhi), with a stamp in their licence booklet putting this on record (important when lawyers are required to show their licences to clients or the authorities). Two consecutive assessments as 'incompetent' may result in gradated disciplinary punishments, including permanent disbarment. The criteria of compliance are elastic and include professional ethics and political probity. For law firms, they include 'thought and political education' and 'praise or complaints of their professional practice activities by the clients, concerned departments or the masses.'[17] The duties of a licensed lawyer include, according to the oath of loyalty they are required to swear upon taking up their licence, 'to uphold the leadership of the Chinese Communist Party and the socialist system'.[18] In practice, lawyers have the fear of not winning their licences back hanging over them all the time. Human rights lawyers have provided ample testimony about being pressurized and penalized with disbarment for their advocacy. A prominent example is that of lawyers Liu Wei and Tang Jitian, captured in the film *Disbarment* by He Yang, for forcefully defending a Falun Gong practitioner.[19]

Once a lawyer becomes known as a 'rights lawyer', or a journalist as a trouble-making investigative muckraker, they, along with other 'targets of stability maintenance' (*weiwen duixiang*), will typically also draw the attention of the police or Public Security Ministry and subordinate agencies, in particular, of the so-called domestic security or *guobao* divisions within it,[20] the Ministry of State Security or *guo'an*, as well as a number of other flexibly established Party-State offices and agencies dealing with 'social stability' and 'national security' issues.[21] They then face control measures ranging from surveillance, tracking and following, travelling and foreign travel bans, informal house arrest or 'soft detention', to criminal, administrative and judicial detention and criminal prosecution, as well as, more rarely, forced disappearance and torture and (in quite rare cases) psychiatric incarceration.[22] These measures and their effects are, in many ways, identical with those described in chapter 3.

Gao Zhisheng, the first lawyer to use online open letters to protest the torture of Falun Gong practitioners, experienced all of the above, except for psychiatric incarceration (so far as has been possible to ascertain). He was not only disbarred, professionally ostracized (with help from the ACLA), convicted of inciting subversion, given a suspended sentence in 2006, and sent to prison when the suspension was revoked a few years later. From about 2005, he was largely kept under house arrest with his family, who were also severely harassed; and from August 2007 he was repeatedly disappeared and very cruelly tortured. As of this writing, he remains under strict control in his home village in Shaanxi, worlds apart from his former colleagues in Beijing.[23] In addition to these deprivations of liberty, Gao and other rights defenders have also, of course, been censored.

For years, the authorities seemed primarily intent on targeting rights defenders individually, hiding and obscuring what they were doing to human rights advocates, treating them as a potential threat and warning to colleagues who might engage in similar advocacy, but also as a problem to be denied as far as the wider public were concerned. As a consequence, some of these defenders were better known internationally than domestically. But, while the authorities might succeed in preventing them from becoming widely known, Gao and his colleagues remained hard to convict in the court of public opinion. Meanwhile, in the first decade of the twenty-first century, lawyers started coordinating and publicizing their activities in unprecedented ways, making use of new means of communication discussed in chapter 4.

Civil society organization

To make full sense of how rights defence lawyers came to be perceived as a threat, we need to appreciate the wider civil society context in which they operate and in which, increasingly, they came to assert a civic identity.[24] In China, the expression *gongmin shehui*, 'citizens' society', evokes the juxtaposition of *gongmin*, the citizen, and *renmin*, 'the people' considered collectively. The term *renmin* belongs to China's communist era – it is part of an illiberal conception of the individual person's role and status in society. By contrast, *gongmin* is a liberal idea. The classic, liberal political conception of civil society is often traced back to Tocqueville's account of the eighteenth-century North America. According to Tocqueville, the United States excelled in having many associations, formed freely and voluntarily for non-commercial purposes, to serve some aspect of the common good, in the civic or 'civil' spirit to be found in democratic political systems.[25] Taking up this basic thought, Adam Michnik, some 150 years later, argued that a move 'toward civil society' could change totalitarian (or post-totalitarian society) for the better because civil society was based on the idea of equal rights.[26]

Michnik's and Havel's ideas resonate with Chinese rights defenders, not least because of obvious affinities between the twentieth-century Eastern Europe and the illiberal and corporatist organization of society in the People's Republic today. As noted earlier, the Chinese system imposes strict limitations on association; and, while the advent of a 'socialist market' economy dissolved many previously existing economic structures, corporatist patterns of social organization survived in the form of Party-controlled official organizations such as the All China Lawyers Association, All China Trade Union Federation (ACFTU), All China Women's Federation (ACWF), All China Environment Federation, and so on. The existence of these large organizations, as well as a regulatory framework limiting civil society organizations to one per topic of concern have long prevented the rise of state-recognized independent advocacy associations,[27] while the ACLA and other official federations and associations have acted as tools to spread Party messages and implement Party directives.

For example, take a campaign called, in typical jargon, *Two-Study-One-Be* (*liang xue yi zuo*). It exhorts all Party members to *study* the Party Charter and regulations, to *study* the serialized speeches of high-ranking party members, especially Xi Jinping, and to *be* a good Party member. As of October 2016, the home websites of the ACFTU and ACWF displayed campaign banners and/or links to materials on the *Two-Study-One-Be* campaign, and the ACLA and its subordinate websites carried reports about *Two-Study-One-Be* training sessions,[28] as did various Party websites.[29] A typical text might read:

ACWF will never forget that to keep marching forward, it must firmly establish the Fourfold Consciousness [another slogan, referring to 'consciousness of politics, consciousness of the big picture, consciousness of the Core, and consciousness of the (Party Central) line']. In its thinking, its political governance and its actions, it will strive to identify with Party Central under General Secretary Xi Jinping to the highest degree, and lead all women in listening to the Party and following the Party.[30]

And so on. Texts like these may contrast oddly with the highly sophisticated videographic materials mentioned in chapter 4. But one should not underestimate their power. The Party, these messages say, is everywhere. It drives and controls all official professional organizations. Whatever protection you may seek from, or support you may give to, ACFTU, ACLA or ACWF is also support given to, or protection sought from, the Party. Groups representing particular interests or views must be subordinated to the Party, led by Xi Jinping, newly styled as 'Core'.[31] In principle, not only organizations of long-standing such as ACWF, but also more recently created government-organized non-governmental organizations ['GONGOs'] – entities whose inherently contradictory description captures their lack of meaningful independence from government – are subject to these principles.

Given their professions of strict subordination to the Party, it does not surprise that government-controlled organizations, on occasion, become instruments of repression of human rights advocates amongst their membership, rather than providers of support or protection. This was shown briefly in the context of ACLA just above. Even more dramatically, ACFTU has, in some cases, been drafted into efforts to suppress labour protests, with ACFTU members directly physically clashing with striking workers.[32] In the context of women's rights, ACWF is involved in 'persuading' women to have abortions so as to comply with the birth planning policies of the Party-State, for example, a role that can take on repressive and human-rights-violating aspects.[33]

The constraints imposed by official organizations run on corporatist principles[34] led to rights defence and rights advocacy being organized in informal ways to circumvent these strictures. Anthony Spires, conducting research on civil society in Guangdong Province, for example, found that the estimated number of informal entities outnumbered by far that of officially registered ones.[35] They might be registered as commercial non-profit enterprises or simply not registered at all. Spires has argued that the many organizations situated in the grey zone of toleration and risk largely exist in 'contingent symbiosis' with the Party-State: allowed to undertake services that helped the Party-State satisfy popular need, but always facing the possibility of limitations, persecution and closure. Such NGOs included advocacy organizations focusing on issues that were deemed somewhat sensitive without being the most sensitive – these included, for example, advocacy on behalf of the rights of ethnic minorities, such as Uighurs and Tibetan activists, and forceful, principled criminal defence of Falun Gong members.

One of the most important types of independent human rights advocacy groups emerging in this context were independent groups to help workers, especially migrant workers disadvantaged by the household registration system, as well as social discrimination.[36] Many operated in Guangdong Province, which has long had the reputation of taking more open and liberal approaches, and which could benefit from the proximity of the Hong Kong-based support groups, but which has also been the site of significant labour unrest.[37] Examples of such groups are Dagongzhe in Shenzhen and Panyu Workers' Centre in Guangzhou, as well as the Laowei law firm led by lawyer Duan Yi.[38] Gradually, they became involved in defending workers not only in individual disputes, but also in the defence of workers' rights to collective labour action.[39] Their work was somewhat related to anti-discrimination groups such as Yirenping, successfully advocating against, for example, employment discrimination against carriers of Hepatitis B.[40] For a long time, environmental NGOs could also be regarded as relatively 'safe' within a zone of toleration.[41] Environmentalists could establish an environmental law clinic, led by Professor Wang Canfa, at China University of Politics and Law,[42] widely known for its relatively liberal position; and this clinic became a leading advocate for using litigation on behalf of environmental pollution victims. Similarly, women's rights defenders formed semi-official organizations such as the Women's Rights Centre, established by lawyer Guo Jianmei within Peking University Law School, and successfully advocated, *inter alia*, for changes to help victims of domestic violence;[43] and Wuhan University established a law clinic focusing on a number of mainly rural rights issues, to give another example.

For rights defenders unable to operate under the protective umbrella of a university or similar institution, the choice not to register invariably placed them in a grey zone between toleration and persecution and at risk of being forced to distort their mission and activities to conform to government limitations. Such groups drew financial support from various sources, including foreign governments and organizations; and domestic civil society organizations collaborated with foreign NGOs, of which some 7,000 were thought to operate in China as of 2016.[44] They also attracted the attention of a new generation of law students and young lawyers who often saw such work as a meaningful and relatively safe way of helping their country reform.

Throughout this period of growth, the authorities maintained policies of selective repression that ensured that advocacy remained segregated into different areas, intensifying divisions caused more naturally by different expertise and career paths, and fostering anxiety and mutual distrust. The more sensitive the topics covered, vocal the advocacy or stronger the support by foreign organizations, the greater the likelihood of suffering persecution.[45] Well-known examples of rights advocacy and research organizations that ventured beyond what was thought to be the limits of official toleration included the Open Constitution

Initiative (Gongmeng),[46] the Transition Institute[47] and China Against Death Penalty.[48] They were the first to face pressure. For example, the advocacy NGO Gongmeng's director Xu Zhiyong was targeted for 'tax evasion',[49] Guo Yushan, the founder of the Transition Institute and various members of the NGO were held in criminal investigation detention and reportedly tortured in 2013–14.[50] The co-founder of Gongmeng and China Against Death Penalty, Teng Biao, suffered many years of persecution, including forced disappearance and torture in 2011, before going into exile in 2014.[51]

By the time Xu, Guo and Teng left or were imprisoned, and organizations still operating had come under increased pressure, however, an important shift was underway in China's human rights advocacy movement.

'Organization-less' but coordinated actions and initiatives

Important human rights advocacy causes remained well outside what was understood as a tolerated zone of organized civil society activity, and expected incremental human rights progress failed to materialize or was marred by regression in other respects.[52] As civil society actors and organizations working on the more 'sensitive' issues realized that their ability to work within NGOs to defend human rights was going to remain limited, they became more vocal in articulating demands and coordinating activities outside these organizational contexts, for example, by participating in demonstrations protesting against housing and education rights violations.[53] But, as they became more vocal, the authorities became more nervous and repressive. Thus, precariously situated, but increasingly better able to communicate and associate, the most outspoken civil society actors took to creating what, as Clay Shirky argues,[54] one might call 'organization-less' advocacy initiatives.

The so-called New Citizen Movement, which was initiated in May 2012, is a good example. Its name made conscious reference to a normatively rich and ambitious concept of citizenship, drawing on China's indigenous liberal tradition,[55] as well as the European enlightenment era[56] and official legal language also used in the context of rights defence and dissent.[57] As the scholar and rights advocate Xu Zhiyong explained at a 'civic meal' in late 2012, the concept

> reflects what sort of system the State should have, what the relationship between the State and its citizens should be, and [the idea of] civil society as an independent and free entity.[58]

The initiative was started, he also explained, because the achievements of NGO advocacy, including those of the group Gongmeng he had directed, had been limited. Case-by-case work, the typical pattern of lawyers' human rights advocacy over the past decade, had only led them so far; and a wider, more inclusive kind of action was now required.[59]

The advocacy goals of the New Citizen Movement were both political and pedestrian. Rather like a political party platform and quite unlike Charter 08,[60] they identified mass grievances and developed specific demands that could theoretically be implemented without system change. Thus the New Citizen Movement asked for asset disclosure by public officials, a demand getting at the issue of widespread corruption. It also campaigned for equal education rights for migrant worker children, drawing on the experience and migrant parent networks developed by Gongmeng over several years.

These demands could be counted on to be understood and supported by large numbers of people. Everybody is against corruption, at least in principle, and education inequality is a widely shared concern amongst the disadvantaged social groups.[61] The initiative's advocacy strategies were also calculated to allow wide participation. They included, for example, so-called 'civic meal' meetings organized at the same time in different locations across the nation, as well as 'flash mob' demonstrations:

flash-like gatherings of supporters unfurling a banner, followed by the dissemination of pictures showing the same message in a variety of urban locations all over China. Thus, the initiative coordinated flash mob demonstrations by migrant worker parents holding up banners asking for equal education rights in front of the Ministry of Education building in Beijing.[62] These actions were fluid in their organization, and did not rely on clearly visible structures. Some of the initiatives also posed a low threshold of participation. Participating in a demonstration (however small-scale and brief) might be risky; but what could be wrong or dangerous about gathering for a joint meal? In the south of China, even more explicitly political initiatives emerged, including flash mob demonstrations to demand that China finally ratify the ICCPR[63] and a campaign for 'peaceful non-cooperation' to achieve democracy in China.[64]

None of these initiatives succeeded in setting off a wide-scale movement, largely because, within months, their main (co-)initiators were detained and, for the most part, prosecuted, convicted and imprisoned. Even then, rights defenders like Guo Feixiong, Xu Zhiyong and Tang Jingling, as well as the criminal defence lawyers representing them, were generally able to produce and disseminate final statements defending their beliefs and actions. Xu Zhiyong even managed to smuggle a video-clip out from a police detention centre. It showed him, wearing an orange detention centre jacket, behind bars, delivering a defiant campaign message that was immediately disseminated further via social media platforms in China and via news websites overseas.[65] Thus rights defenders were able to use their own unfair trials and unjust punishment for civic advocacy purposes.

In sum, human rights advocacy during the post-Mao Reform and Opening era evolved from the acts of a daring few to more coordinated actions making use of new technologies to associate, communicate and express rights-based demands. It evolved from being confined to institutional channels, such as the official media and formal legal mechanisms of litigation, petitioning and 'review' requests, which were used in the early years of the Sun Zhigang Incident, to action in the streets and online. Rights advocacy thus became a practice that includes very different quests for justice, with petitioners, journalists, lawyers and NGO workers coming together in coordinated action. Most importantly, in reaction to intransigence, exclusion and persecution, this kind of advocacy became more consciously and explicitly political-legal in its messages. While failing in what might, for a long time, be thought its stated goal of incremental, top-down change, it succeeded in conveying the political message of liberal-democratic reform – perhaps the better, the less it found itself limited by the perceived need to persuade and placate current powerholders, albeit at enormous cost to the advocates. The advocates remained able to operate, despite a feeling that the system was closing in on them. 'Hai you kongjian' – 'there is still some space' – became a much-used phrase among rights defenders.

THE CONSEQUENCES OF AUTHORITARIAN REVIVAL

With the establishment of Xi Jinping in central power, some previously existing trends became more pronounced as the system reverted to greater concentration of power and more assertive methods of control, and the possibility of reform and further opening came into question. In 2013, an anti-liberal shift of rhetoric and attitude exemplified by the Party-issued Document No. 9 dismissed the very idea of universal values and portrayed 'civil society' as a concept and force used by China's enemies,[66] while references to the 'People' and 'Masses' became more prominent. In 2014, the Party announced that 'Party Leadership and Socialist Rule of Law are identical',[67] a position echoing attempts by conservative nationalist scholars, such as Jiang Shigong, to explain Party leadership as a fact foundational to, rather than disturbing, the constitutional order.[68]

Simultaneously, a combination of repressive measures targeting individual persons and organizations which had played prominent advocacy roles, and changes in the regulatory framework governing the liberal professional communities and civil society organizations, were rolled out rather as though they followed a carefully coordinated programme. The crackdowns, it soon became clear, no longer targeted only those working in the most 'sensitive' areas. Well-known and until then relatively safe advocacy groups such as Yirenping came under pressure; or they were forced out of their protective institutional affiliation, as in the case of the Zhongze centre led by Guo Jianmei;[69] and five feminist activists were subjected to criminal investigation detention and abuses in March 2015 for planning to commemorate International Women's Day and protest patriarchy and authoritarianism.[70] This in some cases led to flight and exile from China.[71] The crackdown on lawyers discussed below was to be followed by a selective crackdown on labour rights activists and the NGOs they had created.[72] The initial detentions of the Xi era followed established patterns; but the global diplomatic and social media backlash created, especially, by the detention of the Feminist Five,[73] led the authorities to redesign their methods, in ways discussed in the following,

Visible repression, anti-liberal rules

On 10 July 2015, a young lawyer was on a business trip when he heard another crackdown on human rights lawyers had just started. He went to an internet café to check on his WeChat messages.

> When I opened my account, the first message I saw read 'Flee at once'. As I flicked through the messages they all read: 'disappeared' – 'disappeared' – 'disappeared' – over a hundred messages like that. And out of nine people reported disappeared, seven were good friends of mine, really close friends. I knew it took only three minutes, no more than

five, to locate someone [via their account]; so I immediately closed it down again.[74]

The author of this brief narrative had been told to flee, but where could he have gone to? By 2015, the system's means and mechanisms of surveillance were very far developed; and escaping the grasp of the security apparatus and its many co-opted helpers as a known human rights defender would have been difficult. Within a few days, hundreds of lawyers all over China were rounded up.[75] Many were released after being warned against advocacy, but some remain in custody and have effectively disappeared as of this writing, as they are completely cut off from family and counsel. Named after the date the crackdown began (9 July) with the night-time detention of lawyers Wang Yu and Bao Longjun and their sixteen-year-old son, Bao Zhuoxuan, the '7-09 Crackdown' mainly targeted rights lawyers and assistants connected to the law firm Fengrui, to veteran human rights lawyer Li Heping and to a group around the activist Hu Shigen, which included rights lawyers, as well as more 'grassroots' human rights defenders. In comparison with past crackdowns, 7-09 affected a much larger number of lawyers. It was also more openly acknowledged and more widely advertised by the Party-State compared to their other repression of human rights advocates since at least the 1990s.

Lawyer Wang Yu was taken away from her home shortly after alerting her friends by text message about the disappearance of her teenage son and husband on their way to the airport, on the night of 9 July 2015. She and her husband were held for over a year without access to independent counsel on 'suspicion of state subversion'. Only once were the two to be seen in over twelve months following their detention. After some friends tried to help smuggle their son out of the country, the authorities caught up with him in Myanmar and returned him to China. They then showed Wang Yu and her husband on national television, devastated and in tears on getting this news.[76] Then, on 1

August 2016, a Hong Kong television station screened her in an 'interview' upon her 'release on bail'. Speaking against a backdrop of summery greenery and soft, pleasant music, she renounced her former advocacy, denounced two foreign organizations[77] for awards given to her earlier that year and thanked and praised the authorities. Reports described her as released; yet none of her family or friends were able to contact Wang Yu or to determine her whereabouts. There was no mention of why her lawyers had not been allowed to see her. In the days following, several other '7-09' advocates were displayed confessing and repenting their 'crimes' of subversion in court.[78] For the most part, the authorities described the detentions that had preceded these statements as measures of 'residential surveillance in a designated location', making use of Criminal Procedure Law reforms enacted in 2012.

Enhancing the effects of the televised 'confessions', officially circulated video-clips cast human rights advocates as enemies, visually associating them with images of US warfare in Iraq and Syrian refugees stranded in Europe, suggesting that human rights advocates were part of a US-based plot to subvert China.[79] Furthermore, some months earlier, in January 2016, the authorities had detained a Swedish NGO worker. Peter Dahlin, too, was shown on national television incriminating himself over working with some of the '7-09' detainees, while held under 'residential surveillance in a designated place'. Using a phrase well known to diplomats who criticize China about human rights violations, he said,

> I violated Chinese law through my activities here. *I have caused harm to the Chinese government and have hurt the feelings of the Chinese people.* I apologize sincerely for this and am very sorry that this ever happened.[80] (Emphasis added.)

Released and sent back to his home country after a few days, he told a reporter about sleep deprivation and being forced to hear one of his colleagues being tortured during his detention in the same building.[81] A few months later, lawyer Li Chunfu was released after over 500 days 'residential surveillance in a designated location' with signs of serious mental illness;[82] and lawyer Xie Yang, finally able to meet his defence lawyer, provided a detailed account of his torture to this lawyer, who decided to publish the news.[83]

From 2013 onwards, the Party-State had imposed stricter rules and limitations on lawyers, journalists and academics.[84] For example, new rules were introduced to tighten the limitations of courtroom human rights advocacy. Article 309 of the Criminal Law, as revised in 2015, prohibits 'insulting, defaming or threatening judicial personnel or litigation participants, and not heeding the court's admonitions, seriously disrupting courtroom order.'[85] The revised rules governing the administration of law firms, issued by the Ministry of Justice in 2016, prohibit lawyers from a range of activities and hold law firms responsible for preventing infraction of these rules through the 'management' and 'education' of its lawyers. It prohibits lawyers, *inter alia*, from

> Disturbing the public order or endangering public safety by illegal methods such as inciting, abetting or organizing litigants or other persons to go to the legal authorities or other relevant department to stage sit-ins, hold placards or banners, shout slogans, voice support, or look on; [as well as] otherwise mobilizing people to stir up trouble, create an influence, or exert pressure on relevant departments; producing distorting or misleading accounts of and comments on cases handled by themselves or other lawyers; or maliciously hyping up cases, publishing or disseminating speech denying the fundamental political system and basic principles established by the Constitution, or endangering national security [and] using networks and media to provoke dissatisfaction with the party and government, or initiating or participating in organizations that endanger national security.[86]

Holding law firms responsible for their staff in this way creates what one human rights lawyer called 'collective punishment' rules,[87] designed to take the chilling effect of speech crimes right into the core activities of the legal profession.

The authorities also further concentrated control over NGOs and sought to exclude extraneous factors and influences that were not under Party contol. Already since 2000, the Ministry of Civil Affairs' Provisional Measures for Banning Illegal Social Organizations provided a tool to control organizations trying to exist without registration.[88,89] A new Charity Law restricts domestic funding sources; and a Foreign NGO Management Law treats foreign organizations, including NGOs, as in principle suspect entities, subordinating them to police control, requiring them to submit detailed activity plans, and take guidance even on personnel matters from the police bureaux in charge.[90] More widely, legislative reforms included the 2015 National Security Law, framing the struggle for security as one against foreign and domestic enemies, including perceived 'enemy forces' within wider Chinese society, as well as those considered disloyal within the Party.

The authorities have taken measures not only to tighten advocacy spaces for rights lawyers. They have also sought to co-opt lawyers in ways that would prevent them from becoming human rights advocates. For example, a Party 'Opinion' issued in late 2015[91] announced that lawyers should henceforth be recruited to volunteer their services in litigation-related petitioning work. Depending on the case, such lawyer-volunteers would be expected 'to help petitioners get a correct understanding of the opinions of the authorities regarding the lawful handling of the case *and persuading them to submit to the decision and stop bringing complaints*'; or at most, if there was any mistake, to 'make *suggestions to the governmental and legal authorities* so as to propitiate the matter getting resolved through the [proper] legal procedure' (emphases added).[92] If implemented, such a scheme would distort what should be a relationship between the lawyer and their client, shifting the lawyer's responsibility from being mainly towards their client to being primarily towards the Party-State authorities. It could thus co-opt lawyers and law firms, drafting them into helping the government silence petitioners, rather than being their legal advocates and defenders. Rules of this kind encroach further upon the autonomy of the legal profession, which governments are under obligation to protect, *inter alia*, under the UN Basic Principles on the Role of Lawyers.[93]

Viewed together, the Xi-style high-visibility crackdowns and rules, more explicitly requiring lawyers to collaborate with the Party-State in suppressing rights defence and rights advocacy, signal a clear shift away from the mode of (limited) liberal transition towards rule of law through reform that was a legitimate point of reference through most of the post-Mao era.

A neo-totalitarian turn?

The changes discussed above indicate a move towards an, in ambition if not in reality, totalist or (neo-)totalitarian political model. Clearly, its idea is that all realms of societal life are parts of one organic body which functions well only if there is coordination and a high degree of centralist direction. Organizations conceived in this corporatist way are naturally both instruments of control and themselves controlled by the central State;[94] and the sole purpose of their existence is to be part of one whole. This, evidently, reflects a way of thinking not only about organizations such as environmental groups or the ACWF, but also a way of envisioning the entire nation. The corporatist view is also one that relegates and rejects those who do not form parts of the nation's body to the place of possible threats, of possible enemies of the People. If, in the early 2000s, it could persuasively be argued that China was transitioning towards a more pluralist, diverse and open conception of society, that it was moving, in scholar Merle Goldman's words, *From Comrade to Citizen*,[95] the preceding selective discussion of more recent changes suggests a further shift. The main shift is not so much one back to 'comrades' as it is one towards 'the people', 'the masses' and 'the nation'.

As the crackdowns on human rights defenders discussed above illustrated, the shift from 'citizens' to 'the people' relies centrally on the creation of a narrative that serves to enhance the role of the state as protector from dangerous enemies. Yet there is little concern with the plausibility, let alone veracity, of the narrative. The statements that the detained human rights lawyers suffered no rights violations is straightforwardly false, considering that they were denied fair trials on multiple grounds. But, rather like in Havel's greengrocer example, the official narrative offers an opportunity to those who wish or need to take it up to 'conceal from themselves the low origins of their obedience'.[96] It allows – and even invites – viewers to join a comforting pretence, which, once it has been joined, triggers its own efforts of make-believe and which can turn into further complicity.[97] The narrative also enacts the subjection of crackdown targets and intimidates sympathizers, and it conveys a nationalistic defensiveness towards outside attackers.[98]

In some ways, such narratives and accompanying propaganda replicate the twentieth-century totalitarian mockery of and contempt for legal forms. They appear to draw on Schmitt's influential definition of the concept of the political by reference to the polity's enemies. They seem aimed at ensuring, if not unanimity of opinion, at least a uniformity of expressed views. They use the production of fear to achieve this goal, and, in doing so, to further indicate the move towards a more 'totalist'[99] or totalitarian or Orwellian form.

However, it is not clear how effective such rules and measures can be, considering the nature of the twenty-first-century's global communication platforms and general interconnectedness. As noted in the Introduction, society is less 'atomistic', ideology is less strong, and state–society relations are far more differentiated than in the previous century. Moreover, there is thus far no indication that the embattled human rights defender movement has been vanquished, even though it is clearly embattled. On the contrary, as seen in the context of the '7-09' crackdown, and accompanying changes in rules and practices, every restrictive or repressive move of the Party-State triggers almost immediate challenges from this community. As public discourse is far less streamlined than in the totalitarian twentieth-century societies, these challenges continue to be disseminated and discussed in wider circles, within China and beyond its borders.

CONCLUSION

This chapter has traced the emergence of civil society and human rights advocacy, and its increasingly severe repression. The development described here seems to follow an in-built logic of rights defence in authoritarian (or indeed neo-totalitarian) settings. As established in chapter 2, the system sees a point in granting some official recognition to human rights norms and principles, especially when, after the great crisis of the Cultural Revolution, the idea of 'ruling the country in accordance with law' appears attractive. Yet, the system also depends on systematically preventing human rights from becoming effective in restricting public power. Accordingly, it sets up mechanisms to regulate, control and – ultimately – repress rights defenders. These systems tend to identify human rights advocates with the victims they work with, and by persecuting them, further aggravate human rights problems.

It is a reflection of this logic that in the space of some fifteen years, human rights lawyers and other relevant actors have barely made any dent in the system that continues to work as a remarkably repressive and intransigent set of institutions. They have effected little institutional change for the better. Under Xi Jinping, the system's repressiveness has become more articulated and visible than it was before. It has more clearly rejected the liberal transition paradigm than any other post-Mao leadership; and the Xi era is also the first time that the authorities have very publicly portrayed – and persecuted – human rights defenders as enemies of the People.

And yet, the account is not entirely bleak. The authorities would not have gone to such lengths branding human rights defenders 'enemies', had it not been for some realization that the defenders do pose challenges to the system. They are right. Despite not winning cases in court or achieving institutional change of political accountability, the work of human rights defenders has affected China's public sphere. Their work has effected a broad shift towards more vocal, more fluid and diverse expressions of human rights claims and a widening variety of strategies. Human rights defenders' achievement is reflected, for instance, in ordinary people's ready ability to use human rights language when complaining about injustices. It is also reflected in the vast amount of information and insight they have been able to collect and disseminate (in China and abroad). Even under the great pressure of persecution and the dismantling of the professions that support them, they continue to operate, living by a principle of hope without expectation, or, in Havel's phrase, of not reckoning with success.[100]

Conclusion

This book has assessed human rights in China as a set of social practices involving different actors, including domestic and international actors situated 'inside' and 'outside' the system.[1] It is now time to return to the task of assessing the impact of China's authoritarian system on the human rights considered, the impact of these rights on the system, and further consequences of the dynamic between them. As set out in summary below, the legal-political system's disregard for and routine violation of many human rights has to some extent been counteracted by expanding rights advocacy efforts which, in turn, have led to intensified government repression. Both advocacy and repression, it will be argued here, have transnational dimensions that cannot be ignored.

It must be appreciated, first, that the Party-State has given some recognition to some human rights, but that human rights have not fundamentally changed the nature of the institutions of the Party-State. This was discussed with regard to three major groups of human rights. China's recognition of the rights of liberty and integrity of the person, the right not to be tortured, and the right to life has led to some protection from arbitrary violations of these rights through national laws and further regulations; and there are some legal mechanisms that allow citizens and advocates to seek protection of these rights. Systematic violations remain. China's authoritarian system has not overcome the problem of systematic torture as a common feature of 'law enforcement'. If one detention system is abolished, others will be created to serve the system's 'need' to incarcerate and torture; and abolition of the death penalty remains at this point a merely theoretical prospect. Even the legislative reforms meant to eradicate systematic rights violations on occasion are found to have created new ones, and consolidated old ones into 'legal' mechanisms. Yet, because there are mechanisms to challenge violations, these rights are major causes of contention between citizens and the Party-State.[2]

By contrast, the system lacks any credible mechanism to protect freedom of speech and thought, despite the *prima facie* recognition of freedom of expression and related rights found in the Constitution. The Party-State argues that its denial of freedom of speech is in nature similar to the limitations imposed by other countries; but this argument is flawed. It conveniently overlooks the fact that in systems with meaningful (if limited) protection of free speech, some limitations are unacceptable, and freedom of speech is justiciable. The Party-State's restrictive, paternalistic approach to the idea of freedom of thought, moreover, deeply divides it from any justification of speech limitations that a liberal-democratic system might offer; as do its intolerant attitude towards peaceful political criticism of the government, its (compared to the earlier post-Mao era) increasingly intolerant attitude towards manifestation of faith, and its arrogated mission to rectify political thought.[3]

Also, while there have been great rises in prosperity, the fulfilment of socio-economic rights is systematically thwarted, not only through the denial or malfunctioning of mechanisms of accountability. It is thwarted even more decisively by the refusal to treat socio-economic rights such as the right against forced eviction *as rights* that implicitly require the State to afford respect and legal protection to individuals, and to do more than just raising welfare in the aggregate, or raising the GDP. While some discrimination-based legal advocacy has been successful, challenges based on socio-economic and cognate rights are not tolerated, even where the Party-State's claimed utilitarian approach would counsel that the complaints were in line with the Party-State's own goals.[4] Moroeever, all human rights advocacy has met with intensified repression under the Xi Jinping leadership.[5]

Together, these findings not only urge the conclusion that the overall human rights situation is poor; they also make it impossible to accept the system's frequently reiterated claim that it operates under the rule of law – if we accept that systemic arbitrariness in the use of coercive power is incompatible with rule of law, and that a complete denial of the human right to be treated as a person whose dignity matters could upset a state's authority.[6] Exactly how bad the damage to the Party-State's authority is from its systemic human rights violations is hard to tell, because the assessment here certainly does not suggest that there is a 'complete denial' of people's human rights and the need to protect them.[7] There are many laws, some of which are meant to safeguard rights, and there is a general sense that the law should be followed. But the principle of legality is routinely ignored or even explicitly suspended in the human rights-sensitive areas examined here. At times, there is control or abuse without basis in law – as in the limitations of the internet and many limitations of the liberty and integrity of the person.[8] Other times, the Party-State ordains exceptions from ordinary legality that purport to allow rights-infringing practices.[9] Yet other times, it makes policies that claim to benefit people in the aggregate but require the positive subjection of the individual to the will of the Party-State as custodian of a greater good.[10] These findings suggest a duality of law-based, normative and law-denying, prerogative Party-State actions. As Fraenkel has pointed out, such a system cannot achieve genuine rule of law.[11]

In so far as exemptions from ordinary legality, and with them the prerogative state, have expanded in recent years, as argued in chapter 6, this assessment also directly challenges the assumption that the system is – must be – moving towards improved rule of law and human rights; an assumption which continues to frame many intergovernmental and civil society exchanges,[12] but which each of the preceding chapters has called into question. The clearest commitment to human rights values, and efforts to protect human rights, in the system as discussed here are perhaps in criminal justice. Yet precisely in this area, we observed antagonistic trends.

Second, these reflections do not deny the possibility of liberal progress, or of change for the better. They merely challenge a Fukuyama-esque belief in it being the only alternative left.[13] Belief in progress is compatible with liberal principles only if it takes seriously the possibility that people, and governments, can make choices either way and that systems can deteriorate and turn more authoritarian as a result of such choices. Indeed, the Party-State and its admirers increasingly hold out the 'Chinese model' as an example of an alternative to a flawed 'western' liberal-democratic order.[14] Leaders of some previously liberal-democratic countries, such as Hungary, now say that China, along with Russia and Turkey, could be superior models of 'illiberal democracy' to be emulated,[15] and China and other authoritarian systems are seeking to weaken human rights at the UN level,[16] and this is only one of the problems besetting the institutions of international human rights law, whose impending demise has often been reported.[17] These are manifestations of a global authoritarian resurgence;[18] but such a resurgence can only heighten the importance of human rights as a focal point of state–citizen contention.

This book has discussed human rights as a social practice that is not entirely dependent on formal institutions and that is partly taking place outside the institutions of the Party-State. It has shown how human rights are exercised and defended when citizens choose to speak freely despite rules and control practices limiting and threatening them. It has discussed the forcefulness and daring with which citizens challenge unlawful detentions, document and criticize abusive practices including torture, and undertake complex advocacy in death penalty cases. It has also discussed how important socio-economic rights and social grievances are in driving the bottom-up engagement with the idea of rights as a powerful tool of those who resist dispossession and exploitation. In all these contexts, the presence and voice of citizens has become a political factor that clearly needs to be taken into account. Ignatieff has argued that human rights is 'a driver language behind values triggering political change'.[19] Writing in 2000, he said:

> Human rights has gone global not because it serves the interests of the powerful but primarily because it has advanced the interests of the powerless. Human rights has gone global by going local, imbedding itself in the soil of cultures and world views independent of the West, in order to sustain ordinary people's struggles against unjust states and oppressive social practices.[20]

In the same way, 'human rights as politics' is a powerful driver of demands for change in China today. The authorities' repressive reactions to the rise of independent legal-political human rights advocacy merely serve to underline the deeply political nature of the struggle for human rights.

The fact that the political struggle for human rights in China is also part of a global struggle increases its complexities in ways particularly important to those of us outside China, because it changes the nature of the difference between inside and outside. China's engagement with transnational civil society, especially from the 1990s onwards, has been of great importance in driving the 'vernacularization' of human rights. More widely, there has been a shift from traditional diplomatic, government-to-government relations to engagement with transnational conglomerates; NGOs large and small; universities and other educational institutions with their staff and students; media entities, freelance journalists, writers and film-makers; hospitals, retail chains of all kinds; lawyers and law firms; tourists and other travellers; and so on. These changes have strengthened but also complicated human rights advocacy. In the words of Kerry Brown, they have made all of us diplomats.[21]

Yet, third, we must appreciate that as a consequence of these changes, not only human rights advocacy has 'gone global'. Increasingly, repression has, too. The shadows of China's authoritarianism are growing longer, also because repression has acquired a more clearly transnational dimension. An example of direct and active transnational repression of rights advocacy and dissent was that of the Swedish NGO worker Peter Dahlin, held and interrogated in Beijing in 2016, until he was ready to make a public TV 'confession' of unspecified crimes.[22] In the cases of several Hong Kong booksellers and publishers, also in 2016, the authorities showed detainees abducted across the border from Hong Kong and Bangkok stating that they had voluntarily gone to mainland China, either to assist with police enquiries, or to turn themselves in. This was as implausible as the domestic 'TV confessions' considered earlier;[23] and after his return to Hong Kong, one of the booksellers confirmed that he, too, had been coerced to make statements.[24] The result of such cross-border acts of repression is not only that the individual advocates are stopped. Rather, such measures have further intimidatory effects on wider circles of critics and advocates from outside China. Legislation such as the Foreign NGO Management Law, considered in chapters 4 and 6, as well as national security and anti-espionage laws have similar effects. They reflect a style of governance by engendering fear that is at least as much a cause for concern as incidental examples of immediate, physical coercion.

By engaging with China's repressive system, the transnational actors mentioned above – actors from government, civil society, the media, education, business, law, art, and so on – are compelled to make decisions that can sometimes help to extend and amplify the effects of the system's human rights violations. NGOs with offices or operations in China, for instance, are not merely concerned about their projects, but naturally also about employees and the partners they interact with. Each civil society organization has to make daily decisions about whom to approach, whom to engage with and work with, and what projects and topics to touch. Can a 'sensitive' rights defender be invited along to a seminar on rule of law that involves established academics? Will there be a problem with funding a group whose members have previously been abducted? Will our own employees be 'invited for chats' with the authorities? If yes, how to protect them? If someone is detained, how to find lawyers for them (should these be 'rights lawyers' or professionals with good connections?), and how to negotiate matters with the family of the detained, who may be in extremely vulnerable positions? Finally, when is it time to leave China? Amalgamated from many conversations held over several years, these are typical questions an NGO working in or with China may face. It can be no surprise if, facing such pressures, they feel inclined to hold on to an axiomatic belief in incremental improvement; if it seems that the best, safest, most acceptable way of referring to the rule of law situation will be by reference to 'advancement' and 'reform'.

Transnational advocacy and repression have thus generated their own dynamic and perils. Once offices have been established, programmes have been set up, and funding has been granted and invested in such programmes, the risk of seeing them collapse is an understandable concern that may lead to self-censorship on the part of a foreign or transnational organization. To give an example, when, in 2016, the American Bar Association (ABA) hesitated to make a statement on the '7-09' crackdown on human rights lawyers, it was hard to resist the conclusion that it took into account the risks to its established 'Rule of Law in China' programme; and this impression was compounded when rights defender Teng Biao, by then in exile in the US, reported that the ABA had withdrawn its original offer to publish his book on self-censorship grounds.[25] When, later, following public criticism, the ABA awarded lawyer Wang Yu its human rights prize, the authorities produced her on national television, publicly rejecting the award and declaring that she felt herself used by foreign organizations, thus trying to draw foreign supporters and observes into cycles of self-censorship that domestic rights defenders have long been aware of.[26] A similar dynamic can play out in the context of Party-State-set taboos, such as that on Falun Gong, the spiritual group, whose members featured in some of the narratives in this book,[27] and some of whom had also been among Wang Yu's clients. Be it in reaction to official instructions or hints, or because open discussion of their plight could trigger further persecution, or in order to avoid causing trouble to domestic interlocutors and partners, or for other reasons, transnational civil society and even media organizations can seem reluctant to work on this topic. Like other actors engaging with China, they may end up being drawn into reluctant complicity with efforts to marginalize this important human rights issue.

The gradual expansion of the system's reach thus challenges any complacent assumption that the system's human rights violations will continue to be contained within its geographical or jurisdictional boundaries. If ever we could, we can now no longer think of them as merely other people's problems. Some twenty-five years after China initiated its rapprochement with the international human rights regime in the wake of the June Fourth crackdown, its rights abuses are being brought closer to the world, urging us to address human rights as an increasingly transnational responsibility.

Notes

Introduction

1 State Council Information Office, White Paper on Human Rights (November 1991), Preface, available at <http://china.org.cn/e-white/7/index.htm> [last accessed 30 October 2016]; Sun Pinghua, *Human Rights Protection System in China* (Heidelberg, Berlin: Springer Verlag, 2014), at p. 35.

2 Cf. Andrew Nathan, 'China and international human rights – Tiananmen's paradoxical impact', in Jean-Philippe Béja (ed.), *The Impact of China's 1989 Tiananmen Massacre* (Abingdon: Routledge, 2009), 207–20; Robert Weatherley, *Making China Strong: The Role of Nationalism in Chinese Thinking on Democracy and Human Rights* (Basingstoke: Palgrave Macmillan, 2014) at p. 148f.

3 Discussed in chapter 2.

4 Discussed in chapter 2.

5 Discussed in chapter 5.

6 Discussed in chapter 1.

7 Camilla Ruz, 'Human rights: What is China accused of?', BBC News, 21 October 2016, available at <http://www.bbc.co.uk/news/magazine-34592336> [last accessed 13 November 2016].

8 Such as reports issued by the US State Department and Congressional-Executive Commission on China; the Swedish government and the UK government.

9 For example, the artist-activist Ai Weiwei recreated scenes from his own experience of enforced disappearance in the Royal Academy of Arts in London. A digital audio-visual tour of the exhibition is available at <https://www.royalacademy.org.uk/exhibition/ai-weiwei-360> [last accessed 10 November 2016].

10 An important exponent of this type of argument in the field of legal scholarship is Randall Peerenboom. See Randall Peerenboom, *China's Long March Toward Rule of Law* (Cambridge: Cambridge University Press, 2002).

11 Randall Peerenboom, 'Fly high the banner of socialist rule of law with Chinese characteristics! What does the 4th Plenum decision mean for legal reforms in China?', *Hague Journal on the Rule of Law*, 7:1 (2015) 49–74.

12 Zhang Weiwei, 'The allure of the Chinese model', *International Herald Tribune*, 2 November 2006, available at <http://www.sinoptic.ch/textes/articles/2006/20061102_zhang.weiwei_chinese.model-en.pdf> [last accessed 12 November 2016].

13 For various reasons, some important international human rights NGOs have explicitly committed to being non-political. The best-known example is Amnesty International. Amnesty International European Institutes Office, 'Frequently Asked Questions', available at <http://www.amnesty.eu/en/about-amnesty-international/faq/#faq1>.

14 James Nickel, 'Human rights', in *Stanford Encyclopaedia of Philosophy*, 2014, <https://plato.stanford.edu/entries/rights-human/>.

15 For a discussion of 'rights language' and its critics, see Leif Wenar, 'Rights', *Stanford Encyclopaedia of Philosophy*, 2015, <https://plato.stanford.edu/entries/rights/>.

16 Ronald Dworkin, *Justice for Hedgehogs* (Cambridge, MA: Harvard University Press, 2010); and Ronald Dworkin, *Law's Empire* (Cambridge, MA: Harvard University Press, 1986). On human rights as 'lingua franca', see Michael Ignatieff, 'Human rights as politics / Human rights as idolatry', The Tanner Lectures, Princeton, 4–7 April 2000, available at <http://tannerlectures.utah.edu/_documents/a-to-z/i/Ignatieff_01.pdf> [last accessed 10 November 2016]. On human rights as a social practice, see 'Isabel Trujillo and Francesco Viola, *What Human Rights Are Not* (Hauppauge, NY: Nova Science Publishers, 2014).

17 Allen Buchanan, *The Heart of Human Rights* (Oxford: Oxford University Press, 2013), ch. 1. Buchanan makes a stronger claim about the authority of international human rights law practice.

18 W.B. Gallie, 'Essentially Contested Concepts', *Proceedings of the Aristotelian Society*, 56 (1955–6) 167–98.

19 Chapter 4 will argue that recognition of freedom of expression and cognate rights is almost absent in China.

20 The fieldwork has included loosely structured conversations with lawyers, other human rights defenders, academics, petitioners, citizen journalists and videographers, as well as observation of gatherings, workshops, seminars and discussions, conducted mainly between October 2010 and February 2017. Some ninety per cent of these conversations were conducted in mainland China, mostly in urban and semi-public settings, such as coffee-shops and

parks. All quoted passages have been anonymized, using standard social science techniques, and bearing in mind the fact that the interlocutors are at high risk of government abuses. To illustrate: I conducted recorded conversations with about eighty rights lawyers and about forty non-lawyer rights defenders between October 2010 and February 2017. Of these interlocutors, as of November 2016, some nine lawyers and four non-lawyers have been criminally convicted for their advocacy. Some twenty-two have suffered detention without trial, including forced disappearances; and well over half have reported suffering physical violence, including torture. The lawyers who were interlocutors for this project include many of those targeted in the so-called '7-09' crackdown on lawyers discussed in chapter 6.

21 Ronald Dworkin, *Justice for Hedgehogs* (Cambridge, MA: Harvard University Press, 2010).

22 John Tasioulas, 'Human rights', in *Routledge Companion to the Philosophy of Law* (London: Routledge, 2012), which juxtaposes orthodox and political accounts.

23 For example, chapter 3 quotes Teng Biao on a connection between the death penalty and 'having enemies'.

24 Discussed in chapters 2 and 6.

25 Elena Consiglio, 'The doctrines of human rights in China', unpublished manuscript on file with author.

26 Anonymous (匿名), '法理学研究会2016年度工作计划 [2016 Annual Working Plan of the Legal Theory Association]', 10 May 2016, available at <http://www.lawinnovation.com/index.php/Home/Xuejie/artIndex/id/13458/tid/1.html> [last accessed 10 April 2017].

27 Teng Biao (滕彪), 'The political meaning of the crime of "subverting state power"', in Jean-Philippe Béja, Fu Hualing and Eva Pils (eds), *Liu Xiaobo, Charter 08, and Challenges of Political Reform in China* (Hong Kong: Hong Kong University Press, 2012).

28 Others have used concepts such as deliberative or consultative democracy or meritocracy to capture what the Chinese system is – or what it strives to be. Daniel Bell, *The China Model: Political Meritocracy and the Limits of Democracy* (Princeton, NJ: Princeton University Press, 2015).

29 P.S. Sondrol, 'Totalitarian and authoritarian dictators: A comparison of Fidel Castro and Alfredo Stroessner', *Journal of Latin American Studies*, 23:3 (2009) 599.

30 Klaus Müller, 'East European studies, neo-totalitarianism and social science theory', TIPEC Working Paper 03/7, available at <www.trentu.ca/tipec/3muller7.pdf> [last accessed 10 November 2016].

31 Juan Linz, *Totalitarian and Authoritarian Regimes* (Boulder, CO: Lynne Rienner Publishers, 2000), at p. 67.

32 On responsive authoritarianism, see e.g. Robert P. Weller, 'Responsive authoritarianism and blind-eye governance in China', in Nina Bandelj and Dorothy J. Solinger (eds), *Socialism Vanquished, Socialism Challenged: Eastern Europe and China, 1989–2009* (Oxford: Oxford University Press, 2012).

33 Hannah Arendt, *The Origins of Totalitarianism* (New York: Harcourt, Brace, Jovanovich, 1973).

34 The approach taken here is sympathetic to Umberto Eco's account of 'ur-fascism', which emphasizes that there is no definitive list of criteria that can be ticked off to determine if a system is fascist. Umberto Eco, 'Ur-fascism', *New York Review of Books*, 22 June 1995, available at <http://www.nybooks.com/articles/1995/06/22/ur-fascism/> [last accessed 10 November 2016].

35 Emphasizing the uniqueness of the Chinese system, and avoiding entanglement in pre-established terminology, Ringen has come up with the term 'control-o-cracy' to characterize the Chinese system. Stein Ringen, *The Perfect Dictatorship: China in the 21st Century* (Hong Kong: Hong Kong University Press, 2016).

36 This dimension is revisited in the Conclusion.

Chapter 1: Human Rights and Competing Conceptions of Justice, Law and Power

1 He Yang (何杨), 应急避难场所 [*Emergency Shelter*], independent documentary (2010), available at <http://vimeo.com/12677411> [last accessed June 2016].

2 The role of the Supreme People's Procuratorate is discussed in chapter 2.

3 He Yang (何杨), above, n. 1.

4 In Chinese, *Yuan you tou zhai you zhu* 冤有头债有主. Sometimes also translated as 'Every injustice has its perpetrator and every debt its debtor', for example, at Proz.com, available at <http://www.proz.com/kudoz/chinese_to_english/slang/1855352-%E5%86%A4%E6%9C%89%E5%A4%B4%E5%80%BA%E6%9C%89%E4%B8%BB.html> [last accessed June 2016]. Ye is commenting on the killing of police officers by a petitioner, Yang Jia.

5 For discussions of the way in which 'social stability' discourse can lead to the repression of rights-based complaints, see Sarah Biddulph, *The Stability Imperative: Human Rights and Law in China* (Vancouver: University of

British Columbia Press, 2015); Sarah Biddulph, Elisa Nesossi, Flora Sapio and Susan Trevaskes, *The Politics of Law and Stability in China* (Aldershot: Edward Elgar, 2014).

6 He Yang (何杨), above, n. 1.

7 Václav Havel, *Moc Bezmocných* ['The Power of the Powerless'] (Prague, 1978) published in translation by Jan Vladislav (ed,), *Living in Truth* (London: Faber and Faber, 1986).

8 On law as an interpretive social practice, see Ronald Dworkin, *Justice for Hedgehogs* (Cambridge, MA: Harvard University Press, 2010); and *Law's Empire* (Cambridge, MA: Harvard University Press, 1986). On human rights as a social practice, see Isabel Trujillo and Francesco Viola, *What Human Rights Are Not* (Hauppauge, NY: Nova Science Publishers, 2014), p. xii.

9 On human rights as an interpretive social practice, see Introduction. The position adopted here is that the possibility of objectively right answers to moral questions is not defeated by merely showing that people disagree on these questions.

10 The question of how many human rights ought to be recognized is important in a general way, but not important to this book, which can only address a few central rights in a minimalist fashion.

11 Alexander Cooley, 'Authoritarianism goes global: Countering democratic norms', *Journal of Democracy*, 26 (2015) 49–63. See also Andrew Nathan, 'China's authoritarian challenge', *Journal of Democracy*, 26 (2015), 156–70.

12 See the website of the Xiyuan Action Project, available at <http://www.xiyuanwang.net/> [last accessed June 2016]. For a more in-depth discussion of this group, see Jue Jiang, 'Legal and political rights advocacy in wrongful conviction death penalty cases in China: A study of the Leping case of injustice', *Columbia Journal of Asian Law*, 29 (2016) 96–145.

13 This is documented, for example, in Zhao Liang's (赵亮) documentary *Petition* (上访, Beijing, 2009), a documentary made over a period of twelve years, portraying the petitioner community in Beijing. Of course, the expression is sometimes used with sarcasm.

14 Albert Chen, 'The legal history of traditional China', in *An Introduction to the Legal System of the People's Republic of China*, 4th edn (LexisNexis, 2011).

15 Confucius, *Analects*, II.3. 子曰:道之以政，齐之以刑，民免而无耻。道之以德，齐之以礼，有耻而格。Available at <http://www.guoxue.com/gxrm/gxrm-24.htm> [last accessed 23 October 2013]. The expression here translated as 'law and punishment' is represented by the single character *xing* (刑) whose central meaning is legal punishment (as in *xingfa*, penal or criminal

law). Translation by Liu Shu-Hsien, in *Understanding Confucian Philosophy: Classical and Sung-Ming* (Westport, CT: Praeger, 1998), at p. 20.

16 An enduring account of this tradition is provided in Derk Bodde and Clarence Morris, *Law in Imperial China* (Cambridge, MA: Harvard University Press 1967).

17 Michael Ignatieff, 'The right to have rights: Refugees, migrants and citizens', Fulbright Lecture, King's College London, 8 June 2016; Devin T. Stewart, 'In search of a global ethic', Carnegie Council, 21 April 2016, available at <http://www.carnegiecouncil.org/publications/articles_papers_reports/777> [last accessed 10 June 2016].

18 Classical accounts of rights juxtapose interest and choice theories. See Nigel Simmons, 'The Analysis of Rights', in *Central Issues in Jurisprudence*, 3rd edn (London: Sweet & Maxwell, 2008).

19 Jonathan D. Spence, *The Search for Modern China* (New York: W.W. Norton, 1999).

20 Robert Weatherley, *The Discourse of Human Rights in China* (Basingstoke: Macmillan, 1999) at p. 69f. (with reference to Liang Qichao).

21 Du Gangjian (杜鋼建), 中國近百年人權思想 [translated as *Thoughts on Human Rights in Twentieth-Century China*] (Chinese University of Hong Kong Press, 2011).

22 Marina Svensson, *Debating Human Rights in China: A Conceptual and Political History* (Lanham, MD: Roman & Littlefield, 2002).

23 At this point, three concepts transliterated as *li* have been introduced – they are separate concepts as would be clear from the Chinese characters used to write them: *li* 礼 for propriety, *li* 理 for reason, and *li* 利 for interest.

24 Stephen C. Angle, *Human Rights in Chinese Thought: A Cross-Cultural Inquiry* (Cambridge: Cambridge University Press, 2002).

25 Liang Qichao, 'On rights consciousness (1902)', in Marina Svensson and Stephen C. Angle (eds), *The Chinese Human Rights Reader: Documents and Commentary, 1900–2000* (Armonk, NY: M.E. Sharpe, 2002).

26 A movement led under the quickly out-manoeuvred Emperor Guangxu, who died in suspicious circumstances ten years later. The 1908 Draft Constitution (钦定宪法大纲) is discussed in Marina Svensson, *Debating Human Rights in China: A Conceptual and Political History* (Lanham, MD: Roman & Littlefield, 2002). See also Jenny Leung Larson and Feng Chongyi, 'Charter 08's Qing Dynasty precursor', *Asia Pacific Journal*, 9:2 (2011) 1–16.

27 The draft contains the provisions: 'The subject shall be granted freedom to express himself through the spoken and written word and in publications within the limits of the law' (臣民於法律範圍以內, 所有言論、著作、出版及集會、結社

等事，均准其自由) and 'the subject shall not be arrested, confined or punished except as prescribed by law' [臣民非按照法律所定，不加以逮捕、監禁、處罰, quoted in Lin Feng (林峰) 百年憲政與中國憲政的未來: *100 Years of Constitutionalism and the Future of Constitutionalism in China* (Hong Kong: Hong Kong City University Press, 2011), p. 79.

28 Xia Yong, *The Philosophy of Civil Rights in the Context of China* (Leiden: Martinus Nijhoff, 2011), 63ff. The translators, Jim Welden and Bi Xiaoqing, persuasively translate *minquan* as 'civil rights', but the author discusses various ways in which the idea differs from liberal, individualist ideas of civil rights. The expression can also be translated as 'people power'.

29 See also ch. 4 ('Sun Zhongshan's human rights thought'), in Du Gangjian, above, n. 21, at 77–86.

30 Marina Svensson, 'Human rights in China as an interdisciplinary field: History, current debates and new approaches', in Thomas Cushman (ed.), *Handbook of Human Rights* (London: Routledge), 685–701.

31 Discussed, with different emphases, by Elena Consiglio, 'The doctrines of human rights in China', unpublished manuscript on file with author; Samuli Seppänen, *Ideological Conflict and the Rule of Law in Contemporary China: Useful Paradoxes* (Cambridge: Cambridge University Press, 2016), 115–23.

32 Jonathan Benney, *Defending Rights in Contemporary China* (Abingdon: Routledge, 2012), especially ch. 2.

33 Eva Pils, 'Taking *yuan* (冤) seriously', *Temple International and Comparative Law Journal*, 25 (2011) 285–327.

34 Sally Engle Merry, *Human Rights and Gender Violence: Translating International Law into Local Justice* (Chicago, IL: Chicago University Press, 2005).

35 An overview of human rights as a global, international movement is provided in Aryeh Neier, *The International Human Rights Movement: A History (Human Rights and Crimes Against Humanity)* (Princeton, NJ: Princeton University Press, 2013), ch. 1 ('The movement').

36 Andrew Nathan, 'China's challenge', *Journal of Democracy*, 26:1 (2015) 156–70.

37 Bodde and Morris, above, n. 16.

38 Section 386 of the Great Qing Code [大清律例] reads: (不应为): 凡不应得为而为之者答四十事理重者杖八十. An excerpt of the Great Qing code is available at <http://www.dushu.com/showbook/101196/1042017.html> [last accessed June 2016].

39 Famously, the principle of *nullum crimen* was called into question by the Nuremberg trial: see Henry J. Steiner, Philip Alston and Ryan Goodman, *International Human Rights in Context: Law, Politics, Morals*, 3rd edn (Oxford: Oxford University Press, 2008), at p. 123. A shorthand (not wholly accurate)

way of describing the liberal perspective is that what has not been (explicitly) prohibited, is allowed.

40 Bodde and Morris, above, n. 16.

41 Chang Wejen, 'Classical Chinese jurisprudence and the development of the Chinese legal system', *Tsinghua Law Review*, 2 (2010) 217–272, at p. 255.

42 Confucius, *Analects*, section 12:10 (子曰：「聽訟，吾猶人也 。必也，使無訟乎！ 」).

43 Introduction to Sarah Biddulph, Elisa Nesossi, Flora Sapio and Susan Trevaskes, *The Politics of Law and Stability in China* (Aldershot: Edward Elgar, 2014).

44 Yu Yingshi (余英时), 'The Chinese Communists are not Confucians', translated by Ai Ru, interview published at *ChinaChange* (1 July 2015), available at <http://chinachange.org/2015/07/01/the-chinese-communists-are-not-confucianists/> [last accessed 19 October 2016].

45 Even if, as Angle has proposed, this will require contemporary Confucians to abandon some long-held positions (as Christian churches have had to): Stephen Angle, *Contemporary Confucian Political Philosophy* (Cambridge: Polity, 2012), 17f.

46 Such as the Hong Kong protest movement, which Professor Yu supported, promptly leading to the banning of his books in mainland China. See Fei Chang Dao, 'State media reports Yu Yingshi's books banned, his books disappear from online bookstores', blog, 13 October 2014, available at <http://blog.feichangdao.com/2014/10/state-media-reports-yu-yingshis-books.html> [last accessed 16 April 2017].

47 Arlif Dirlik, 'Mao Zedong in contemporary Chinese official discourse and history', *China Perspectives*, 2 (2012) 17–27.

48 It bears some affinities with other philosophical perspectives on law, such as Jeremy Bentham's classical rejection of the idea of inalienable natural rights.

49 People's Daily, 'Completely smash the feudal capitalist and revisionist legal system', *Chinese Law & Government*, 2:4 (1969–1970). English translation available at <http://mesharpe.metapress.com/link.asp?id=rpw84w8w70644l15> [last accessed June 2016].

50 Ibid.

51 Article 2 of 中华人民共和国国家安全法 [National Security Law of the People's Republic of China], passed on 1 July 2015 at the 15th meeting of the Standing Committee of the 12th National People's Congress.

52 Minxin Pei, *China's Crony Capitalism: The Dynamics of Regime Decay* (Cambridge, MA: Harvard University Press, 2016).

53 For a detailed and nuanced discussion, see Barry Naughton, 'Is China social-ist?', *Journal of Economic Perspectives*, 31:1 (2017) 3–24.

54 Teng Biao, 'A hole to bury you', *Wall Street Journal*, 28 December 2010, available at <http://www.wsj.com/articles/SB10001424052970203731004576045152244293970> [last accessed June 2016].

55 Conversation # 2 2012 –1.

56 CCP Central Committee Decision concerning Some Major Questions in Comprehensively Moving Governing the Country Forward According to the Law (28 October 2014) (党的领导和社会主义法治是一致的，社会主义法治必须坚持党的领导，党的领导必须依靠社会主义法治).

57 Xi Jinping (习近平), 党大还是法大是伪命题 [*Excerpts from Xi Jinping on Comprehensively Ruling the Country in accordance with law*] (15 April 2015), available at <http://opinion.haiwainet.cn/n/2015/0430/c456318-28688962.html> [last accessed June 2016]: 'The relationship between the Party and the Law is a central reflection of the relationship between political governance [*zhengzhi*] and legal governance [*fazhi*]. There is political governance in legal governance; there is no legal governance that could escape political governance.'

58 Flora Sapio, 'Carl Schmitt in China', The China Story blog, 7 October 2015, available at <https://www.thechinastory.org/2015/10/carl-schmitt-in-china/> [last accessed June 2016].

59 These would threaten to establish what Schmitt, with reference to eighteenth-century Enlightenment philosophers, calls a 'dictatorship of enlightened reason': Carl Schmitt, *Dictatorship: From the Origin of the Modern Concept of Sovereignty to Proletarian Class Struggle*, translated by M. Hoelzl and G. Ward (Cambridge: Polity, 2014). Chapter 4 discusses the instruction, issued to education institutions, to stop discussing 'so-called "universal values"' in 2013.

60 Sapio, above, n. 58.

61 Samuli Seppänen discusses Jiang Shigong's 'irrationalist turn', above, n. 31, at pp. 159–62. So far as they embrace Carl Schmitt, one might describe these scholars as anti-rationalist.

Chapter 2: Institutional Avenues of Human Rights Advocacy

1 Amnesty International, 'Annual Report – China 2015/16', 23 February 2016, available at <https://www.amnesty.org/en/countries/asia-and-the-pacific/china/report-china/> [last accessed 27 October 2016]; Human Rights Watch, 'China (Country Report) (2016)', available at <https://

www.hrw.org/world-report/2016/country-chapters/china-and-tibet> [last accessed 27 October 2016].

2 Freedom House, 'Country Report: China (2016)', available at <https://freedomhouse.org/report/freedom-world/2016/china> [last accessed 27 October 2016].

3 For example, the reports produced by the Swedish government and those produced by the US State Department and Congressional-Executive Committee on China.

4 State Council Information Office Assessment Report on the Implementation of the National Human Rights Action Plan of China (2012–2015) (16 June 2016), available at <http://www.chinahumanrights.org/html/2016/NHRAPC_0614/5056.html> [last accessed 27 October 2016]; State Council Information Office, 'National Human Rights Action Plan of China (2016–2020)' (29 September 2016), available at <http://www.chinahumanrights.org/html/2016/POLITICS_0929/5844.html> and <http://news.xinhuanet.com/english/2016-09/29/c_135722183.htm> [last accessed 27 October 2016].

5 See, for example, China Society for Human Rights Studies, 'US no better than China on women's rights', available at <http://www.chinadaily.com.cn/opinion/2016-10/14/content_27058849.htm> [last accessed 16 April 2017]; China Society for Human Rights Studies, 'China eases household registration in urbanisation drive', available at <http://english.gov.cn/news/top_news/2016/10/14/content_281475466178735.htm> [accessed 16 April 2017]; China Society for Human Rights Studies, 'China opposes British interference in internal affairs', available at <http://english.cctv.com/2016/10/13/ARTIj1oOJ0U6w0bjIJt9XYeT161013.shtml> [last accessed 16 April 2017].

6 This is discussed in chapter 6.

7 Beth A. Simmons, 'Conclusion' in *Mobilizing for Human Rights: International Law in Domestic Politics* (Cambridge: Cambridge University Press, 2009), at p. 360.

8 Kenneth G. Lieberthal and David M. Lampton (eds), *Bureaucracy, Politics and Decision-making in Post-Mao China* (Berkeley, CA: University of California Press, 1992).

9 Pitman B. Potter, *China's Legal System* (Cambridge, MA: Polity, 2013), ch. 1.

10 Wu Tiaohe (吴调和), '党是人民利益的代表 [The Party is the Representative of the People's Interests]', *Shi Dai Chao Magazine* (时代潮), 3 (2006), available at <http://www.people.com.cn/GB/paper83/16850/1480483.html> [last accessed 10 November 2016].

11 PRC Law on Legislation [中华人民共和国立法法], promulgated 15 March 2000, effective 1 July 2000, available at <http://www.gov.cn/test/2005-08/13/content_22423.htm> [last accessed 27 October 2016].

12 Ernest Caldwell, 'Horizontal rights and Chinese constitutionalism: Judicialization through labor disputes', *Chicago-Kent Law Review*, 88 (2012) 63, argues that labour rights have acquired horizontal effects in China and are protected through mediation. See also discussion of the – later revoked – Qi Yuling decision and of mediation below.

13 An overview with further links can be found on the website of the OHCHR: OHCHR, 'The Core International Human Rights Instruments and their monitoring bodies', available at <http://www.ohchr.org/EN/ProfessionalInterest/Pages/CoreInstruments.aspx> [last accessed 27 October 2016].

14 International Covenant on Economic, Social and Cultural Rights (adopted 16 December 1966, entered into force 3 January 1976) 993 UNTS 3 (ICESCR).

15 International Covenant on Civil and Political Rights (adopted 16 December 1966, entered into force 23 March 1976) 999 UNTS 171 (ICCPR).

16 Andrew Neal, 'Implementing ILO Labour Rights in China', in Ulla Liukkunen and Yifeng Chen (eds) *Fundamental Labour Rights in China – Legal Implementation and Cultural Logic* (Heidelberg: Springer, 2016), 30f; China Labour Bulletin, 'China and the ILO, Introduction', 28 February 2001, available at <http://www.clb.org.hk/en/content/china-and-ilo-introduction>.

17 Convention on the Elimination of All Forms of Discrimination against Women (adopted 18 December 1979, entered into force 3 September 1981) 1249 UNTS 13 (CEDAW).

18 Convention on the Elimination of All Forms of Racial Discrimination (adopted 21 December 1965, entered into force 4 January 1969) 660 UNTS 195 (CERD).

19 Convention against Torture and Other Cruel, Inhuman or Degrading Treatment or Punishment (1984) 1465 UNTS 85.

20 Convention on the Rights of the Child (adopted 20 November 1989, entered into force 2 September 1990), 1577 UNTS 3 (CRC).

21 Convention on the Rights of Persons with Disabilities (adopted 30 March 2007, entered into force 3 May 2008), 2515 UNTS (CRPD).

22 Convention on the Protection of the Rights of All Migrant Workers and Members of Their Families (adopted 18 December 1990, entered into force 1 July 2003) 2220 UNTS 3 (CPRM).

23 International Convention for the Protection of All Persons from Enforced Disappearance (adopted 20 December 2006, entered into force 23 December 2010) 2716 UNTS 3.

24 中华人民共和国宪法 [PRC Constitution], passed on 4 December 1982, promulgated and effective as of 4 December 1982, last revised on 14 March 2004.

25 Rights previously safeguarded but omitted in the 1982 Constitution are discussed in chapter 5.

26 Björn Ahl, 'Chinese law and international treaties', *Hong Kong Law Journal*, 39 (2009) 735, at p. 751; Congyan Cai, 'International law in Chinese courts', *American Journal of International Law*, 110:2 (2016) 269, at p. 282f.

27 Huang, Songyou (黄松有), '宪法司法化及其意义—从最高人民法院今天的一个 "批复"谈起 [The judicialization of the Constitution and its significance – a discussion proceeding from the SPC's approving response today]', *People's Court Gazette* (人民法院报), 13 August 2013, available at <http://www.gongfa.com/huangsyxianfasifahua.htm>.

28 Thomas E. Kellogg, 'The death of constitutional litigation in China?' *China Brief*, 9:7 (2009), available at <http://www.jamestown.org/uploads/media/cb_009_7_02.pdf> [last accessed 18 February 2017]; Willy Lam, 'The politicisation of China's law-enforcement and judicial apparatus', *China Perspectives*, 2 (2009), 42–51, available at <http://chinaperspectives.revues.org/4805> [last accessed 27 October 2016].

29 For a more detailed assessment, see Otto Malmgren, 'Article 37: The right to liberty of person under the Chinese constitution', *China-EU Law Journal*, 2:1 (2013) 35–67.

30 PRC Criminal Procedure Law [中华人民共和国刑事诉讼法], passed on 1 July 1979, promulgated on 7 July 1979, effective as of 1 January 1980, last revised on 14 March 2012, available at <http://www.gov.cn/flfg/2012-03/17/content_2094354.htm> [last accessed 27 October 2016]; Joshua Rosenzweig, Flora Sapio, Jue Jiang, Biao Teng and Eva Pils, 'The 2012 revision of the Chinese Criminal Procedure Law', in Mike McConville and Eva Pils (eds), *Criminal Justice in China: Comparative Perspectives* (Cheltenham: Edward Elgar, 2011).

31 The argument here relies on the non-positivistic understanding of rights developed in the Introduction.

32 Chinese Human Rights Defenders, 'Joint Civil Society Report Submitted to UN Committee against Torture – October 2015', available at <https://www.nchrd.org/2015/11/joint-civil-society-report-submitted-to-un-committee-against-torture-october-2015/> [last accessed 27 October 2016].

33 Rosenzweig et al., above, n. 30.

34 中华人民共和国立法法 [PRC Law on Legislation], promulgated 15 March 2000, last revised 15 March 2015, available at <http://

www.npc.gov.cn/npc/dbdhhy/12_3/2015-03/18/content_1930713
.htm>; translation by ChinaLawTranslate available at <http://www
.chinalawtranslate.com/2015lawlaw/?lang=en#_Toc414358117> [last accessed
27 October 2016].

35 Keith Hand, 'Using law for a righteous purpose: The Sun Zhigang incident
and evolving forms of citizen action in the People's Republic of China', *The
Columbia Journal of Transnational Law*, 45 (2006), 138.

36 Teng Biao, 'The Sun Zhigang incident and the future of constitutionalism:
Does the Chinese constitution have a future?', CRJ Occasional Paper, 30
December 2013, available at <https://www.law.cuhk.edu.hk/en/research/
crj/download/papers/2013-tb-szg-constitutionalism.pdf> [last accessed 27
October 2016].

37 Ibid.

38 中华人民共和国立法法 [PRC Law on Legislation], promulgated
15 March 2000, last revised 15 March 2015, available at <http://
www.npc.gov.cn/npc/dbdhhy/12_3/2015-03/18/content_1930713
.htm>; translation by ChinaLawTranslate available at <http://
www.chinalawtranslate.com/2015lawlaw/?lang=en#_Toc414358117>.

39 Wang Zhenmin (王振民) argues, in 中国违宪审查制度 [*Constitutional Review
in China*] (Beijing: Chinese University of Politics and Law Press, 2004) that
the entity that produced a legal norm must be in charge of reviewing its
conformity with other legal standards (谁制定谁审查).

40 Chinese scholars in the academic establishment have emphasized that com-
plementarity of rights and duties is a socialist principle. Elena Consiglio, 'The
doctrines of human rights in China', ch. V of PhD dissertation (University
of Palermo), on file with author.

41 Written out of the current Constitution but not therefore non-existent,
according to the non-positivist view taken here. Cf. Article 12 ICCPR.

42 The practice of *shuanggui* and the problems with torture it involves are discussed, with further references, in chapter 3.

43 A former prosecutor whose experience included interrogating former *shuanggui* detainees explained they had to be interrogated all over again because
the Procuracy could take no official notice of *shuanggui*. Conversation #69
12-01.

44 Human Rights Watch, 'Special measures: Detention and torture in the
Chinese Communist Party's special measures system', 6 December 2016,
available at <https://www.hrw.org/report/2016/12/06/special-measures/
detention-and-torture-chinese-communist-partys-shuanggui-system> [last
accessed 10 April 2017].

45 Lieberthal and Lampton, above, n. 8.

46 Adam Pzreworski, 'Ruling against rules', in Tom Ginsburg and Alberto Simpser (eds), *Constitutions in Authoritarian Regimes* (Cambridge: Cambridge University Press, 2014), 21–35.

47 Will Waluchov, 'Constitutionalism', in *Stanford Encyclopedia of Philosophy* (2010), sections 1–3, available at <http://plato.stanford.edu/entries/constitutionalism/#ConLawVerConCon>.

48 For example, Zhang Qianfan (张千帆), 宪法学讲义 [*Lectures on Constitutional Law*] (Beijing: Peking University Press, 2011); Zhang Qianfan, *The Constitution of China: A Contextual Analysis* (Portland, OR: Hart Publishing, 2012); He Weifang, *In the Name of Justice: Striving for the Rule of Law in China* (Washington, DC: Brookings Institute Press, 2013).

49 Jiang Shigong (强世功), 'Written and unwritten constitutions: A new approach to the study of constitutional government in China [中国宪法中的不成文宪法——理解中国宪法的新视角]', *Modern China*, 36:1 (2010), 12–46, available at <http://www.lishiyushehui.cn/modules/topic/detail.php?topic_id=282> [last accessed 27 October 2016].

50 Allen Habib, 'Promises', in *Stanford Encyclopaedia of Philosophy*, last revised 2014, available at <https://plato.stanford.edu/entries/promises/>. See, in particular, 'Normative Power Views' (5.1).

51 Political scientists studying complaints behaviour have emphasized differences between 'rules consciousness' and 'rights consciousness'. See, for exanple, Lianjiang Li, 'Rights consciousness and rules consciousness in contemporary China', *The China Journal* 64 (2010) 47–68. From the perspective taken here, the use of *yuan* and cognate concepts shows that an overarching value of justice, connected to rule-following as well as to rights, clearly also plays a role. See also Kevin J. O'Brien and Li Lianjiang, *Rightful Resistance in Rural China* (Cambridge: Cambridge University Press, 2006).

52 Liu Wei, in He Yang, *Disbarment* (吊照门) (independent documentary film, 2010). Also: Mathew Robertson and Yaxue Cao, 'The vilification of lawyer Wang Yu and violence by other means', available at https://chinachange.org/2015/07/27/the-vilification-of-lawyer-wang-yu-and-violence-by-other-means/ [last accessed 27 October 2016]; CCTV 13, 北京锋锐律所"维权"黑幕利益链调查 (19 July 2015), available at <http://news.sina.com.cn/c/2015-07-19/023932122718.shtml> [last accessed 27 October 2016]. According to some lawyers, there is greater tolerance for letting lawyers speak about these issues in the South, especially in Guangdong. Conversation #3 2012-1.

53 He Yang, above, n. 52.

54 Lon Fuller, 'The forms and limits of adjudication', in Michael Freeman (ed.), *Alternative Dispute Resolution* (New York: New York University Press, 1995), ch. 1.

55 David Luban, 'Settlements and the erosion of the public realm', *Georgetown Law Journal*, 83 (1995) 2619.

56 Emphasized also by the President of the Supreme People's Court at <http://xhpfm.mobile.zhongguowangshi.com:8091/v210/newshare/674595?channel=weixinp&from=timeline&isappinstalled=0> [last accessed 27 October 2016].

57 Frank K. Upham, 'Who will find the defendant if he stays with his sheep? Justice in rural China', *Yale Law Journal*, 114 (2005) 1675, at pp. 1680f.

58 Xinhua Net, '最高法:我国法官人数已近20万人 [SPC: Nationwide number of judges approximates 200,000]', 25 July 2013, available at <http://news.xinhuanet.com/legal/2013-07/25/c_116690034.htm>. No later public figures could be found.

59 Xinhua Net, '我国执业律师人数已突破30万 [Number of professional lawyers surpasses 300,000]', 9 January 2017, <http://news.xinhuanet.com/politics/2017-01/09/c_1120275319.htm>.

60 Li Ling, 'The Chinese Communist Party and People's Courts: Judicial dependence in China', *American Journal of Comparative Law*, 64:1 (2016), 4.

61 Every year, the Annual Work Report by the Supreme People's Court President (such as Zhou Qiang (周强), '最高人民法院工作报告——2017年3月12日在第十二届全国人民代表大会第五次会议上 [Supreme People's Work Report – submitted at the Fifth Plenary Meeting of the Twelfth NPC on 12 March 2017]', available at <http://www.npc.gov.cn/npc/xinwen/2017-03/15/content_2018938.htm> [accessed 16 April 2017]) includes a rundown of disciplinary procedures, investigations, prosecutions and convictions for judicial corruption-related crimes, such as 'bending the law' and bribe-taking; and professional judges have been quitting in rather large numbers. See Sina.com, '法官离职潮背后:丰满的理想抵挡不住现实骨感 [What lies behind the wave of judges quitting: fine ideals cannot withstand sense of realism]' (24 July 2016), available at <http://news.sina.com.cn/c/nd/2016-07-24/doc-ifxuhukz0907342.shtml> [last accessed 27 October 2016].

62 On the problems ordinarily affecting the defence in criminal trials, see Mike McConville et al., *Criminal Justice in China: An Empirical Enquiry* (Cheltenham: Edward Elgar, 2011), at p. 317.

63 See Gu Li (古莉), 中国人大听取"两高报告" 去年中国700多人以恐怖或分裂罪获刑, 13 March 2015, at <http://www.chinainperspective.com/ArtShow.aspx?AID=40721>, calculating a conviction rate of 99.3% on the basis

of the Supreme People's Procuracy Work Report (2015); Andrew Jacobs, 'Conviction rates count more in Chinese justice than innocence', *The New York Times*, 13 May 2015, available at <http://www.nytimes.com/2015/05/13/world/asia/conviction-rates-count-more-in-chinese-justice-than-innocence.html?_r=0>.

64 律师事务所管理办法 [Regulation on the Management of Law Firms], promulgated by edict 133/2016 of the Ministry of Justice on 6 September 2016, available at <http://www.gov.cn/gongbao/content/2016/content_5109321.htm>.

65 Benjamin L. Liebman, 'Legal reform: China's law-stability paradox', *Daedalus*, 143:2 (2014) 96–109; Carl F. Minzner, 'China's turn against law', *American Journal of Comparative Law*, 59 (2011) 935.

66 Chapter 4 discusses some limitations of this option due to censorship.

67 On the role of court mediation in other, especially rural settings, see Stéphanie Balme, *China – les visages de la justice ordinaire* [The faces of ordinary justice in China] (Paris: Presses de Sciences Po, 2016), 187–202; Frank Upham, above, n. 57.

68 Discussed in Benjamin L. Liebman, 'Article 41 and the Right to Appeal', Columbia Public Law Research Paper No. 14-407 (2014).

69 中华人民共和国国务院信访条例 [State Council Regulation on Letters and Visits], promulgated on 10 January 2005, effective as of 1 May 2005, available at <http://theory.people.com.cn/GB/41179/41181/3127789.html> [last accessed 27 October 2016].

70 Eva Pils, 'Land disputes, rights assertion and social unrest: A case from Sichuan', *Columbia Journal of Asian Law*, 19 (2006) 365, reprinted as Hauser Global Law School Working Paper 07/05 and in Perry Keller (ed.), *Obligations and Property Rights in China* (Farnham: Ashgate Publishing, 2012).

71 Xiao Han (萧瀚), '子虚乌有的诈骗——有关夏霖案案情 [Trumped-up fraud cases – cases related to that of [Lawyer] Xia Lin]', *Epoch Times*, 25 September 2016, available at <http://www.epochtimes.com/gb/16/9/25/n8335874.htm> [last accessed 10 April 2017].

72 Eva Pils, above, n. 70.

73 Carl F. Minzner, 'Xinfang: An alternative to the formal Chinese legal system', *Stanford Journal of International Law*, 42 (2006) 103.

74 Li Li, 'Judicial independence should come first', interview with Professor He Weifang, 10 November 2005, available at <http://chinadigitaltimes.net/2005/11/judicial-independence-should-come-first-li-li/> [last accessed 27 October 2016].

75 Yang Fan (扬帆), 中国信访据称2015年上访量下降 访民反驳系因维稳力度强, Radio Free Asia, 26 January 2016, available at <http://www.rfa.org/mandarin/yataibaodao/renquanfazhi/yf3-01252016105302.html> [last accessed 10

April 2017]. See also 张璁, '2015年全国信访总量下降7.4%', 25 January 2016, available at <http://paper.people.com.cn/rmrb//html/2016-01/26/nw.D110000renmrb_20160126_5-06.htm> [last accessed 10 April 2017]. Neither article mentions absolute figures.

76 For example, visits are not allowed by groups larger than five persons, and 'jumping levels' in petitioning (*yueji shangfang*) is not allowed: Mr Liu could not have gone straight from Zigong to Beijing, according to these rules.

77 Carl F. Minzner, above, n. 73.

78 Flora Sapio, 'Legal erosion and the policing of petitions', in Mike McConville and Eva Pils (eds), *Comparative Perspectives on Criminal Justice in China* (Cheltenham: Edward Elgar, 2013). Discussed in chapter 3.

79 The documentary *Petition* portrays the fate of one victim of this practice. See also chapter 3 for further references on psychiatric incarceration. Zhao Liang (赵亮), *Petition* [上访], independent documentary, Beijing, 2009 [copy on file with author].

80 The plan is mentioned in the Introduction.

81 Yaxue Cao, 'The life and death of Cao Shunli', China Change, 18 March 2014, available at <https://chinachange.org/2014/03/18/the-life-and-death-of-cao-shunli-1961-2014/> [last accessed 27 October 2016].

82 UPR Info, 'China prevents moment of silence in memory of human rights defender', 26 March 2014, available at <https://www.upr-info.org/en/news/china-prevents-moment-silence-memory-human-rights-defender> [last accessed 10 April 2017].

83 Du Bin (杜斌), see book cover.

84 Conversation #23 2013-1.

85 Picture on file with author. Lawyer Shi Qing (石青律师) [pen name], '营口中院非法剥夺律师阅卷权 [The Intermediate Court of Yingkou illegally refuses lawyers access to files]', 20 April 2013 at <http://news.boxun.com/news/gb/china/2013/04/201304040209.shtml>.

86 Conversation #52 2011-1. On such effects in the case of court petitioning, see also He Xin and Feng Yuqing, 'Mismatched discourses in the petition offices of Chinese courts', *Law and Social Inquiry*, 41 (2016) 212–41.

87 A topic to be further discussed in chapter 6, which addresses the trajectory of the China's rights defence movement.

88 Beth A. Simmons, *Mobilizing for Human Rights: International Law in Domestic Politics* (Cambridge: Cambridge University Press, 2009).

89 Simmons discusses this with regard to the examples of Israel as an 'embattled democracy' and Chile as a country in transition to liberal democracy, addressing compliance with the Convention Against Torture, in ibid., ch. 7.

Chapter 3: Liberty and Life

1 黑龙江省农垦总局法制教育中心（俗称"青龙山洗脑班"以下简称"黑监狱"）[Legal Education Centre of the Heilongjiang Province General Bureau of Farm Reclamation (popularly known as Qinglongshan Brainwashing Class)], available at <http://wqw2010.blogspot.co.uk/2014/04/blog-post_2873.html> [last accessed 10 November 2016].

2 Celia Hatton, 'Lawyer: I was tortured by Chinese Police', BBC World News, 15 November 2015, available at <http://www.bbc.co.uk/news/world-asia-34794712> [last accessed 10 November 2016].

3 建三江维权全程24天日志 [Jiansanjiang, a 24-day Diary], Human Rights in China, 14 April 2014, available at <http://www.hrichina.org/chs/gong-min-yan-chang/jian-san-jiang-wei-quan-quan-cheng-24tian-ri-zhi> [last accessed 10 November 2016].

4 中国维权律师关注组谴责黑龙江建三江农垦公安对维权律师施以酷刑非法拘禁公民 [China Human Rights Lawyers Concern Group condemns Heilongjiang Province Jiansanjiang Land Reclamation Police for torture and false imprisonment of human rights lawyers and (other) citizens]', China Human Rights Lawyers Concern Group, 8 April 2014, available at <http://www.chrlawyers.hk/zh-hant/20140408_2> [last accessed 10 November 2016].

5 Discussed in chapter 6. On the Jiansanjiang Incident, see also Elisa Nesossi, 'Political opportunities in non-democracies: The case of Chinese *weiquan* lawyers', *The International Journal of Human Rights*, 19:7 (2015) 961–78, at p. 967f.

6 John Stuart Mill, *On Liberty*, 4th edn (London: Longman, Roberts & Green, 1869).

7 Under public international law, the right to liberty of the person includes freedom from arbitrary detention and forced disappearance, as well as security of the person. It is inherently connected to the right to a fair trial, especially in criminal justice contexts. Article 9 UDHR, Article 9 ICCPR and the IPPED are discussed in Sangeeta Shah, 'Detention and trial', in Daniel Moeckli, Sangeeta Shah and Sandesh Sivakumaran (eds), *International Human Rights Law*, 2nd edn (Oxford: Oxford University Press, 2014), 259–85.

8 The right to integrity of the person includes the right to life, as well as the right not to be tortured or treated inhumanely. See Nigel Rodley, 'Integrity of the person', in Daniel Moeckli, Sangeeta Shah and Sandesh Sivakumaran (eds), *International Human Rights Law*, 2nd edn (Oxford: Oxford University Press, 2014), 174–94.

9 This system is discussed in chapter 5.

10 Fu Hualing, 'Re-education Through Labour in historical perspective', *The China Quarterly*, 184 (2005) 811–30.

11 Chris Smith and Ngai Pun, 'The dormitory labour regime in China as a site for control and resistance', *The International Journal of Human Resource Management*, 17:8 (2006) 1456–70. Also observations at various Beijing university campuses in 2003.

12 Chinese Human Rights Defenders, 'The Darkest Corners: abuses of involuntary psychiatric commitment in China', 22 August 2012, copy on file with author, available at <https://www.amnesty.org.uk/blogs/countdown-china/%E2%80%9C-darkest-corners%E2%80%9D-abuses-involuntary-psychiatric-commitment-china>; Eva Pils, 'Taking *Yuan* (冤) seriously', *Temple International and Comparative Law Journal*, 25 (2011) 285–327.

13 Human Rights Watch, 'An alleyway in hell: China's abusive "black jails"', 12 November 2009, available at <http://www.hrw.org/en/reports/2009/11/12/alleyway-hell-0> [last accessed 10 November 2016].

14 The use of 'detention' and 'arrest' in English follows established translation conventions also reflected in translations of the Criminal Procedure Law. For a discussion of Article 37, see Otto Malmgren, 'Article 37: The right to liberty of person under the Chinese constitution', *China-EU Law Journal*, 2:1 (2013) 35–67.

15 Article 238 of the PRC Criminal Law [中华人民共和国刑法], passed on 1 July 1979, promulgated on 6 July 1979, effective as of 1 January 1980, last revised on 29 August 2015, available at <http://www.chinalawtranslate.com/%E4%B8%AD%E5%8D%8E%E4%BA%BA%E6%B0%91%E5%85%B1%E5%92%8C%E5%9B%BD%E5%88%91E6%B3%95%EF%BC%882015%E5%B9%B4%E4%BF%AE%E6%AD%A3%EF%BC%89/?lang=en?lang=en> [last accessed 16 April 2017].

16 For a discussion of the arguments challenging the constitutionality of the now-abolished Custody and Repatriation system, see Keith Hand, 'Using law for a righteous purpose: The Sun Zhigang Incident and evolving forms of citizen action in the People's Republic of China', *The Columbia Journal of Transnational Law*, 45 (2006) 138. The law cited is 中华人民共和国立法法 [PRC Law on Legislation], promulgated by the Standing Committee of the National People's Congress, 15 March 2000, effective 1 July 2000, available at <http://www.gov.cn/test/2005-08/13/content_22423.htm> [last accessed 10 November 2016].

17 International Covenant on Civil and Political Rights (adopted 16 December 1966, entered into force 23 March 1976) 999 UNTS 171 (ICCPR).

18 Fu Hualing, 'The varieties of law in China', Human Rights in China, 18 July 2011, available at <http://www.hrichina.org/en/crf/article/5422> [last accessed 10 November 2016].

19 For a classical account of the role of law in Mao era, see Jerome A. Cohen, *The Criminal Process in the People's Republic of China, 1949–1963: An Introduction* (Cambridge, MA: Harvard University Press, 1968).

20 Routine detention of criminal suspects (in the absence of a right to bail since *qubao houshen* is understood as a restrictive measure imposed at the discretion of the police) is in tension with Article 9(3) of the ICCPR. Mike McConville et al., *China's Criminal Justice: An Empirical Enquiry* (Cheltenham: Edward Elgar, 2011), 44ff., especially at 56ff. on low bail rates.

21 Keith Hand, above, n. 16.

22 Amnesty International, 'Changing the soup but not the medicine? Abolishing Re-education Through Labour in China' (London: Amnesty International Publications, 2013), available at <https://www.amnesty.org/en/documents/ASA17/042/2013/en/> [last accessed 10 November 2016].

23 Decision-making panels been introduced, but, as they did not take a fully judicial format, they were, according to lawyers, not effective in reducing the power of the police.

24 For a critical discussion and appeals to abolish RTL, see Mao Yushi et al., 'Open letter suggesting the abolition of Re-education Through Labour', 2007, available at <http://www.aboluowang.com/2007/1204/65722.html> [last accessed 29 December 2013]; Reuters, 'China's Re-education Through Labour system', Reuters, 20 December 2007, available at <http://www.reuters.com/video/2007/12/20/chinas-re-education-through-labour?videoId=73011> [last accessed 10 November 2016]; Donald C. Clarke, 'The famous hukou editorial', Chinese Law Prof Blog, 26 March 2010, available at <http://lawprofessors.typepad.com/china_law_prof_blog/2010/03/the-famous-hukou-editorial.html> [last accessed 10 November 2016].

25 'Statement on abolition of RTL and related problems by Chinese lawyers for the protection of human rights', Siweiluozi's Blog, 19 November 2013, available at <http://www.siweiluozi.net/2013/11/statement-on-abolition-of-re-education.html> [last accessed 10 November 2016]; Amnesty International, above, n. 22; Donald Clarke, 'Why Chinese needs a good word for "irony", and why it's too soon to bid farewell to re-education through labour', Chinese Law Prof Blog, 28 November 2013, available at <http://lawprofessors.typepad.com/china_law_prof_blog/2013/11/why-chinese-needs-a-good-word-for-irony-and-why-its-too-soon-to-bid-farewell-to-re-education-through.html> [last accessed 10 November 2016].

26　'Statement on abolition of RTL', above, n. 25.

27　Teng Biao, Presentation on the topic of 'Extra-judicial detention', copy on file with author; Sarah Biddulph, 'The production of legal norms: A case study of administrative detention in China', *UCLA Pacific Basin Law Journal*, 20 (2003) 217–77. See also Article 11(2), Administrative Litigation Law.

28　Hu Jia and Zeng Jinyan, 'Prisoners in Freedom City', independent documentary (2006), available at <https://www.youtube.com/watch?v=l2zvJItBCN8> [last accessed 10 November 2016]. See also Elisa Nesossi, 'An interview with Zeng Jinyan 曾金燕', The China Story, 27 May 2013, available at <https://www.thechinastory.org/2013/05/an-interview-with-zeng-jinyan-%E6%9B%BE%E9%87%91%E7%87%95/> [last accessed 10 November 2016]. Many of the conversations mentioned in the Introduction were conducted in settings of *ruanjin*.

29　Article 2, International Convention for the Protection of All Persons from Enforced Disappearance, available at <http://www.ohchr.org/EN/HRBodies/CED/Pages/ConventionCED.aspx> [last accessed 10 November 2016]; Universal Declaration of Human Rights.

30　Article 2, Constitution of Communist Party of China, adopted on 14 November 2012, available at <http://www.china.org.cn/china/18th_cpc_congress/2012-11/16/content_27138030_2.htm> [last accessed 10 November 2016]. See also Chapter VII of the Charter on 'Party Discipline'. Clearly, the duty to abide by the laws of the state (see also Article 38) is not extended to requiring the CCDI to respect the criminal law prohibition of false imprisonment. As of this writing, efforts to redesign the Party discipline and inspection system are underway. See Jun Mai, 'New Communist Party rules call on top Chinese cadres to inform on each other', *South China Morning Post*, 3 November 2016, available at <http://www.scmp.com/news/china/policies-politics/article/2042440/new-communist-party-rules-call-top-chinese-cadres> [last accessed 10 April 2017].

31　See chapter 2 on the possible creation of a new Party-State Supervision Committee.

32　Human Rights Watch, 'Special measures: Detention and torture in the Chinese Communist Party's *Shuanggui* system', 6 December 2016, available at <https://www.hrw.org/report/2016/12/06/special-measures/detention-and-torture-chinese-communist-partys-shuanggui-system> [last accessed 10 April 2017]; Flora Sapio, 'Shuanggui and Extralegal Detention in China', *China Information*, 22:1 (2008) 7–37; Larry Catá Backer, 'Communist Party and State discipline in China: Exploring Shuang gui 双规 and Shuang kai', Law at the End of the Day, 2 August 2011, available at

<http://lcbackerblog.blogspot.co.uk/2011/08/communist-party-and-state-discipline-in.html> [last accessed 10 November 2016]; Pu Zhiqiang, 'Ningyuan Shuanggui', Vimeo, February 2014, translated by HKU Media Project and ChinaChange, available at <https://vimeo.com/104070378> [last accessed 10 November 2016]. Original with Chinese subtitles: 双规噩梦 —湖南永州宁远双规访谈实录, available at <https://www.youtube.com/watch?v=ovpCJR8Ciho> [last accessed 10 November 2016].

33 Human Rights Watch, above, n. 13.

34 Donald Clarke, above, n. 25; Teng Biao, 'What is a "legal education center" in China', *ChinaChange*, 3 April 2014, available at <https://chinachange.org/2014/04/03/what-is-a-legal-education-center-in-china/> [last accessed 10 April 2017].

35 Jiang Tianyong, Tang Jitian, Wang Cheng and Zhang Junjie (江天勇、唐吉田、王成、张俊杰), '建三江被拘四律师获释后的联合声明 [Joint statement by the four lawyers detained in Jiansanjiang following their release]', 13 April 2014, available at <http://www.hrichina.org/en/citizens-square/joint-statement-four-lawyers-detained-jiansanjiang-following-their-release> [last accessed 10 November> 2016].

36 江天勇四律师被拘留前对"建三江黑监狱"受害者的调查记录 [Jiang Tian-yong's records on the victims of the Jiansanjiang Black Prison prior to the four lawyers' detention]', Weiquanwang, 3 April 2014, available at <http://wqw2010.blogspot.co.uk/2014/04/blog-post_2873.html> [last accessed 10 November 2016]. Many lawyers have testified to the use of torture in all contexts of custody imposed on Falun Gong members, including 'legal education centres' – see, for example, Conversation #28 2013-1.

37 Wang Xing (王星), '北京"黑监狱"截访案10人获刑 [10 persons criminally punished in the case of the Beijing "Black Prison" for retrieving petition-ers]', *Southern Metropolis Daily*, (南方都市报), 6 February 2013, available at <http://news.sohu.com/20130206/n365654524.shtml> [last accessed 29 December 2013].

38 Ibid.

39 Chinese Human Rights Lawyers Group, 'Solemn declaration on illegal deten-tion of four lawyers and many citizens by Heilongjiang authorities', Human Rights in China, 21 March 2014, available at <http://www.hrichina.org/en/citizens-square/solemn-declaration-illegal-detention-four-lawyers-and-many-citizens-heilongjiang> [last accessed 10 April 2017].

40 'Urgent complaint filed before the Heilongjiang Supreme People's Procuratorate against Sui Fengfu, Party Secretary of the General Bureau of Farm Reclama-tion of Heilongjiang and other persons for abduction, illegal detention, and

other crimes', Human Rights in China, 28 March 2014, available at <http://www.hrichina.org/en/citizens-square/urgent-complaint-filed-heilongjiang-supreme-peoples-procuratorate-against-sui-fengfu> [last accessed 10 November 2016].

41 Zhang Lei, 'Administrative complaint submitted to Heilongjiang Provincial High People's Court against Qixing Sub-branch of the Jiansanjiang Farm Reclamation Public Security Bureau', Human Rights in China, 4 April 2014, available at <http://www.hrichina.org/en/citizens-square/administrative-complaint-submitted-heilongjiang-provincial-high-peoples-court-0> [last accessed 10 November 2016].

42 Joshua Rosenzweig, 'Disappearing justice: Public opinion, secret arrest and criminal procedure reform in China', *The China Journal*, 70 (2013) 73–97; Joshua Rosenzweig, Flora Sapio, Jiang Jue, Teng Biao and Eva Pils, 'The 2012 revision of the Chinese Criminal Procedure Law: (Mostly) old wine in new bottles', in Mike McConville and Eva Pils (eds), *Comparative Perspectives on Criminal Justice in China* (Cheltenham: Edward Elgar, 2013). The longest period for such non-residential residential surveillance is twice six months, according to the rules (Conversation #93 2013-1 describes an earlier such case).

43 Rosenzweig et al., ibid.

44 Terence C. Halliday and Sida Liu describe criminal procedure reform as occurring in 'recursive cycles', driven by attempts to liberalize, as much as by resistance against liberalization: *Criminal Defence in China: The Politics of Lawyers at Work* (Cambridge: Cambridge University Press, 2016), ch. 2.

45 He Yang (何杨), *Conversation with Lawyer Zhu Mingyong on torture* (专访朱明勇律师—黑打); Anonymous, '乐平一案两凶之真凶 [*The True Murderer of Leping*]', independent documentary film (September 2013).

46 He Yang (何杨), '应急避难场所 [*Emergency Shelter*]', independent documentary film (2010).

47 Pu Zhiqiang, above, n. 32.

48 Du Bin, *Above the Ghosts' Heads: The Women of Masanjia Labor Camp*, independent documentary (2013), available at <https://www.youtube.com/watch?v=sFEl7oophB0> [last accessed 10 November 2016].

49 'Stephen Sackur interviews Ai Weiwei: "In prison, nothing protects you"', BBC *Hardtalk*, 17 March 2014, available at <https://www.youtube.com/watch?v=1Ach0sc4yI8> [last accessed 10 April 2017]; ChinaAid, 'Interview with Gao Zhisheng', 23 September 2015, available at <https://www.youtube.com/watch?v=DflUjveJNGU> [last accessed 10 November 2016].

50 More extensive descriptions can be found, for example, in the above-quoted report by Amnesty International; see Amnesty International, above, n. 22. For a historical account, see Albert Chen Hongyi (陈弘毅), '古今中外酷刑现象的反思 [Reflections on the phenomenon of torture in China and abroad]', 31 August 2013, available at <http://www.aisixiang.com/data/67217.html> [last accessed 10 November 2016]. See also Eva Pils, *China's Human Rights Lawyers: Advocacy and Resistance* (Abingdon: Routledge, 2014), ch. 6.

51 Article 1, Convention against Torture and Other Cruel, Inhuman or Degrading Treatment or Punishment (1984) 1465 UNTS 85.

52 Articles 238, 247 and 248 of中华人民共和国刑法 [PRC Criminal Law], above, n. 15; Articles 18, 50 and 54 of中华人民共和国刑事诉讼法 [PRC Criminal Procedure Law], passed on 1 July 1979, promulgated on 7 July 1979, effective as of 1 January 1980, last revised on 14 March 2012, translation available at <http://www.cecc.gov/resources/legal-provisions/criminal-procedure-law-of-the-peoples-republic-of-china> [last accessed 10 November 2016].

53 Committee Against Torture, 'Concluding observations on the fifth periodic report of China (advance version)', 9 December 2015, available at <http://www.savetibet.org/wp-content/uploads/2015/12/CAT_C_CHN_CO_5_22477_E.pdf> [last accessed 10 November 2016].

54 Flora Sapio, 'Coercive interrogation', in Flora Sapio (ed.), *Sovereign Power and the Law in China* (The Hague: Brill, 2010), 207–18; further references are provided below.

55 Chinese Human Rights Defenders, 'Joint Civil Society Report Submitted to UN Committee against Torture – October 2015', available at <https://chrdnet.com/2015/11/joint-civil-society-report-submitted-to-un-committee-against-torture-october-2015/> [last accessed 10 November 2016]; Amnesty International, 'No end in sight: Torture and forced confessions in China', 12 November 2015, available at <https://www.amnesty.org/en/documents/asa17/2730/2015/en/> [last accessed 10 November 2016]; Human Rights Watch, 'Tiger chairs and cell bosses: Police torture of criminal suspects in China', 13 May 2015, available at <https://www.hrw.org/report/2015/05/13/tiger-chairs-and-cell-bosses/police-torture-criminal-suspects-china> [last accessed 10 November 2016]; Chen Youxi, 'Torture in China: Fact or fiction', translated by Duihua Foundation, 2 August 2010, available at <http://www.duihuahrjournal.org/2010/08/translation-commentary-torture-in-china.html> [last accessed 10 November 2016].

56 Conversation #28 2013-1.

57 Human Rights Watch, above, n. 55.

58 Mike McConville, 'Comparative empirical coordinates and the dynamics of criminal justice in China and the West', in Mike McConville and Eva Pils

(eds), *Comparative Perspectives on Criminal Justice in China* (Cheltenham: Edward Elgar, 2013), p. 23 (partly quoting Leo and Koenig).

59 Jiang Jue, 'Legal and political rights advocacy in wrongful conviction death penalty cases in China: A study of the Leping case of injustice', *Columbia Journal of Asian Law*, 29:2 (2016), available at <http://cjal.columbia.edu/article/ legal-and-political-rights-advocacy-in-wrongful-conviction-death-penalty- cases-in-china-a-study-of-the-leping-case-of-injustice/> [last accessed 10 November 2016].

60 Human Rights Watch, above, n. 55, discusses persistent procedural flaws and indicating that evidence was excluded in only 6% of cases where torture was alleged. See also Jeremy Daum, 'Tortuous progress: Early cases under China's new procedures for excluding evidence in criminal cases', *NYU Journal of International Law and Policy*, 43 (2011) 699–712; Margaret K. Lewis, 'Controlling abuse to maintain control: The exclusionary rule in China', *NYU Journal of International Law and Politics*, 43 (2011) 629.

61 Chen Youxi, above, n. 55.

62 Conversation #95 2013-3.

63 Joshua D. Rosenzweig, above, n. 42. Jiang Jue discusses complaints as one of the institutional motivations for 'criminal reconciliation', i.e. settling criminal cases between victim and perpetrator (or their families) often on the basis of a payment. See Jiang Jue, *Criminal Reconciliation in Contemporary China: An Empirical and Analytical Enquiry* (Cheltenham: Edward Elgar, 2016). See also Zhang Xianming (张先明), '最高法院发布意见防范刑事冤假错案 [SPC issues Opinion on preventing wrongful criminal cases]', *People's Court Gazette* (人民法院报), 22 November 2013, avalable at <http://www.chinacourt.org/ article/detail/2013/11/id/1148623.shtml> [last accessed 10 November 2016].

64 Conversation #69 2012-1. Similar attitudes towards torture are discussed by Ira Belkin. See Ira Belkin, 'China's tortuous path toward ending torture in criminal investigation', *Columbia Journal of Asian Law*, 24 (2010–11) 273.

65 Darius Rejali, 'Ice water and sweatboxes', *Slate*, 17 March 2009, available at <http://www.slate.com/id/2213959/> [last accessed 10 November 2016].

66 Conversation #101 2011-1.

67 'Accept supervision' is a phrase used, for example, in 'accepting supervision from the media'.

68 Conversation #120-16-1.

69 Cited in chapter 1.

70 Jeremy Waldron, *Torture, Terror and Trade-Offs: Philosophy for the White House* (Oxford: Oxford University Press, 2010), ch. 7, p. 224. On the argument that democratic systems created a 'lingua franca of modern torture' through

their use of white or clean torture techniques, see Darius Rejali, *Torture and Democracy* (Princeton, NJ: Princeton University Press, 2007).

71 Conversation #25 2013-3.

72 Article 6, International Covenant on Civil and Political Rights (1966) 999 UNTS 171.

73 Human Rights Committee, 'General Comment No. 6: Article 6 (Right to Life)' (1982) UN Doc No. HR1/GEN/1/Rev.1.

74 PRC Criminal Law [中华人民共和国刑法], avove, n. 15. There is no crime for which death is the only mandatory form of punishment.

75 BBC, 'China executes corrupt Hangzhou and Suzhou officials', BBC News, 19 July 2011, available at <http://www.bbc.co.uk/news/world-asia-pacific-14197485>. According to Deutsche Welle, no Communist Party officials have been executed since Xi came into office. See 'China allows death penalty for "extremely serious" corruption cases', Deutsche Welle, 18 April 2016, available at <http://www.dw.com/en/china-allows-death-penalty-for-extremely-serious-corruption-cases/a-19195292> [last accessed 10 November 2016].

76 Article 252 of中华人民共和国刑事诉讼法 [PRC Criminal Procedure Law], passed on 1 July 1979, promulgated on 7 July 1979, effective as of 1 January 1980, last revised on 14 March 2012, translation available at <http://www.cecc.gov/resources/legal-provisions/criminal-procedure-law-of-the-peoples-republic-of-china> [last accessed 10 November 2016].

77 Børge Bakken, 'Capital punishment reform, public opinion, and penal elitism in the People's Republic of China', in Surya Deva and Roger Hood (eds), *Confronting Capital Punishment in Asia: Human Rights, Politics and Public Opinion* (Oxford: Oxford University Press, 2013), 192. See also Yu Jiang (俞江), '中国刑法史上的"杀人偿命" ["A life for a life" in the Chinese history of criminal law]', 3 May 2012, available at <https://commondatastorage.googleapis.com/letscorp_archive/archives/23228> [last accessed 10 November 2016].

78 Borge Bakken, 'The norms of death: Capital punishment in China', presentation at the Australian National University, uploaded 5 December 2010, available at <https://www.youtube.com/watch?v=D6dC7Zcv198> [last accessed 10 November 2016].

79 Dietrich Oberwittler and Shenghui Qi, 'Public opinion on the death penalty in China: results from a general population survey conducted in three provinces in 2007/08', Max Planck Institute for Foreign and International Criminal Law, available at <https://www.mpicc.de/files/pdf2/forschung_aktuell_41.pdf> [last accessed 10 November 2016]. However, on corruption, see Zachary Keck, 'China overwhelmingly supports death penalty for corrupt officials', *The*

Diplomat, 7 November 2014, available at <http://thediplomat.com/2014/11/china-overwhelmingly-supports-death-penalty-for-corrupt-officials/> [last accessed 10 November 2016].

80 Ibid.; some 29% versus 23%.

81 Ibid. For the example of post-World War II (Western) Germany, see Yvonne Hotzel, *Debatten um die Todesstrafe in der BRD* [Death Penalty Debates in the Federal Republic of Germany] (Berlin: de Gruyter, 2010).

82 For a brief presentation of the argument against cultural relativism, see James Rachels, 'The challenge of cultural relativism', in James Rachels (ed.), *The Elements of Moral Philosophy*, 3rd edn (New York: Random House, 1999), 20–36; Bernard Williams, *Morality: An Introduction to Ethics* (New York: Harper & Row, 1972).

83 Zhang Xiaohu (张小虎), '刑事法学旧派与新派的犯罪学思想比较研究 [A comparative study of the criminological ideas of old and new schools of criminal law thought]', undated, available at <http://www.hflib.gov.cn/law/law/falvfagui2/XF/LWJ/1104.htm> [last accessed 10 November 2016] (briefly introducing Beccaria's and Bentham's arguments against the death penalty). See below on the argument that the death penalty is undemocratic.

84 Sue Trevaskes, 'China's death penalty: The Supreme People's Court, the suspended death sentence and the politics of penal reform', *British Journal of Criminology*, 53 (2013) 482–99.

85 For a sympathetic, yet critical discussion, see Liu Renwen, 'Recent reforms and prospects in China', in Surya Deva and Roger Hood (eds), *Confronting Capital Punishment in Asia: Human Rights, Politics and Public Opinion* (Oxford: Oxford University Press, 2013), 107–22.

86 Shan Yuxiao and Li Rongde, 'Supreme Court procedure reduces death sentences by 60%', *Caixin Magazine*, 13 September 2016, available at <http://english.caixin.com/2016-09-13/100988191.html> [last accessed 10 November 2016].

87 Trevaskes, above, n. 84, at 487; China Against Death Penalty (北京兴善研究所), '中国死刑报告/China Death Penalty Report' (2012), available at <https://www.worldcoalition.org/media/resourcecenter/CADP2012report-ZH.pdf> [last accessed 10 November 2016], 12–13; Mao Yushi (茅于轼), '死刑信息的公开化 [Publicising information about the death penalty]', Mao Yushi's Blog [茅于轼的博客], 9 August 2007, available at <http://blog.sina.com.cn/s/blog_49a3971d01000bbh.html> [last accessed 10 April 2017].

88 Dietrich Oberwittler and Shenghui Qi, 'Public opinion on the death penalty in China: results from a general population survey conducted in three provinces

in 2007/08', Max Planck Institute for Foreign and International Criminal Law, available at <https://www.mpicc.de/files/pdf2/forschung_aktuell_41.pdf> [last accessed 10 November 2016], at p. 18.

89 Jiang Jue, above, n. 59.

90 Rosenzweig et al., above, n. 42, at p. 33f.

91 UNGA, 'Report of the Special Rapporteur on extrajudicial, summary or arbitrary executions' ('Summary of Cases Transmitted') (2013) UN Doc A/HRC/17/28/Add.1.

92 Elizabeth Lynch, 'China's first test of the new exclusionary rules – A dog without a bite', *China Law & Policy Blog*, 30 September 2010, available at <http://chinalawandpolicy.com/tag/fan-qihang/> [last accessed 10 April 2017].

93 Oberwittler and Qi, above, n. 88.

94 For a critical discussion, see Rosenzweig et al., above, n. 41 (section on criminal reconciliation). For a discussion favouring this argument, see Liu Renwen (刘仁文), '死刑案件不应排除和解 [In death penalty cases, reconciliation should not be ruled out]', in 死刑的温度 [*The Temperature of the Death Penalty*] (Beijing: SDX Joint Publishing Company, 2014), 338–41.

95 Joshua Rosenzweig, 'Public opinion, criminal justice, and incipient popular liberalism in China', The China Story, 17 March 2014, available at <https://www.thechinastory.org/2014/03/public-opinion-criminal-justice-and-incipient-popular-liberalism-in-china/> [last accessed 10 November 2016] (on the Xia Junfeng case); Teng Biao, 'Politics of the death penalty in China', *ChinaChange*, 16 January 2014, available at <https://chinachange.org/2014/01/16/politics-of-the-death-penalty-in-china/> [accessed 10 November 2016].

96 AL Caplan, Gabriel Danovitch, Michael Shapiro, Jacob Lavee and Miran Epstein, 'Time for a boycott of Chinese science and medicine pertaining to organ transplantation', *The Lancet*, 378 (2011).

97 Didi Kirsten Tatlow, 'China bends vow on using prisoners' organs for transplants', *The New York Times*, 16 November 2015, available at <http://www.nytimes.com/2015/11/17/world/asia/china-bends-vow-using-prisoners-organs-for-transplants.html> [accessed 10 November 2016].

98 Oberwittler and Qi, above, n. 93.

99 Falun Gong practitioners channelled through the criminal process are usually convicted of 'using an evil cult to undermine the implementation of the law' (Section 300 of the Criminal Law), a crime that does not carry the death penalty.

100 James Griffiths, 'Report: China still harvesting organs from prisoners at a massive scale', CNN, 23 June 2016, available at <http://edition.cnn.com/2016/06/23/asia/china-organ-harvesting/> [accessed 10 November 2016]; David Kilgour,

David Matas and Ethan Guthman, 'Bloody Harvest/The Slaughter: An Update', 22 June 2016, available at <http://endorganpillaging.org/wp-content/uploads/2016/06/Bloody_Harvest-The_Slaughter-June-23-V2.pdf> [accessed 10 November 2016].

101 UNGA, above, n. 91, item 36.

102 Teng Biao, above, n. 95.

103 'China ushers in non-residential residential surveillance', available at <http://www.duihuahrjournal.org/2013/01/china-ushers-in-non-residential.html> [last accessed 17 April 2017].

Chapter 4: Expression and Thought

1 Roderick Hills, 'Academic freedom in NYU-Shanghai versus NYU-NYC', PrawfsBlawg, 5 October 2016, available at <http://prawfsblawg.blogs.com/prawfsblawg/2016/10/last-week-the-gao-issued-a-report-on-academic-freedom-at-campuses-operated-by-american-universities-in-china-the-report-ha.html> [last accessed 11 November 2016].

2 Zhang Xiong, 'Yu Jianrong is all the rage', *Contemporary Chinese Thought*, 45:4 (2014) 72–81, at 80.

3 He Yini, 'China's mobile users hit 1.3 billion in 2015', *China Daily*, 26 January 2016, available at <http://www.chinadaily.com.cn/business/2016-01-26/content_23261207.htm> [last accessed 11 November 2016].

4 Freedom House, 'Country Report: China (2016)', available at <https://freedomhouse.org/report/freedom-world/2016/china> [last accessed 11 November 2016].

5 The practices keep changing, as reflected in a wealth of scholarly work.

6 Chapter 1 discusses the anti-institutional view of contemporary Confucians such as Yu Yingshi.

7 '臣民於法律範圍以內，所有言論、著作、出版及集會、結社等事，均准其自由', quoted in Lin Feng (林峰) 百年憲政與中國憲政的未來: *100 Years of Constitutionalism and the Future of Constitutionalism in China* (Hong Kong: Hong Kong City University Press, 2011), at 79.

8 Universal Declaration of Human Rights (adopted 10 December 1948), UN Doc A/810, at 71 (1948).

9 International Covenant on Civil and Political Rights (adopted 16 December 1966, entered into force 23 March 1976), 999 UNTS 171 (ICCPR).

10 'China's Charter 08', translated by Perry Link, *New York Review of Books*, 15 January 2009, available at <http://www.nybooks.com/articles/2009/01/15/chinas-charter-08/> [last accessed 11 November 2016].

See also '《08宪章》全文 [Charter '08 Full Text]', available at <http://www.bannedbook.org/forum2/topic2716.html> [last accessed 11 November 2016].

11 Ibid.

12 On the connection between these rights, see Kevin Boyle and Sangeeta Shah, 'Thought, expression, association, and assembly', in Daniel Moeckli, Sangeeta Shah and Sandesh Sivakumaran (eds), *International Human Rights Law* (Oxford: Oxford University Press, 2014), 217–37.

13 中华人民共和国宪法 [PRC Constitution], passed on 4 December 1982, promulgated and effective as of 4 December 1982, last revised on 14 March 2004.

14 There is much debate within liberal-democratic systems as to where the boundaries of free speech are and what kinds of restriction are justified. See Ian Hare, 'Extreme speech under international and regional human rights standards', in Ivan Hare and James Weinstein (eds), *Extreme Speech and Democracy* (Oxford: Oxford University Press, 2009), ch. 3.

15 Human Rights Council Resolution 12/16 on the Promotion and Protection of All Human Rights, Civil, Political, Economic, Social and Cultural Rights, Including the Right to Development, 12 October 2009, para. 5(p)(i). See also UN Human Rights Committee, 'General Comment No. 34, Article 19, Freedom of Opinion and Expression', 12 September 2011, CCPR/C/GC/34, para. 2, stating that restrictions on freedom of expression specified in Article 19(3) 'may not put in jeopardy the right itself'.

16 Chapter 2 discusses, *inter alia*, the reliance on Party norms and 'red letterhead documents' of mixed Party-State authorship.

17 Freedom House, 'Country Report: China (2016) – Freedom of the Press', available at <https://freedomhouse.org/report/freedom-press/2016/china> [last accessed 11 November 2016].

18 By contrast, there is, as of October 2016, a State Council Religious Affairs Regulation for which a draft revision has been published. Article 1 of the Regulation affirms the general principle of freedom of religion. Note, however, that the Constitution affirms the freedom only of the *normal* exercise of religion – see Article 36. See 'Religious Affairs Regulations Draft Revisions (Deliberation Draft)', ChinaLawTranslate, 9 August 2016, available at <http://chinalawtranslate.com/religious-regulations/?lang=en> [last accessed 11 November 2016].

19 As discussed in chapter 2.

20 For early instances of this type of constitutional argument, using freedom of conscience and freedom of speech arguments, see Li Heping, Teng Biao et al., 'The supremacy of the constitution and freedom of religion: Joint defense plea

in the case of Wang Bo, Wang Xinzhong and Liu Shuqin', in Stacy Mosher and Patrick Poon (eds), *A Sword and a Shield: China's Human Rights Lawyers* (Hong Kong: China Human Rights Lawyers Concern Group, 2009), 70–88; Jerome Cohen and Eva Pils, 'Hu Jia in China's legal labyrinth', *Far Eastern Economic Review*, May (2008) 52–4.

21 In addition to the above note 6, one might, in this respect, mention the case of the authors of the book *Investigation into China's Peasantry*. The authors were charged with defamation of a local official, but, due to Lawyer Pu Zhiqiang's masterful handling of courtroom advocacy, the court hearing in this civil matter was converted into effectively putting the official on trial. Philip Pan, 'In China, turning the law into the people's protector', *Washington Post*, 27 December 2004, available at <http://www.washingtonpost.com/wp-dyn/articles/A30146-2004Dec27.html> [last accessed 11 November 2016].

22 Article 293 Criminal Law, CECC, translation available at <http://www.cecc.gov/pages/newLaws/criminalLawENG.php> [last accessed 11 November 2016]. See also Mindy Kristen Longanecker, 'No room for dissent: China's laws against disturbing social order undermine its commitment to free speech and hamper the rule of law', *Pacific Rim Law & Policy Review*, 18:2 (2009) 375–403.

23 Article 111 Criminal Law, CECC translation available at <http://www.cecc.gov/pages/newLaws/criminalLawENG.php> [last accessed 11 November 2016]. Human Rights in China, 'State secrets: China's legal labyrinth' (2009), available at <http://www.hrichina.org/sites/default/files/PDFs/State-Secrets-Report/HRIC_StateSecrets-Report.pdf> [last accessed 27 December 2013].

24 Article 105 (2) Criminal Law, CECC translation available at <http://www.cecc.gov/pages/newLaws/criminalLawENG.php> [last accessed 11 November 2016]. Teng Biao (滕彪), 'The political meaning of the crime of "subverting state power"', in Jean-Philippe Béja, Fu Hualing and Eva Pils (eds), *Liu Xiaobo, Charter 08 and Challenges of Constitutional Reform in China* (Hong Kong: Hong Kong University Press, 2012).

25 Article 243 Criminal Law, CECC translation available at <http://www.cecc.gov/pages/newLaws/criminalLawENG.php> [last accessed 11 November 2016]. See also Joshua D. Rosenzweig, 'China's battle over the right to criticize', *Far Eastern Economic Review*, 5 May 2009.

26 Article 246 Criminal Law, CECC translation available at <http://www.cecc.gov/pages/newLaws/criminalLawENG.php> [last accessed 11 November 2016].

27 Article 300 Criminal Law, CECC translation available at <http://www.cecc.gov/pages/newLaws/criminalLawENG.php> [last accessed 11 November 2016].

28 Article 296 CL <http://www.cecc.gov/resources/legal-provisions/criminal-law-of-the-peoples-republic-of-china> [last accessed 11 November 2016].

29 Benjamin Liebman, 'Innovation through intimidation: An empirical account of defamation litigation in China', *Harvard International Law Journal*, 47 (2006) 33.

30 Yik Chan Chin, 'Privilege and public opinion supervision defences in China's right to reputation litigation', *Media and Arts Law Review*, 19 (2014) 276–99.

31 Perry Link comments along the same lines. See Changingsociety, 'China's Charter 08', interview with Professor Perry Link, January 2009, available at <http://media.nybooks.com/010509-link.mp3> [last accessed 11 November 2016].

32 'We wish to share the responsibility with Liu Xiaobo', open letter available at <http://www.hrichina.org/en/content/3217> [last accessed 11 November 2016].

33 Liu Xiaobo's 1st and 2nd instance defence statements, available at <http://www.hrichina.org/en/content/3206> and <http://www.hrichina.org/en/content/3210> [last accessed 11 April 2017]; Mo Shaoping et al., 'Criminal defense in sensitive cases: Yao Fuxin, Yang Jianli, Jiang Lijun, Du Daobin, Liu Xiaobo, and Others', in Jean-Philippe Béja, Fu Hualing and Eva Pils (eds), *Liu Xiaobo, Charter 08 and Challenges of Constitutional Reform in China* (Hong Kong: Hong Kong University Press, 2012), ch. 2; Joshua Rosenzweig, 'The sky is falling: Inciting subversion and the defense of Liu Xiaobo', in Jean-Philippe Béja, Fu Hualing and Eva Pils (eds), *Liu Xiaobo, Charter 08 and Challenges of Constitutional Reform in China* (Hong Kong: Hong Kong University Press, 2012), ch. 3; Liu Xiaobo (刘晓波), 'I have no enemies: my final statement/ 我没有敌人:我的最后陈述', available in English and Chinese in Human Rights in China, 'Freedom of speech on trial in China', *China Rights Forum*, 2010:1 (2010) 116–21.

34 Article 105(2) Criminal Law, CECC translation available at <http://www.cecc.gov/pages/newLaws/criminalLawENG.php> [last accessed 1 November 2016].

35 Perry Link, 'The Passion of Liu Xiaobo', *New York Review of Books*, 13 July 2017, <http://www.nybooks.com/daily/2017/07/13/the-passion-of-liu-xiaobo/>.

36 Teng Biao (滕彪), above, n. 24.

37 See the discussions in chapters 1 and 2. On the last point, Barry Naughton, 'Is China socialist?', *Journal of Economic Perspectives*, 31:1 (2017) 3–24.

38 Li Xiaorong, 'Testimony by Li Xiaorong for the Congressional-Executive Commission on China, December 6, 2011, hearing', available at <http://www.cecc.gov/sites/chinacommission.house.gov/files/documents/hearings/2011/CECC%20Hearing%20Testimony%20-%20Li%20Xiaorong%20-%2012.6.11.pdf> [last accessed 1 November 2016].

39 The defence statement for Liu Xiaobo, available at <http://www.hrichina.org/en/content/3206> [last accessed 1 November 2016]: Section III D argues that 'there are no convincing criteria for making a rigorous and scientific distinction between this crime and the citizens' freedom of speech.'

40 'Beijing court upholds Liu Xiaobo's initial sentence', available at <http://news.xinhuanet.com/english2010/china/2010-02/11/c_13172103.htm> [last accessed 1 November 2016]; '专家谈刘晓波煽动颠覆国家政权案 [Experts discuss the incitement of subversion case of Liu Xiaobo]', *Zhongpingshe Beijing*, 11 February 2010, available at <http://www.cenews.eu/?p=21974> [last accessed 17 April 2017]. See also (with comments from Zhao Bingzhi) '所谓"因言获罪"是对刘晓波案判决的误读 [The so-called "criminalisation of speech" is a misreading of the verdict against Liu Xiaobo]', Xinhua News, 25 October 2010, available at <http://news.xinhuanet.com/world/2010-10/25/c_12698346.htm> [last accessed 1 November 2016].

41 The idea of 'Three Represents' 三个代表 was put forward by then President Jiang Zemin in 2000: The Party 'represents the development trends of advanced productive forces. It represents the orientations of an advanced culture. It represents the fundamental interests of the overwhelming majority of the people of China.' For an official explanation, see China Internet Information Center, 'What is "Three Represents" CPC Theory', available at <http://www.china.org.cn/english/zhuanti/3represents/68735.htm> [last accessed 11 April 2017].

42 The term 'Harmonious Society' 和谐社会 was first used prominently in a resolution by the Party Central meeting of October 2006 and quickly became a dominant political slogan. See Xinhua News, '中共中央关于构建社会主义和谐社会若干重大问题的决定 [Party Central Resolution on the Construction of a Socialist Harmonious Society]', 18 October 2006, at <http://news.xinhuanet.com/politics/2006-10/18/content_5218639.htm> [last accessed 11 April 2017].

43 For various formulations of the Scientific Development Perspective 科学发展观 by President Hu Jintao and Premier Wen Jiabao, see <http://news.xinhuanet.com/ziliao/2005-03/16/content_2704537.htm> [last accessed 11 April 2017].

44 Teng Biao (滕彪), above, n. 24. This was drafted before and completed after the forced disappearance and torture the author suffered in this context.

45 See also chapter 6.

46 In 2015, the Criminal Law was amended to punish whoever 'fabricates or deliberately spreads on media, including on the Internet, false information regarding dangerous situations, the spread of diseases, disasters and police information, and who seriously disturb social order'. See Human Rights

Watch, 'China: New ban on "spreading rumors" about disasters', 2 November 2015, available at <https://www.hrw.org/news/2015/11/02/china-new-ban-spreading-rumors-about-disasters> [last accessed 1 November 2016].

47 Chris Luo, 'Police arrest 16-year-old boy in Gansu for spreading internet "rumours"', *South China Morning Post*, 19 September 2013, available at <http://www.scmp.com/news/china-insider/article/1313136/police-arrest-16-year-old-boy-gansu-spreading-internet-rumours> [last accessed 1 November 2016].

48 Patrick Boehler, 'Is a 16-year-old boy's release a victory for netizens in China's internet crackdown?', *South China Morning Post*, 23 September 2013, available at <http://www.scmp.com/news/china-insider/article/1315878/teenagers-release-rare-victory-chinas-internet-crackdown> [last accessed 1 November 2016].

49 Luo, above, n. 47: In Yang Hui's case, it was pointed out that one of the images he posted showed him wearing a T-shirt with the defiant English slogan 'Make The Change'.

50 Perry Link, 'China: the anaconda in the chandelier', *New York Review of Books*, 11 April 2002, available at <http://www.nybooks.com/articles/2002/04/11/china-the-anaconda-in-the-chandelier/> [last accessed 7 November 2016].

51 Simon Denyer and Luna Lin, 'The absurd face of China's censorship: Bookstore tears out Taiwan page from Webster's', *Washington Post*, 13 October 2016, available at <https://www.washingtonpost.com/news/worldviews/wp/2016/10/13/the-absurd-face-of-chinas-censorship-bookstore-tears-out-taiwan-page-from-websters/> [last accessed 1 November 2016].

52 The CECC distinguishes legislative, political, psychological and technological prior restraints at <https://www.cecc.gov/prior-restraints> [last accessed 11 April 2017].

53 Wenming Dai, '"Hybrid journalists" – Chinese journalists in an era of reform: Their values and challenges', Reuters Foundation Scholarship Paper, University of Oxford, 2013, available at <https://reutersinstitute.politics.ox.ac.uk/sites/default/files/Hybrid%20Journalists-Chinese%20Journalists%20in%20an%20era%20of%20reform%20-%20their%20values%20and%20challenges.pdf>.

54 David Bandurski, 'News ethics, media controls, and investigative journalism', *China Digital Times*, 25 November 2015, available at <http://chinadigitaltimes.net/2015/11/news-ethics-media-controls-and-investigative-journalism/> [last accessed 1 November 2016]; David Bandurski and Martin Hala, *Investigative Journalism in China* (Hong Kong: Hong Kong University Press, 2010); Marina Svensson and Elin Saether, *Chinese Investigative Journalists' Dreams* (Lanham, MD: Lexington Books, 2014).

55 Susan Shirk, 'Changing media, changing China', in Susan Shirk (ed.), *Changing Media, Changing China* (New York: Oxford University Press, 2011) at p. 21.

56 David Bandurski and Xiao Qiang, 'China's emerging public sphere: the impact of media commercialization, professionalism and the internet in an era of transition', in Susan Shirk (ed.), *Changing Media, Changing China* (New York: Oxford University Press, 2011); Sebastian Veg, 'China's embryonic public sphere', *Current History*, September 2015, 203–9, available at <http://www.currenthistory.com/VEG_CurrentHistory.pdf> [last accessed 1 November 2016]; Yang, Guobin, *The Power of the Internet in China: Citizen Activism Online* (New York: Columbia University Press, 2009).

57 Marina Svensson, 'Rule of law and public accountability: Can investigative journalism promote social justice and human rights?', in I. Karlsson and K. Röing de Nowina (eds), *Utsikt mot utveckling – Meeting Global Challenges in Research Cooperation* (Uppsala: Uppsala Centre for Sustainable Development, 2009), 183–91.

58 Michael Forsythe, 'China clamps down on online news reporting', *The New York Times*, 26 July 2016, <http://www.nytimes.com/2016/07/26/world/asia/china-media-sina-sohu-netease-phoenix.html> [last accessed 11 November 2016].

59 He Huifeng, 'WeChat red envelopes help drive online payments use in China', *South China Morning Post*, 19 February 2016, available at <http://www.scmp.com/tech/article/1913340/wechat-red-envelopes-help-drive-online-payments-use-china> [last accessed 11 November 2016]. On citizen journalists using microblogging, see Jiao Bei, 'How Chinese journalists use Weibo microblogging for investigative reporting', Reuters Foundation Scholarship Paper, 2013, available at <https://reutersinstitute.politics.ox.ac.uk/sites/default/files/How_Chinese_journalists_use_Weibo_microblogging_for_investigative_reporting(1).pdf> [last accessed 11 November 2016]; Wenming Dai, above, n. 53. See also Cindy, 'China's new media pushing political boundaries', *China Digital Times*, 15 October 2016, available at <http://chinadigitaltimes.net/2016/10/chinas-new-media-pushing-political-boundaries/> [last accessed 11 November 2016].

60 See Gary King, Jennifer Pan and Margaret Roberts, 'How censorship in China allows government criticism but silences collective expression', *American Political Science Review*, 107:2 (2013) 1–18.

61 China Correspondent, 'The Great Firewall of China', *Open Democracy*, 15 March 2013, available at <https://www.opendemocracy.net/china-correspondent/great-firewall-of-china> [last accessed 11 April 2017].

62 For example, Emily Feng, 'China blocks Economist and Time websites, apparently over Xi Jinping articles', *The New York Times*, 8 April 2016, available at <http://www.nytimes.com/2016/04/09/world/asia/china-blocks-economist-time.html> [last accessed 11 April 2017].

63 Howard French, 'Bloomberg's folly', *Columbia Journalism Review*, May/June 2014, available at <http://www.cjr.org/feature/bloombergs_folly.php?page=3> [last accessed 11 April 2017].

64 Yu Yingshi, 'The Chinese Communists are not Confucianists', translated by Ai Ru, *ChinaChange*, 1 July 2015, available at <http://chinachange.org/2015/07/01/the-chinese-communists-are-not-confucianists/> [last accessed 11 November 2016]. The Chinese original was initially available as 余英时：大陆提倡儒家是儒家的死亡之吻 [Yu Yingshi: Mainland advocacy of Confucianism is its kiss of death]', 12 June 2015, available at <http://mp.weixin.qq.com/s?__biz=MjM5NzcwNTc4Nw==&mid=208206390&idx=3&sn=2620600c7f5159e5b1c56f378f3a97bc&scene=1#rd>; but later, this link resulted in the message quoted in the main text. A screen-grab of the site that used to carry the article in Chinese [last accessed 11 November 2016], as well as a copy of the Chinese language article are on file with the author. In the wake of Hong Kong's Umbrella Revolution, Yu Yingshi's works were banned. See NTDTV, 'CCP bans works of Yu Yingshi and Jiu Badao for HK support', October 2014, available at <http://www.ntd.tv/en/programs/news-politics/china-forbidden-news/20141013/233691-ccp-bans-works-of-yu-yingshi-and-jiu-badao-for-hk-support.html> [last accessed 11 November 2016]; Fei Chang Dao, 'State media reports Yu Yingshi's books banned, his books disappear from online bookstores', blog, 13 October 2014, available at <http://blog.feichangdao.com/2014/10/state-media-reports-yu-yingshis-books.html> [last accessed 16 April 2017].

65 For a database, see China Digital Times, 'GreatFire.org launches VPN information database', *China Digital Times*, 5 July 2016, available at <http://chinadigitaltimes.net/2016/07/greatfire-launches-vpn-information-database/> [last accessed 11 November 2016].

66 Consider, for example, the sheer uncertainty about this issue as expressed in an online discussion, available at <https://www.reddit.com/r/China/comments/2tgear/punishment_for_using_vpn_in_china/> [last accessed 11 November 2016].

67 UN Human Rights Council Resolution on the promotion, protection and enjoyment of human rights on the Internet (27 June 2016, A/HRC/32/L.20), available at <https://www.article19.org/data/files/Internet_Statement_Adopted.pdf> [last accessed 11 November 2016].

68 Sophie Beach, 'Fang Binxing navigates around Great Firewall', *China Digital Times*, 5 April 2016, available at <http://chinadigitaltimes.net/2016/04/fang-binxing-skirts-great-firewall-foreign-media-dont/#fang-binxing> [last accessed 11 November 2016].

69 Li Jing, 'China blocks VPN services that let users get round its "Great Firewall" during big political gatherings in Beijing', *South China Morning Post*, 9 March 2016, available at <http://www.scmp.com/news/china/policies-politics/article/1922677/china-blocks-vpn-services-let-users-get-round-its-great> [last accessed 11 November 2016].

70 See above on the Draft UN Resolution on online freedom of speech.

71 Freedom House, above, n. 4.

72 In the case of Liu Xiaobo, by contrast, it seems unlikely that many ordinary Chinese citizens would have known about his case, as information about his case was rather effectively suppressed from the start.

73 '党和政府主办的媒体必须姓党 [The Party- and Government-sponsored media must bear the Party surname]', Sina.com, 19 February 2016, available at <http://news.sina.com.cn/c/nd/2016-02-19/doc-ifxprucu3024202.shtml> [last accessed 11 November 2016]; Josh Rudolph, 'Xi's state media tour: "News must speak for the Party"', *China Digital Times*, 19 February 2016, available at <http://chinadigitaltimes.net/2016/02/191569/> [last accessed 11 November 2016].

74 Ibid.

75 To quote Mao Zedong (毛泽东): 'It is man's social being that determines his thinking. Once the correct ideas characteristic of the advanced class are grasped by the masses, these ideas turn into a material force which changes society and changes the world.' See Mao Zedong, 'Where do correct ideas come from?', *Selected Work of Maio Tse-tung* (1963), available at <http://www.marxists.org/reference/archive/mao/selected-works/volume-9/mswv9_01.htm> [last accessed 11 November 2016].

76 Forsythe, above, n. 58.

77 David Bandurski, 'Mirror, mirror on the wall', *China Media Project*, 20 February 2016, available at <https://medium.com/china-media-project/mirror-mirror-on-the-wall-fde286bba78a#.cb12103x1> [last accessed 11 April 2017].

78 Daniela Stockmann and Mary Gallagher, 'Remote control: How the media sustain authoritarian rule in China', *Comparative Political Studies*, 44:4 (2011) 436–67.

79 On what they call 'strategic distraction', see Gary King, Jennifer Pan and Margaret Roberts, 'How the Chinese government fabricates social media

posts for strategic distraction, not engaged argument', draft available at <http://gking.harvard.edu/files/gking/files/50c.pdf>.

80 Ai Weiwei, 'China's paid trolls: Meet the Fifty-cent Party', *The New Statesman*, 17 October 2012, available at <http://www.newstatesman.com/politics/politics/2012/10/china%E2%80%99s-paid-trolls-meet-50-cent-party> [last accessed 11 November 2016].

81 Bandurski, above, n. 77.

82 ChinaFile, 'Document No. 9: a ChinaFile Translation', *ChinaFile*, 11 August 2013, available at <http://www.chinafile.com/document-9-chinafile-translation> [last accessed 11 November 2016].

83 Patrick Boehler and Vanessa Piao, 'Xi Jinping's speech on the arts is released, one year later', *The New York Times*, 15 October 2015, available at <http://sinosphere.blogs.nytimes.com/2015/10/15/xi-jinping-speech-arts-culture/> [last accessed 11 November 2016].

84 The image of these heroes is being protected with new vigour. See ChinaLawTranslate, 'Not heroes of free speech', 21 October 2016, available at <http://chinalawtranslate.com/not-heroes-of-free-speech/?lang=en> [last accessed 11 November 2016].

85 Communist Party's First Public Service TV Ad, 27 July 2016, available at <https://www.youtube.com/watch?v=gSr9bLXzd1A> [last accessed 11 November 2016].

86 Article 3 (3) of 中国共产党章程 [Chinese Communist Party Charter], available at <http://english.cpc.people.com.cn/206972/206981/8188065.html> [last accessed 11 April 2017].

87 Articles 18 and 19 of the ICCPR are arguably engaged here.

88 See chapter 6.

89 '颜色革命/ Color Revolution', available at <https://www.youtube.com/watch?v=8qBt-i9ErSY> [last accessed 11 November 2016], at 2′02″. The producer of the clip is named as 'Beijing Dujia Jingshi Culture and Media Ltd' (北京读家经世文化传媒有限公司), but the clip was released via the Supreme People's Procuracy's official micro-blog. See Cindy, 'Video warns of foreign-backed Color Revolution', *China Digital Times*, 3 August 2016, available at <http://chinadigitaltimes.net/2016/08/hk-activist-branded-us-backed-separatist-govt-video/> [last accessed 11 November 2016] (which also provides an English translation). The release coincided with some of the '7-09' trials (see chapter 6).

90 Ibid.

91 Bai Mo (白墨), '观察：习近平"媒体姓党"下新闻人的选择 [Observation: The selection of news media people under Xi Jinping's "the media must bear

the Party surname" principle]', BBC News: Chinese Desk, 16 March 2016, available at <http://www.bbc.com/zhongwen/simp/china/2016/03/160329_ana_china_media_free_speach> [last accessed 11 November 2016]: this shows a picture of the form with Yu Shaolei's (余少镭) handwritten explanation, '无法跟着你们姓'. See also Tom Phillips, "'Love the party, protect the party": How Xi Jinping is bringing China's media to heel', *The Guardian*, 28 February 2016, available at <https://www.theguardian.com/world/2016/feb/28/absolute-loyalty-how-xi-jinping-is-bringing-chinas-media-to-heel> [last accessed 11 November 2016].

92 For a classic account of the role of propaganda in China, see Anne-Marie Brady, *Marketing Dictatorship: Propaganda and Thought Work in Contemporary China* (Lanham, MD: Rownman & Littlefield, 2008). On Propaganda's ability to influence even when it does not persuade, see Huang Haifeng, 'Propaganda's signalling function', *Comparative Politics*, 47:4 (2014) 419–37.

93 See William Davies, 'The age of post-truth politics', *The New York Times*, 24 August 2016, available at <http://www.nytimes.com/2016/08/24/opinion/campaign-stops/the-age-of-post-truth-politics.html> [last accessed 11 April 2017]; 'Yes I'd lie to you', *The Economist*, 10 September 2016, available at <http://www.economist.com/news/briefing/21706498-dishonesty-politics-nothing-new-manner-which-some-politicians-now-lie-and> [last accessed 11 November 2016].

94 China Copyright and Media, 'State Council guiding opinions concerning establishing and perfecting incentives for promise-keeping and joint punishment systems for trust-breaking, and accelerating the construction of social sincerity', 18 October 2016, translation by Rogier Creemers, available at <https://chinacopyrightandmedia.wordpress.com/2016/05/30/state-council-guiding-opinions-concerning-establishing-and-perfecting-incentives-for-promise-keeping-and-joint-punishment-systems-for-trust-breaking-and-accelerating-the-construction-of-social-sincer/> [last accessed 11 November 2016].

95 Simon Denyer, 'China wants to give all of its citizens a score – and their rating could affect every area of their lives', *The Independent*, 22 October 2016, available at <http://www.independent.co.uk/news/world/asia/china-surveillance-big-data-score-censorship-a7375221.html> [last accessed 11 November 2016].

96 Ibid.

97 For example, according to a Kantian approach. Gareth Williams, 'Kant's account of reason', section 2.2, in *Stanford Encyclopaedia of Philosophy*, last

revised March 2014, available at <http://plato.stanford.edu/entries/kant-reason/> [last accessed 11 November 2016].

98 Conversation #100 2011-1. Quoted in chapter 3.

99 Marcia Stepanek, 'The algorithms of fear', *Stanford Social Innovation Review*, 14 June 2016, available at <https://ssir.org/articles/entry/the_algorithms_of_fear> [last accessed 11 November 2016]. In chapter 6, the use of 'televised confessions' made available online as a technique to potentially engender fear is discussed.

100 John Rawls, *The Law of Peoples* (Cambridge, MA: Harvard University Press, 1999), 65.

101 Jeremy Waldron, 'Dignity and defamation: The visibility of hate', *Harvard Law Review*, 123 (2010) 1596.

Chapter 5: Inequality and Socio-economic Rights

1 State Council Information Office, 'Assessment Report on the Implementation of the National Human Rights Action Plan of China (2012–2015)', 16 June 2016, available at <http://www.chinahumanrights.org/html/2016/NHRAPC_0614/5056.html> [last accessed 30 October 2016]. According to China's government records, 99 million people still lived beneath the poverty line as of March 2013. See Liu Chang and He Dan, 'China to increase efforts to alleviate poverty', *China Daily*, 25 March 2013, available at <http://www.chinadaily.com.cn/china/2013-03/25/content_16341128.htm> [last accessed 30 October 2016]: 'over the past 12 months, China's rural population considered to be in poverty declined to about 99 million from 122 million – the first time the country has started to consider those with a yearly net income of less than 2,300 yuan as "destitute".'

2 For representative discussions of this development perspective, see Zhuo Zeyuan, 'Drive of human rights advancement: Development', China Society for Human Rights Studies, 26 November 2014, available at <http://www.chinahumanrights.org/html/2014/PAPERS_1126/1339.html> [last accessed 30 October 2016]; Li Yunlong, 'The development path for human rights with Chinese characteristics', China Society for Human Rights Studies, 26 October 2014, available at <http://www.chinahumanrights.org/html/2014/PAPERS_1126/1343.html> [last accessed 30 October 2016]. Details are complicated not least because the Chinese government uses its own standard for measuring poverty and poverty reduction. See S.C., 'Life at the bottom of the middle kingdom', *The Economist*, 2 December 2011, available at <http://

www.economist.com/blogs/freeexchange/2011/12/chinas-poverty-line> [last accessed 30 October 2016].

3 State Council Information Office, White Paper on Human Rights, November 1991, available at <http://china.org.cn/e-white/7/index.htm> [last accessed 30 October 2016]: see especially section I, 'The Right to Subsistence – the Foremost Human Right the Chinese People Long Fight for'.

4 Henry Shue, 'Correlative duties', in Henry Shue (ed.), *Basic Rights: Subsistence, Affluence, and US Foreign Policy* (Princeton, NJ: Princeton University Press, 1980).

5 Discussed critically in Jeff King, *Judging Social Rights* (Oxford: Oxford University Press, 2012), 1–20f. Virginia Mantouvalou develops an account of the duties of legislatures and courts in 'In support of legalisation', in Conor Gearty and Virginia Mantouvalou, *Debating Social Rights* (Portland, OR: Hart 2011).

6 Isabel Trujillo and Francesco Viola, *What Human Rights Are Not (Or Not Only): A Negative Path to Human Rights Practice* (Hauppauge, NY: Nova Science Publishers, 2016), 79f.

7 Henry Shue, above, n. 4.

8 International Covenant on Economic, Social and Cultural Rights (adopted 16 December 1966, entered into force 3 January 1976) 993 UNTS 3 (ICESCR).

9 These are also addressed by the norms and mechanisms of the ILO.

10 The right to housing and food are part of what the ICESCR defines as an adequate standard of living.

11 ICESCR, Article 2.

12 International Covenant on Civil and Political Rights (adopted 16 December 1966, entered into force 23 March 1976) 999 UNTS 171 (ICCPR). For example, the rights to equal protection and against discrimination in Articles 3 and 26.

13 Convention on the Elimination of All Forms of Racial Discrimination (adopted 21 December 1965, entered into force 4 January 1969) 660 UNTS 195 (CERD).

14 中华人民共和国宪法 [PRC Constitution], passed on 4 December 1982, promulgated and effective as of 4 December 1982, last revised on 14 March 2004. See Articles 42 and 43 (right and duty to work; right to rest); Articles 44 and 45 (livelihood of retired people, right to material assistance, right to healthcare); Article 46 (right and duty to receive education).

15 Article 35, discussed in chapter 4.

16 China Labour Bulletin, 'For Chinese workers, the right to strike is an academic issue', Jennifer's Blog, 12 March 2013, available at <http://www.clb.org.hk/

en/blogs/jennifer/chinese-workers-right-strike-academic-issue> [last accessed 17 April 2017]. The author mentions that the right to strike 'survived' three Constitutions (1954, 1975 and 1978), but was taken out of the 1982 Constitution. Characteristically, this occurred just when the land tenure system was changed too – one might argue that these changes heralded, and were emblematic of, if not necessary to, the 'Reform and Opening' liberalization of the system. However, the 2016 State Council Information Office report (above, n. 3) recognized a right not explicitly enumerated either in ICESCR or in the Constitution, namely that to a healthy environment. More widely on issues of accountability for rights violations as a consequence of environmental degradation, see Malgosia Fitzmaurice, 'Environmental degradation', in Daniel Moeckli, Sangeeta Shah and Sandesh Sivakumaran, *International Human Rights Law*, 2nd edn (Oxford: Oxford University Press, 2014), 590–608. On court attitudes to strikes (work stoppsages), see also Aaron Halegua, 'Who will represent China's workers? Lawyers, legal aid, and the enforcement of labor rights', NYU U.S. Asia Law Institute, 2016, available at <https://usali.org/chinasworkers> [last accessed 17 April 2017], at p. 44f.

17 According to Xuefei Ren, *Urban China* (Cambridge: Polity, 2013), at p. 117, the floating population – people living in a place outside the household registration – was officially at 221 million in 2010. Armstrong states that, as of 2012, it had reached 250 million, with some 160 million of these not properly registered. (In 2012, China's internal migratory population (both inter- and intra-provincial) exceeded 250 million people. Within that population, those without household registration – effectively illegal aliens within their own nation – known as China's 'floating population' (流动人口), exceed 160 million.) See Thomas D. Armstrong, 'China's "floating population"', *Southern California International Review*, 12 October 2013, available at <http://scir.org/2013/10/chinas-floating-population/> [last accessed 30 October 2016]. By 2014, the number is stated to have risen to 274 million. Shannon Tiezzi, 'China's plan for "orderly" hukou reform', *The Diplomat*, 16 February 2016, available at <http://thediplomat.com/2016/02/chinas-plan-for-orderly-hukou-reform/> [last accessed 30 October 2016].

18 You Tien-hsing, *The Great Urban Transformation: Politics of Land and Property in China* (Oxford: Oxford University Press, 2012). Generally, the share of the property market alone in GDP is stated as between 15% and 22%. According to Moody's, as reported in the *Wall Street Journal*, 'the housing market's contribution to the Chinese economy has been falling in recent years. The construction, sale and outfitting of homes contributed to 22% of

China's GDP in 2013, 19.8% in 2014 and 15.1% in 2015.' See Esther Fung, 'China's housing revival buffers economy', *Wall Street Journal*, 16 May 2016, available at <http://www.wsj.com/articles/china-housing-revival-buffers-economy-1463288631> [last accessed 30 October 2016].

19 In most cases, urban property developers could not lawfully acquire such rights from private use rights holders. For example, when they want to build on rural or suburban land, they would not be allowed to buy rural land use rights and build urban houses on them. In fact, there is a grey zone of illegality in which such transactions do happen, often with acquiescence from officials. See Eva Pils, 'Waste no land: Property, dignity and growth in urbanizing China', *Asian-Pacific Law & Policy Journal*, 11:2 (2010) 1–48.

20 Building and land ownership can be split, as is implied by this framework.

21 Boxun, '中华失地农民后援会'公告[Announcement of the 'Support alliance for Chinese landless peasants']', *Boxun* (博讯), 20 April 2012, available at <http://boxun.com/news/gb/party/2012/04/201204032347.shtml#.UzxvYbmPI5o> [last accessed 11 April 2017].

22 The ICESCR mentions, as noted earlier, housing as one of the aspects of adequate living. The right to housing encompasses negative and positive aspects (freedoms and entitlements in the language of UN Habitat), including adequacy of: security of tenure, protection against forced eviction, harassment and other threats; availability of infrastructure; adequacy of provision for basic needs such as drinking water; affordability; habitability, accessibility; adequacy of the location and cultural adequacy of the housing in question. See UN Habitat, 'The right to adequate housing', Fact Sheet No. 21, November 2009, available at <http://unhabitat.org/the-right-to-adequate-housing-fact-sheet-no-21rev-1/> [last accessed 30 October 2016].

23 Yang, Ming (杨明), '北京华远集团董事长任志强:'不存在非公共利益拆迁 只要是城建都是公共利益' [Chairman of Beijing Huayuan Group Ren Zhiqiang says: 'There is no such thing as demolition and relocation that is not in the public interest. As long as it is [for the purpose of] urban construction, it is in the public interest'], *Oriental Outlook Weekly* (瞭望东方周刊), 10 February 2010, available at <http://finance.ifeng.com/opinion/zjgc/20100210/1822226.shtml> [last accessed 11 April 2017].

24 On the relationship between this approach and classical neo-institutional theories of property, see Frank Upham, 'Chinese property rights and property theory', *Hong Kong Law Journal*, 39:3 (2009) 611–26.

25 Eva Pils, 'Land disputes, rights assertion and social unrest: A case from Sichuan', *Columbia Journal of Asian Law*, 19 (2006) 365, reprinted as Hauser

Global Law School Working Paper 07/05 and in Perry Keller (ed.), *Obligations and Property Rights in China* (Farnham: Ashgate Publishing, 2012).

26 I have thus far not found any such decision.

27 Amitai Etzioni, 'Organizational dimensions and their interrelationships: A theory of compliance', in B.P. Indik and F.K. Berrien (eds), *People, Groups, and Organizations* (Columbia, NY: Teachers College Press, 1968).

28 In some places, target rates of 'agreements' of over 90% have reportedly been set by municipal authorities.

29 Kevin O'Brien and Yanhua Deng, 'The reach of the state: Work units, family ties and "harmonious demolition"', *The China Journal*, 72 (2015) 1–17.

30 He Yang (何杨), 应急避难场所 [*Emergency Shelter*], independent documentary film (2010), available at <http://vimeo.com/12677411>.

31 Pollution-related protest might have overtaken land-grab-related protest, but there are no publicly available statistics to assess such comments. See Bloomberg News, 'Chinese anger over pollution becomes main cause of social unrest', 6 March 2013, available at <http://www.bloomberg.com/news/2013-03-06/pollution-passes-land-grievances-as-main-spark-of-china-protests.html> [last accessed 20 October 2016]. See also Eva Pils, 'Resisting dignity takings in China', *Law & Social Inquiry*, 41:4 (2016) 888–916.

32 Chun Peng, 'Taming the dragon: Rural land takings law in modern China', DPhil dissertation, Oxford, forthcoming with Cambridge University Press.

33 Roger Cohen, 'A woman burns', *New York Times*, 25 January 2010, available at <http://www.nytimes.com/2010/01/26/opinion/26iht-edcohen.html?pagewanted=all> [last accessed 20 October 2016]; '唐福珍其人 凤凰卫视/ [Tang Fuzhen as a Person]', Phoenix Television, 15 December 2009, available at <http://v.ifeng.com/documentary/society/201008/931a8e4 b-ce09-44e5-aacd-2e3441272f88.shtml > [last accessed 20 October 2016].

34 Yu Jianrong, 'Do China's Tang Fuzhens regret self-immolation?', translated by Stacy Mosher, *Contemporary Chinese Thought*, 46:1 (2014) 51–4.

35 Eva Pils, above, n. 31.

36 See above, n. 17.

37 Charlotte Goodburn, 'Educating migrant children: The effects of rural-urban migration on access to primary education', in S. Guo and Y. Guo (eds), *Spotlight on China: Changes in Education under China's Market Economy* (Rotterdam: Sense Publishers, 2015), 365–80, citing these numbers with particular reference to how children's right to education is affected.

38 Ian Johnson, 'China's great uprooting: Moving 250 million into cities', *New York Times*, 16 June 2013, available at <http://www.nytimes.com/2013/06/16/world/asia/chinas-great-uprooting-moving-250-million-into-cities.html?pagewanted=all> [last accessed 30 October 2016].

39 Xuefei Ren, *Urban China* (Cambridge: Polity, 2013), at 51f. On legal and political advocacy against this system, see Donald C. Clarke, 'The famous hukou editorial', Chinese Law Prof Blog, 26 March 2010, available at <http://lawprofessors.typepad.com/china_law_prof_blog/2010/03/the-famous-hukou-editorial.html> [last accessed 30 October 2016].

40 Chapters 2 and 3 discussed the Sun Zhigang case.

41 Passed on 9 January 1958 by the NPC (*Hukou dengji tiaoli* 户口登记条例).

42 A quota system was established by individual urban centres. Wang Fei-Ling describes a trend to abolish quotas in the period from 1997 to 2002 in Wang Fei-Ling, 'Reformed migration control and new targeted people: China's *hukou* system in the 2000s', *The China Quarterly*, 177 (2004) 115–32, at p. 119.

43 Goodburn, above, n. 37, at p. 369.

44 Ibid., at p. 370.

45 Ibid., at pp. 371–5 (on general issues with the quality of private migrant worker schools).

46 Zhao Han, 'Rule change forces migrants' children out of Beijing for school', *Caixin Magazine*, 16 February 2015, available at <http://english.caixin.com/2015-02-16/100784599.html> [last accessed 30 October 2016].

47 Chu Chaohai, 'Restrictions on for-profit schools may widen gaps in China's education system', *Caixin Magazine*, 9 November 2016, available at <http://english.caixin.com/2016-11-09/101005791.html>.

48 Xiaojun Sun, Yuan Tian, Yongxin Zhang, Xiaochun Xie, Melissa A. Heath and Zongkui Zhou, 'Psychological development and educational problems of left-behind children in rural China', *School Psychology International*, 36:3 (2015) 227–52; John Sudworth, 'Counting the cost of China's left-behind children', BBC News, 12 April 2016, available at <http://www.bbc.co.uk/news/world-asia-china-35994481> [last accessed 30 October 2016]; César Chelala, 'The plight of China's "left behind" children', *The Globalist*, 14 May 2016, available at <http://www.theglobalist.com/the-plight-of-chinas-left-behind-children/> [last accessed 30 October 2016]. The official figure of *c*.20 million is provided in He Yingchun (贺迎春), 全国中小学在校生农村留守儿童人数达2019万 [Number of elementary and middle school rural left-behind children reaches 20.19 million], 7 July 2016, available at <http://xian.qq.com/a/20160707/012951.htm> [last accessed 30 October 2016]; Han Qing, (桧青), presenter in '中国留守儿童心灵状况 中国官方鼓励男性"为国捐精" [China's "left-behind children" psychological condition/Chinese authorities encourage men to "donate sperm for the Nation"]', Radio Free Asia (Chinese Desk), 29 July 2016, available at <http://www.rfa.org/mandarin/zhuanlan/fuyouluntan/m0729women-07292016144902.html>

[last accessed 30 October 2016] – see for comments on the discrepancy in numbers. This programme also mentions social security discrepancies, providing the example of a peasant who, after deductions, gets a payment of only five RMB per month as social security.

49 Lijun Chen, Dali Yang and Qiang Ren, 'Report on the state of children in China', University of Chicago China Center, 14 May 2016, available at <http://www.chapinhall.org/research/report/report-state-children-china> [last accessed 30 October 2016].

50 Ibid. (citing the official 2010 census).

51 Sudworth, above, n. 48.

52 Ibid. (describing a case of suicide by five siblings, the youngest being of only five years of age).

53 *Locus classicus* of scholarly discussion is Rachel Murphy, 'Turning Chinese peasants into modern citizens: "Population quality", demographic transition, and primary schools', *The China Quarterly*, 177 (2004) 1–20. Low quality is frequently, but not exclusively, ascribed to the rural population.

54 A Google search using the key phrase ('提高农民素质') yielded some 107,000 results on 31 July 2016, with a very recent People's Daily report, available at <http://js.people.com.cn/n2/2016/0729/c360300-28746697.html> [last accessed 31 July 2016].

55 Adam James Smith, '"Re-education" campaigns teach China's new ghost city-dwellers how to behave', *The Guardian*, 6 November 2014, available at <http://www.theguardian.com/cities/2014/nov/06/-sp-china-ghost-city-kangbashi-ordos-re-education-campaign> [last accessed 30 October 2016].

56 Li Cheng, 'Non-discrimination and the reform of the Chinese hukou system in a human rights perspective: A case study of farmer workers', Masters thesis, University of Oslo, 2008, available at <https://www.duo.uio.no/handle/10852/22895> [last accessed 11 April 2017].

57 Xi Wang (希望, a pen name), '中国14名律师要求审计署公布社会抚养费的去向 [14 lawyers seek public disclosure on where social welfare fees have gone from the National Audit Bureau]', 2 September 2013, available at <http://www.rfa.org/mandarin/yataibaodao/renquanfazhi/nu-09022013155348.html> [last accessed 30 October 2016].

58 国务院办公厅关于解决无户口人员登记户口问题的意见国办发〔2015〕96号 [State Council Opinions of the General Office of the State Council on Resolving the Problem of Persons Without Household Registration]', Issued by State Council Development Office (2015) No. 6.

59 Boxun, '揭1300万黑户转正难点:一些地方还存政策性障碍 [Disclosure of difficulties with changing some 13 million from unregistered

to registered status – policy obstacles persist in some locations]', 15 January 2016, available at <http://www.boxun.com/news/gb/china/ 2016/01/201601150918.shtml#.V6CfLE0dw5s> [last accessed 30 October 2016]. For an overview of fines in different provinces, see '各省二胎罚款', available at <http://baike.pcbaby.com.cn/qzbd/1282073.html#ldjc4ta=baby_ tbody1> [last accessed 30 October 2016].

60 Boxun, above, n. 59.

61 Conversation #23 2011-4.

62 Conversation #140 17-1.

63 Alex Wang, 'China's environmental tipping point?' in Timothy Weston and Lionel Jensen (eds), *China in and Beyond the Headlines* (Lanham, MD: Rowman and Littlefield, 2012).

64 Discussed in Daniel Moeckli, Sangeeta Shah and Sandesh Sivakumaran, *International Human Rights Law* (Oxford: Oxford University Press, 2014), at 592ff.; UN 'soft law' on the environment is discussed at 594f. For the role of the Special Rapporteur on Human Rights and the Environment, see OHCHR, 'Special Rapporteur on human rights and the environment (former Independent Expert on human rights and the environment)', available at <http://www.ohchr.org/EN/Issues/Environment/SREnvironment/Pages/ SRenvironmentIndex.aspx> [last accessed 30 October 2016].

65 OHCHR, ibid.

66 Eleanor Albert and Beina Xu, 'China's environmental crisis', Council on Foreign Relations, 18 January 2016, available at <http://www.cfr.org/china/chinas- environmental-crisis/p12608> [last accessed 11 April 2017].

67 Bai Chong'en, Cai Hongbin, Huang Haizhou, Li Bo, Ma Jun, Wei Jianing, Wu Ge, Xu Lin, Yuan Li, Zhou Chengjun and Zhou Hanhua (白重恩、 蔡洪滨、黄海洲、李波、马骏、魏加宁、伍戈、徐林、袁力、周诚君、周 汉华),'土地制度改革与新型城镇化 [Chinese land reform and a new form of urbanization]', published as a draft for discussion at a gathering of a group known as 'China Forum 40' (CF40), 27 May 2013, available at <http:// www.yicai.com/news/2013/05/2734345.html> [last accessed 11 April 2017].

68 Lee Liu, 'Made in China: Cancer villages', *Environment*, March/April 2010, available at <http://www.environmentmagazine.org/Archives/Back%20 Issues/March-April%202010/made-in-china-full.html> [last accessed 30 October 2016]; Cancer Villages Google Maps: Liu argues that cancer villages are connected to 'model city' developments. He mentions the property regime as a factor that renders 'the poor…unable to leave the poisoned land.' See Rob Schmitz, 'Life and death inside a Chinese "cancer village"', *Marketplace*,

19 May 2016, available at <http://www.marketplace.org/2016/05/03/world/life-and-death-inside-chinese-cancer-village> [last accessed 30 October 2016].

69 Human Rights Watch, 'My children have been poisoned: A public health crisis in four Chinese provinces', 15 June 2011, available at <http://www.hrw.org/reports/2011/06/15/my-children-have-been-poisoned-0> [last accessed 30 October 2016]; Tom Phillips, 'Chinese "cancer village" scores rare victory over polluters', *The Telegraph*, 28 August 2014, available at <http://www.telegraph.co.uk/news/worldnews/asia/china/11061201/Chinese-cancer-village-scores-rare-victory-over-polluters.html> [last accessed 30 October 2016].

70 For instance, in some areas in Ningxia I have visited for fieldwork, groundwater is called 'bitter' and widely thought to be the cause of a high prevalence of cancer. Observation (2005, 2008, 2010 in Tongxin County, Ningxia Autonomous Region).

71 Ruby Yang, *The Warriors of Qiugang – a Chinese Village Fights Back*, independent documentary, 2010, available at <http://e360.yale.edu/feature/the_warriors_of_qiugang_a_chinese_village_fights_back/2358/> [last accessed 30 October 2016]. See also RFA, '四川癌症村民抗议垃圾场污染水源与警方爆发冲突', 31 July 2016, available at <http://www.rfa.org/mandarin/yataibaodao/huanjing/xl2-07312016110908.html> [last accessed 30 October 2016].

72 Rachel Stern, 'The political logic of China's new environmental courts', *The China Journal*, 72 (2014) 53–74.

73 China Digital Times, 'Smog journeys: Air pollution inspires film & novel', Greenpeace interview with and film by Jia Zhangke, *China Digital Times*, 27 January 2015, available at <http://chinadigitaltimes.net/2015/01/smog-journeys-air-pollution-inspires-film-novel/> [last accessed 30 October 2016].

74 Mushkat discusses this tension in Roda Mushkat, 'Compliance with international environmental regimes: Chinese lessons', *William & Mary Environmental Law and Policy Review*, 34:2 (2010) at pp. 497f.

75 For an initiative combining legal with political advocacy, see Benjamin Haas, 'We had to sue: the five lawyers taking on China's authorities over smog', *The Guardian*, 13 February 2017, available at <https://www.theguardian.com/cities/2017/feb/13/chinese-lawyers-suing-government-air-pollution> [last accessed 13 February 2017].

76 Chai Jing, *Under the Dome – Investigating China's Smog* [originally titled 柴静雾霾调查：穹顶之下], with English subtitles, available at <https://www.youtube.com/watch?v=T6X2uwlQGQM> [last accessed 30 October 2016].

77 Ben Beaumont-Thomas, 'Smash-hit Chinese pollution doc Under the Dome taken offline by government', *The Guardian*, 9 March 2015, available at <http://www.theguardian.com/film/2015/mar/09/chinese-pollution-documentary-under-the-dome-taken-offline-government> [last accessed 30 October 2016].

78 Human Rights Council, 'Report of the Special Rapporteur on extreme poverty and human rights', 28 April 2016, A/HRC/32/31. See also 'Special Rapporteur on Extreme Poverty and Human Rights presents Thematic Report on Social and Economic Right', 14 June 2016, available at <http://chrgj.org/special-rapporteur-on-extreme-poverty-and-human-rights-presents-thematic-report-on-social-and-economic-rights/> [last accessed 30 October 2016].

79 John Rawls, *A Theory of Justice* (Cambridge, MA: Harvard University Press, 1971) criticizes utilitarianism for its inability to take seriously the difference between persons.

80 State Council Information Office, White Paper on Human Rights (November 1991), available at <http://china.org.cn/e-white/7/index.htm> [last accessed 30 October 2016] (see especially section I, 'The Right to Subsistence – the Foremost Human Right the Chinese People Long Fight for').

81 Conversation # 2014-1. This lawyer continued to comment that 'the government uses violent demolition and relocation, because that helps them bring up the GDP. It's a very simple logic.'

82 Boxun, '阵容庞大：范木根自卫杀人案和维稳拆迁研讨会/视频 [Great turnout: Seminar on the self-defence homicide case of Fan Mugen and stability-preservation style demolition and relocation]', 22 February 2014, available at <http://news.boxun.com/news/gb/china/2014/02/201402220159.shtml#.UzxWtLmPI5p> [last accessed 30 October 2016].

83 UN Special Rapporteur on Extreme Poverty and Human Rights, 'End-of-mission statement on China, by Professor Philip Alston, United Nations Special Rapporteur on extreme poverty and human rights', Beijing, 23 August 2016, available at <http://www.ohchr.org/EN/NewsEvents/Pages/DisplayNews.aspx?NewsID=20402&LangID=E> [last accessed 30 October 2016].

Chapter 6: Rights Defenders

1 The United Nations Declaration on Human Rights Defenders recognizes the role of 'individuals, groups and associations in contributing to, the effective elimination of all violations of human rights and fundamental freedoms of peoples and individuals' and 'the right and the responsibility of individuals, groups and associations to promote respect for and foster

knowledge of human rights and fundamental freedoms at the national and international levels.' United Nations General Assembly, 'Declaration on the Right and Responsibility of Individuals, Groups and Organs of Society to Promote and Protect Universally Recognized Human Rights and Fundamental Freedoms' (8 March 1999), available at <http://www.ohchr.org/Documents/Issues/Defenders/Declaration/declaration.pdf> [last accessed 7 November 2016]. This chapter uses the term 'human rights defenders' in a more inclusive sense than 'advocates', indicating people who advance a cause or case on their own or someone else's behalf.

2 Baidu Online Dictionary, entry on '无告', available at <http://baike.baidu.com/view/908632.htm> [last accessed 7 November 2016]; 汉典帮助 [Chinese Dictionary Help], entry on '无告', available at <http://www.zdic.net/c/0/79/125413.htm> [last accessed 7 November 2016].

3 Eva Pils, *China's Human Rights Lawyers: Advocacy and Resistance* (Abingdon: Routledge, 2014), ch. 5.

4 Beth Simmons, *Mobilizing for Human Rights: International Law in Domestic Politics* (Cambridge: Cambridge University Press, 2009), 31–6 on international civil society. See also Samuel Moyn, *Human Rights in History: The Last Utopia* (Cambridge, MA: Harvard University Press, 2010); Lynn Hunt, *Inventing Human Rights: A History* (New York: W.W. Norton, 2007).

5 United Nations Congress on the Prevention of Crime and the Treatment of Offenders, 'Basic Principles on the Role of Lawyers', 7 September 1990, available at <http://www.ohchr.org/EN/ProfessionalInterest/Pages/RoleOfLawyers.aspx> [last accessed 7 November 2016]; United Nations General Assembly, above, n. 1.

6 On open government information requests and the 'peculiar exemption of social stability' in handling requests, see Yongxi Chen, 'Transparency versus stability: The new role of Chinese courts in upholding freedom of information', *Tsinghua China Law Review*, 9:1 (2016).

7 For a summary discussion of the global role of human rights defenders, see Ilias Bantekas and Lutz Oette, *International Human Rights – Law and Practice* (Cambridge: Cambridge University Press, 2014), ch. 3.

8 Perry Link, 'China: the anaconda in the chandelier', *New York Review of Books*, 11 April 2002, available at <http://www.nybooks.com/articles/2002/04/11/china-the-anaconda-in-the-chandelier/> [last accessed 7 November 2016].

9 Cf. Elisa Nesossi, 'Political opportunities in non-democracies: The case of Chinese *weiquan* lawyers', *The International Journal of Human Rights* 19:7 (2015) 961–78; Terence C. Halliday and Sida Liu, *Criminal Defence in China: The Politics of Lawyers at Work* (Cambridge: Cambridge University Press, 2016).

10 United Nations General Assembly, 'Declaration on Human Rights Defenders', UNGA Res 144 (1998) UN Doc A/RES/53/144, available at <http://www.ohchr.org/EN/Issues/SRHRDefenders/Pages/Declaration.aspx> [last accessed 7 November 2016]. In an authoritarian context, one might adopt a wide definition of human rights defenders than usual, and include, for example, the now imprisoned former Supreme People's Court Vice President Huang Songyou, whose premature attempt to celebrate the Qi Yuling decision as China's *Marbury vs Madison* was mentioned in chapter 2.

11 Discussed in chapter 2.

12 In the manner described at the end of chapter 2.

13 See pictures on file with author and chapter 2.

14 Halliday and Liu, above, n. 9, p. xv. and ch. 5.

15 For example, the style of reporting that developed in the 1990s in newspapers such as *Southern Weekend* (*Nanfang Zhoumo*) and led to the media taking a prominent role in the handling of the 'Sun Zhigang Incident'.

16 Marina Svensson, 'Reporting law and injustices: Investigative journalists and the legal system', in Elin Saether, Marina Svensson and Zhang Zhi'an (eds), *Chinese Investigative Journalists' Dreams: Agency, Autonomy, Voice* (Lanham, MD: Rowman & Littlefield, 2013), 157–77; Marina Svensson, 'Connectivity, engagement and witnessing on China's Weibo', in Avery Goldstein, Jacques DeLisle and Yang Guobin (eds), *The Internet, Social Media, and a Changing China* (Philadelphia, PA: University of Pennsylvania Press, 2016), 49–70.

17 Articles 7–9 of 律师事务所年度检查考核办法 [MoJ Regulation on Annual Law Firm Assessment]. See also 律师执业年度考核规则 [Regulation on Annual Assessment of Lawyers], promulgated by the All China Lawyers Association on 13 August 2010, effective from 1 January 2011, available at <http://2009.lawyers.org.cn/profile/info.jsp?id=12f438db9a4fbb68482443a568fa6448> [last accessed on 7 November 2016].

18 Siweiluozi Blog, 'New pledge of allegiance for Chinese lawyers', 3 March 2012. English translation and link to original, available at <http://www.siweiluozi.net/2012/03/new-pledge-of-allegiance-for-chinese.html> [last accessed 31 December 2013]. See also 关于印发《关于建立律师宣誓制度的决定》的通知 [Notice on Issuance of 'Decision on Oath System for Lawyers'], 3 February 2012, available at <http://baike.baidu.com/view/8206917.htm?fromTaglist> [last accessed 31 December 2013].

19 He Yang (何杨), '吊照门 [*Disbarment*]' (2010), independent documentary film.

20 Public Security Bureaux, 'Internal National Security Protection Squad or 国内安全保卫制度 (*guonei anquan baowei zhidu*', for short *guobao* 国保).

21 The most important of these is the Security Commission of the Party, 中央国家安全委员会 [*Zhongyang guojia anquan weiyuanhui* / Central State Security Commission], established at the 3rd Plenary Session of the 18th Central Committee in November 2013.

22 Discussed with examples in Pils, above, n. 3, ch. 6.

23 'Gao Zhisheng: Chinese lawyer describes "torture"', BBC News, 24 September 2015, <http://www.bbc.co.uk/news/world-asia-china-34341069> [last accessed 7 November 2016]. For an in-depth account of Gao's early activism, see Eva Pils, 'Asking the tiger for his skin: Rights activism in China', *Fordham International Law Journal*, 30 (2007) 1209–87.

24 Different – sociological, political, descriptive, normative – interpretations of 'civil society' are at play in academic discussions of civil society in China. Chan Kin-man (陈建民), '走向公民社会 [*Zou xiang gongmin shehui* / Toward Civil Society]', (Hong Kong: UP Publications, 2010).

25 Alexis de Tocqueville, *De la démocratie en Amérique* (1835), Part I, 391, available at <www.ecole-alsacienne.org/CDI/pdf/1400-0107/14096_TOCQ1.pdf> [last accessed 7 November 2016] and at <www.ecole-alsacienne.org/CDI/pdf/1400-0107/14097_TOCQ2.pdf> [last accessed 7 November 2016].

26 'We want everybody to enjoy the same rights as Jaruzelski, secured by the rule of law.' See Adam Michnik, 'Toward a civil society', in Adam Michnik and Irena Grudzinska Gross (eds), *Letters from Freedom: Post-Cold War Realities and Perspectives* (Berkeley, CA: University of California Press, 1998).

27 Wu Fengshi and Chan Kin-man, 'Graduated control and beyond: The evolving Government–NGO relations', *China Perspectives*, 3 (2012) 9–17.

28 The full slogan is 'Study the Party Charter and Regulations, Study the Serial Speeches, Be a Good Party Member' [学党章党规、学系列讲话，做合格党员], and is explained at <http://cpc.people.com.cn/xuexi/n1/2016/0301/c385474-28162054.html> [last accessed 7 November 2016]. A typical ACLA report is available at <http://www.acla.org.cn/html/gaocengshengyin/20160711/25851.html> [last accessed 7 November 2016]. ACWF devotes a special website to the campaign at <http://www.women.org.cn/col/col616/index.html> [last accessed 7 November 2016].

29 Cf. Zeng Sishi (曾思诗), '基层党员干部应怎样践行"两学一做"? [How should basic level cadres implement "Two Study One Be"?]', People.Cn, 16 October 2016, available at <http://dangjian.people.com.cn/n1/2016/1016/c117092-28781414.html> [accessed 7 November 2016].

30 '全国妇联"两学一做"学习教育专题 [ACWF Special Issue on *Two Study, One Be*]', 30 September 2016, available at <http://www.women.org.cn/art/2016/9/30/art_617_148818.html> [last accessed 7 November 2016].

31 Samuel Wade, 'Xi crowned "core" leader but true strength disputed', *China Digital Times*, 27 October 2016, available at <http://chinadigitaltimes.net/2016/10/xi-crowned-core-leader-true-strength-still-disputed/> [last accessed 7 November 2016].

32 China Labour Bulletin, 'Unity is strength: the workers' movement 2009–2011', 11 October 2011, available at <http://www.clb.org.hk/en/content/unity-strength-workers-movement-china-2009-2011> [last accessed 7 November 2016]. For an earlier, seminal study of labour protest, see Ching Kwan Lee, *Against the Law: Labor Protests in China's Rustbelt and Sunbelt* (Berkeley, CA: University of California Press, 2007).

33 The change from a one-child-policy to a nationwide two-child-policy does not alter this basic model. Han De, 汉德, argues correctly that certain local regulations imposing legal requirements to abort are in convention of higher-ranking law at '强制堕胎三问：是否合法，如何定罪，能否赔偿, Nanfang Zhoumo, 28 June 2012, available at <http://news.ifeng.com/opinion/special/duotai/detail_2012_06/28/15630531_0.shtml> [last accessed 7 November 2016]. Discussed at Su CiCi, 'China's one-child mothers', *Foreign Affairs*, 10 May 2016, available at <https://www.foreignaffairs.com/articles/china/2016-05-10/chinas-one-child-mothers> [last accessed 7 November 2016].

34 See, more widely, Jennifer Hsu and Reza Hasmat, 'The local corporatist state and NGO relations in China', *Journal of Contemporary China*, 23:87 (2014) 516–34.

35 Anthony Spires, 'Contingent symbiosis and civil society in an authoritarian state: Understanding the survival of China's grassroots NGOs', *American Journal of Sociology*, 117:1 (2011) 1–45. For a database, see the China Development Brief, available at <http://chinadevelopmentbrief.cn/directory/> [last accessed 7 November 2016]: this lists 'hundreds' of NGOs.

36 As discussed in chapter 5.

37 Mark Selden and Jenny Chan, 'China's new labour politics', China Policy Institute Analysis Blog, 20 October 2016, available at <https://cpianalysis.org/2016/10/20/chinas-new-labour-politics/> [last accessed 7 November 2016].

38 Chun-Yi Lee, 'Growing or perishing? The development of labour NGOs', in Andreas Fulda (ed.), *Civil Society Contributions to Policy Innovation in China: Environment, Social Development, and International Cooperation* (New York: Palgrave Macmillan 2015), 125–50; Tim Pringle, 'What do labour NGOs in China do?', China Policy Institute Analysis Blog, 17 October 2016, available at <https://cpianalysis.org/2016/10/17/what-do-labour-ngos-in-china-do/> [last accessed 7 November 2016]. For an optimistic assessment of prospects,

see Cynthia Estlund, *A New Deal for China's Workers?* (Cambridge, MA: Harvard University Press, 2017). More sceptically, Anita Chan, 'Introduction: The fallacy of Chinese exceptionalism', in Anita Chan (ed.), *Chinese Workers in Comparative Perspective* (Ithaca, NY: Cornell University Press, 2015).

39 Chris Chan and Elaine Hui, 'The development of collective bargaining in China: From "collective bargaining by riot" to "party state-led wage bargaining"', *The China Quarterly*, 217 (2014) 221–42; John Ruwitch, 'Labor movement "concertmaster" tests Beijing's boundaries', Reuters, 6 December 2014, available at <http://www.reuters.com/article/us-china-labour-lawyer-insight-idUSKBN0JL00T20141207> [last accessed 11 April 2017].

40 For excellent discussions, see Fu Hualing, 'Embedded socio-legal activism in China: The case of Yirenping', *Hong Kong Law Journal*, 12:2 (2014) 6–29; Timothy Webster, 'Ambivalence and activism: Employment discrimination in China', *Vanderbilt Journal of Transnational Law*, 44:3 (2011) 643.

41 Kathinka Fürst and Jennifer Holdaway, 'Environment and health in China: The role of environmental NGOs in policy innovation', in Fulda, above, n. 38, 33–76.

42 Cf. website of 污染受害者法律帮助中心 [Center for Legal Assistance to Pollution Victims] at <http://www.clapv.org/> [last accessed 28 February 2017].

43 Yaxue Cao, 'Guo Jianmei, Zhongze, and the empowerment of women in China', *ChinaChange*, 14 February 2016, at <https://chinachange.org/2016/02/14/guo-jianmei-zhongze-and-the-empowerment-of-women-in-china/>[last accessed 28 February 2017].

44 'China passes new laws on foreign NGOs amid international criticism', BBC News, 28 April 2016, available at <http://www.bbc.co.uk/news/world-asia-china-36157052> [last accessed 7 November 2016].

45 Wu and Chan, above, n. 27.

46 Founded in the wake of the Sun Zhigang Incident. Conversation #2 2013-3; Teng Biao (滕彪), 公盟不死 [Gongmeng is not dead], 17 January 2009, available at <http://blog.qq.com/qzone/622007804/1248271496.htm> [last accessed 11 April 2017].

47 传知行经济研究所 [Transition Institute], <http://www.zhuanxing.cn/> [last accessed 27 December 2013] (original website no longer available; now replaced by a different entity).

48 北京兴善研究所 [China Against Death Penalty], <http://www.cadpnet.org/en/> [last accessed 27 December 2013] (website no longer available).

49 Evan Osnos, 'Where is Xu Zhiyong?', available at <http://lawprofessors .typepad.com/china_law_prof_blog/2009/07/where-is-xu-zhiyong-evan-osnos-in-the-new-yorker.html> [last accessed 7 November 2016].

50 Andrew Jacobs, 'China releases Guo Yushan, scholar who helped activist gain asylum in US', *The New York Times*, 15 September 2015, available at <http://www.nytimes.com/2015/09/16/world/asia/china-releases-scholar-who-helped-activist-gain-asylum-in-us.html> [last accessed 7 November 2016].

51 Teng Biao, 'The West kowtows to China through self-censorship', *The Washington Post*, 28 July 2016, available at <https://www.washingtonpost.com/opinions/ global-opinions/the-west-kowtows-to-china-through-self-censorship/ 2016/07/28/6d2e4ebe-49f8-11e6-bdb9-701687974517_story.html?utm_ term=.5b7742377572> [last accessed 7 November 2016].

52 Chapter 3 addresses the reform of the Criminal Procedure Law as an instance of concurrent progress and regression.

53 Such demonstrations occurred on a regular basis in the larger cities, for example, Beijing. See Teng Biao, 'Rights defence, microblogs, and the surrounding gaze: The rights defence movement online and offline', *China Perspectives*, 2012:3 (2012) 29–41.

54 Clay Shirky, 'Here comes everybody: The power of organising without organisation', Royal Society of Arts book talk, 4 February 2010, available at <http:// www.youtube.com/watch?v=fSJCcDiD-zw> [last accessed 7 November 2016]; Clay Shirky, *Here Comes Everybody: The Power of Organising Without Organisations* (London: Penguin, 2008).

55 For this origin of the calligraphy, see Bei Li's calligraphy, 12 June 2012, available at <https://plus.google.com/107919448256984307579/posts/ UqUxVFoDziD> [last accessed 7 November 2016].

56 Simon Schama, *Citizens: A Chronicle of the French Revolution* (London: Random House, 1989).

57 Merle Goldman, *From Comrade to Citizen: The Struggle for Political Rights in China* (Cambridge, MA: Harvard University Press, 2004), 10f.

58 Xu Zhiyong, '谁把"自由,公义, 爱"当成敌人, 一定是中华民族的敌人/ *Shuei ba "ziyou, gongyi, ai" dangcheng diren, yiding shi Zhonghua minzu de diren!* [Who turns "freedom, justice, love" into an enemy is clearly an enemy of the Chinese nation!]', *Citizen*, Special Issue (公民专刊 *Gongmin zhuankan*), 8 (2013) 76, 78.

59 Xu Zhiyong, recorded intervention at 'The constitution, the media and the chinese rights defence movement: Ten years after the death of Sun Zhigang', Chinese University of Hong Kong, 13 April 2013, available at

<http://www.law.cuhk.edu.hk/en/research/crj/news/20130413-sunzhigang-coverage.php> [last accessed 7 November 2016].

60 Discussed in chapter 4.

61 Discussed in chapter 5.

62 Pictures from various locations are provided in *Citizen*, Special Issue 2013, above, n. 58.

63 Yang Ming (杨明), '公民权利无保障 连署促批准人权公约 [Civil rights lack protection, urging the ratification of the ICCPR]', 3 May 2013, available at <http://www.voachinese.com/content/china-human-right-20130305/1615327.html> [last accessed 7 November 2016].

64 The prosecution detailed part of this campaign in what became the basis for lawyer Tang's conviction. ChinaLawTranslate, 'Guangzhou Public Security Bureau opinion in support of prosecution; Pretrial Doc. (20143 No. 0476)', 25 November 2014, posted in translation 11 December 2014, available at <http://chinalawtranslate.com/en/tangjingling/> [last accessed 7 November 2016].

65 Josh Chin, 'Prominent rights advocate Xu Zhiyong releases jail video', *The Wall Street Journal*, 8 August 2013, available at <http://blogs.wsj.com/chinarealtime/2013/08/08/prominent-chinese-activist-releases-jail-video/?mg=blogs-wsj&url> [last accessed 7 November 2016].

66 ChinaFile, 'Document No. 9: a ChinaFile Translation', 11 August 2013, available at <http://www.chinafile.com/document-9-chinafile-translation> [last accessed 7 November 2016].

67 China Law Translate, 'CCP Central Committee decision concerning several major issues in comprehensively advancing governance according to law', 28 October 2014, available at <http://chinalawtranslate.com/fourth-plenum-decision/?lang=en> [last accessed 7 November 2016].

68 Jiang Shigong (强世功), 'Written and unwritten constitutions: A new approach to the study of constitutional government in China [中国宪法中的不成文宪法——理解中国宪法的新视角]', *Modern China*, 36:1 (2010) 12–46, available at <http://www.lishiyushehui.cn/modules/topic/detail.php?topic_id=282> [last accessed 27 October 2013]; Jiang Shigong (强世功), '图施耐特和"大众宪法 [Tushnet and the "populist" constitutional law]', *Dushu* (读书, 11 (2004) 122–31, available at <http://www.civillaw.com.cn/article/default.asp?id=55048> [last accessed 27 October 2013].

69 Didi Kirsten Tatlow, 'China is said to force closing of women's legal aid center', *The New York Times*, 30 January 2016, available at <https://www.nytimes.com/2016/01/30/world/asia/beijing-women-legal-aid-guo-jianmei.html?_r=0> [last accessed 7 November 2016].

70 Leta Hong Fincher, 'China's feminist five', *Dissent*, Fall 2016, available at <https://www.dissentmagazine.org/article/china-feminist-five> [last accessed 11 April 2017].

71 Orville Schell, 'Crackdown in China: Worse and worse', *New York Review of Books: China File*, 4 April 2016, available at <https://www.chinafile.com/nyrb-china-archive/crackdown-china-worse-and-worse> [last accessed 7 November 2016].

72 Aaron Halegua, Eli Friedman and Jerome A. Cohen, 'Cruel irony: China's Communists are stamping out labor activism', *Washington Post*, 3 January 2016; AFP, 'China labor activists sentenced for helping workers in wage dispute', *The Guardian*, 27 September 2016, <https://www.theguardian.com/world/2016/sep/27/china-labor-activists-sentenced-for-helping-workers-in-wage-dispute> [last accessed 28 February 2017].

73 Fincher, above, n. 70.

74 Conversation #138-16-1.

75 Groups such as the China Human Rights Lawyers Concern Group (CHRLCG) and the Chinese Human Rights Defenders (CHRD) put the total number affected at over 300.

76 Eva Pils, '"If anything happens…": Meeting the now-detained human rights lawyers', ChinaChange, 10 January 2016, available at <http://chinachange.org/2016/01/10/if-anything-happens-meeting-the-now-detained-human-rights-lawyers/> [last accessed 7 November 2016].

77 Namely, the American Bar Association and the Ludovic Trarieux Human Rights Prize Committee.

78 Translated in Chris Buckley, 'Week of TV trials in China signals new phase in attack on rights', *The New York Times*, 5 August 2016, available at <http://www.nytimes.com/2016/08/06/world/asia/china-trial-activists-lawyers.html> [last accessed 7 November 2016].

79 颜色革命Color Revolution, available at <https://www.youtube.com/watch?v=8qBt-i9ErSY> [last accessed 7 November 2016], English translation available at <http://chinadigitaltimes.net/2016/08/hk-activist-branded-us-backed-separatist-govt-video/> [last accessed 7 November 2016].

80 Hong Kong Free Press, 'State TV confession: Peter Dahlin', 20 January 2016, available at <https://www.youtube.com/watch?v=whbgVz4xKww> [last accessed 11 April 2017].

81 Edward Wong, 'Inside China's secret 23-day detention of a foreign non-profit chief', *The New York Times*, 9 July 2016, available at <http://www.nytimes.com/2016/07/10/world/asia/china-ned-ngo-peter-dahlin.html?_r=0> [last accessed 11 April 2017].

82 Wang Qiaoling, 'Chinese rights lawyer Li Chunfu mentally disturbed and physically ruined after abuse in custody', translated by Cao Yaxue, *ChinaChange*, 13 January 2017, available at <https://chinachange.org/2017/01/13/chinese-rights-lawyer-li-chunfu-mentally-disturbed-and-physically-ruined-after-abuse-in-custody/> [last accessed 11 April 2017].

83 Xie Yang and Chen Jiangang, 'Transcript of interviews with lawyer Xie Yang (3) – dangling chair, beating, threatening lives of loved ones, and framing others', translated by Cao Yaxue, *ChinaChange*, 21 January 2017, <https://chinachange.org/2017/01/21/transcript-of-interviews-with-lawyer-xie-yang-3-dangling-chair-beating-threatening-lives-of-loved-ones-and-framing-others/> [last accessed 11 April 2017].

84 On the latter two, see chapter 3.

85 ChinaLawTranslate, 'PRC Criminal Law (amended 2015)', available at <http://www.chinalawtranslate.com/%E4%B8%AD%E5%8D%8E%E4%BA%BA%E6%B0%91%E5%85%B1%E5%92%8C%E5%9B%BD%E5%88%91%E6%B3%95%EF%BC%882015%E5%B9%B4%E4%BF%AE%E6%AD%A3%EF%BC%89/?lang=en> [last accessed 17 April 2017].

86 Excerpted from Article 51 of 律师事务所管理办法 [Measures for the Administration of Law Firms (2016 Revision)], Order No. 133 of the Ministry of Justice, issued 6 September 2016, available at <http://www.gov.cn/gongbao/content/2016/content_5109321.htm> [last accessed 7 November 2016].

87 Yang Fan (扬帆), '中国司法部《律所管理办法》引不满 律师王全平控告部长 吴爱英违法失职 [Chinese Justice Ministry's Measures for the Administration of Law Firms trigger discontent, Lawyer Wang Quanping files unlawful dereliction of duty complaint against Minister Wu Aiying]', Radio Free Asia, 27 October 2016, available at <http://www.rfa.org/mandarin/yataibaodao/renquanfazhi/yf3-10272016111201.html> [last accessed 7 November 2016].

88 取缔非法民间组织暂行办法 [Provisional Measures on Banning Illegal NGOs] issued by the Ministry of Civil Affairs, 10 April 2000, Chinese and English translation available at <http://chinadevelopmentbrief.cn/wp-content/uploads/2014/08/PROVISIONAL-MEASURES-ON-BANNING-ILLEGAL-NGOS.pdf> [last accessed 26 December 2013]. See also Karla Simon, 'The regulation of civil society organisations in China', *International Journal of Civil Society Law*, 9:1 (2011) 55–84. See also Karla Simon, *Civil Society in China: The Legal Framework from Ancient Times to the 'New Reform Era'* (Oxford: Oxford University Press, 2013).

89 Wu and Chan, above, n. 27; Raymond Li, 'Rights groups miss out on easing of registration rules for NGOs', *South China Morning Post*, 12 March 2012,

available at <http://www.scmp.com/news/china/article/1188742/rights-groups-miss-out-easing-registration-rules-ngos> [last accessed 7 November 2016].

90 Stanley Lubman, 'China's new law on international NGOs – And questions about legal reform', *The Wall Street Journal*, China Real Time Blog, 25 May 2016, available at <http://blogs.wsj.com/chinarealtime/2016/05/25/chinas-new-law-on-international-ngos-and-questions-about-legal-reform/> [last accessed 7 November 2016]; Edward Wong, 'Clampdown in China restricts 7,000 foreign organizations', *New York Times*, 28 April 2016, available at <http://www.nytimes.com/2016/04/29/world/asia/china-foreign-ngo-law.html?_r=0> [last accessed 7 November 2016].

91 中央政法委《关于建立律师参与化解和代理涉法涉诉信访案件制度的意见 (试行)》 [Party Central Political-Legal Committee Opinion on Establishing a System for Lawyers to Participate in Resolving and Acting as Representatives in Litigation-Related Petitioning Cases (Trial Version)], 10 November 2015, available at <http://www.moj.gov.cn/index/content/2015-11/10/content_6348175.htm?node=7337> [last accessed 7 November 2016].

92 Ibid.

93 United Nations Congress on the Prevention of Crime and the Treatment of Offenders, 'Basic Principles on the Role of Lawyers', 7 September 1990, available at <http://www.ohchr.org/EN/ProfessionalInterest/Pages/RoleOfLawyers.aspx> [last accessed 7 November 2016].

94 Spires, above, n. 35, 2f.

95 Merle Goldman, *From Comrade to Citizen: The Struggle for Political Rights in China* (Cambridge, MA: Harvard University Press, 2004), 10f.

96 Havel discussed the example of a greengrocer instructed to display a Party slogan in his shop window, arguing that repression works by allowing people some semblance of freedom. See Václav Havel, *Moc Bezmocných* [*The Power of the Powerless*] (Prague: Routledge, 1978), published in translation by Jan Vladislav (ed.), *Living in Truth* (London: Faber and Faber, 1986), 36–122.

97 An example is the human rights lawyer Zhang Kai, who disappeared in the same crackdown, commenting that 'what Wang Yu said merits our respect'. 污点律师张凯取保候审后首次公开谈锋锐所案, 5 August 2016, available at <http://news.china.com/domesticgd/10000159/20160805/23221045.html> [last accessed 7 November 2016].

98 China Digital Times, 'Video warns of foreign-backed "color revolution"', 3 August 2016, available at <http://chinadigitaltimes.net/2016/08/hk-activist-branded-us-backed-separatist-govt-video/> [last accessed 7 November 2016]; Yaxue Cao, 'China smears foreign diplomats in another 4-minute video, as

trials of rights lawyers and activists continue in Tianjin', *China Change*, 4 August 2016, available at <https://chinachange.org/2016/08/04/china-smears-foreign-diplomats-in-another-4-minute-video-as-trials-of-rights-lawyers-and-activists-continue-in-tianjin/> [last accessed 11 April 2017].

99 Robert Jay Lifton, *Thought Reform and the Psychiatry of Totalism: A Study of 'Brainwashing' in China* (New York: W.W. Norton, 1961).

100 Li Xiaorong, 'Václav Havel honors a Chinese prisoner', *The New York Review of Books*, 29 April 2009, available at <http://www.nybooks.com/articles/2009/04/30/vaclav-havel-honors-a-chinese-prisoner/> [last accessed 11 April 2017].

Conclusion

1 In the Chinese terminology introduced in chapter 2.
2 Discussed in chapter 3.
3 Discussed in chapter 4.
4 Discussed in chapter 5.
5 Discussed in chapter 6.
6 Discussed in the Introduction.
7 It would not hinge merely on attitudes found in society but require a normative assessment.
8 Discussed in chapters 4 and 3.
9 The Schmittian influences on the legal system were discussed in chapters 2 and 3.
10 Discussed in chapter 6.
11 Ernst Fraenkel, *The Dual State: A Contribution to the Theory of Dictatorship*, translated by E.A. Shils (New York: Oxford University Press, 1941).
12 A rather typical title for the addresses and speeches given by foreign government officials, for example, is 'Advancing the rule of law in China: A deeper United Kingdom–China partnership'. Title of a speech given by Hugo Swires, then Minister for China, at the Great-Britain–China Centre, 16 March 2016, available at <https://www.gov.uk/government/speeches/advancing-the-rule-of-law-in-china-a-deeper-united-kingdom-china-partnership> [last accessed 10 November 2016].
13 Francis Fukuyama, 'The End of History?', *The National Interest*, Summer 1989, availble at <https://www.embl.de/aboutus/science_society/discussion/discussion_2006/ref1-22june06.pdf> at pp 9–10 [last accessed 17 April 2017].

14 Some therefore regarded the election of Donald J. Trump as US President as a victory for China. James Palmer, 'China just won the US election', *Foreign Affairs*, 9 November 2016, available at <http://foreignpolicy.com/2016/11/09/china-just-won-the-u-s-election-trump-victory/>[last accessed 13 November 2016].

15 A translation of the Hungarian President Orban's widely noted 26 July 2014 speech at Băile Tuşnad (Tusnádfürdő) is available at <http://budapestbeacon.com/public-policy/full-text-of-viktor-orbans-speech-at-baile-tusnad-tusnadfurdo-of-26-july-2014/10592> [last accessed 10 November 2016]. See also Timothy Garton Ash, 'Xi Jinping's China is the greatest political experiment on Earth', *The Guardian*, 1 June 2015, available at <https://www.theguardian.com/commentisfree/2015/jun/01/war-peace-depend-china-domestic-success> [last accessed 11 April 2017].

16 Katrin Kinzelbach, 'Resisting the power of human rights: the People's Republic of China', in Thomas Risse, Stephen C. Ropp and Kathryn Sikkink (eds), *The Persistent Power of Human Rights* (Cambridge: Cambridge University Press, 2013), 164–79.

17 Eric Posner, *The Twilight of Human Rights Law* (Oxford: Oxford University Press, 2014).

18 Alexander Cooley, 'Authoritarianism goes global: Countering democratic norms', *Journal of Democracy*, 26 (2015) 49–63; Larry Diamond, 'Facing up to the democratic recession', *Journal of Democracy*, 26 (2015) 141–55; critically: Steven Levitsky and Lucan Way, 'The myth of democratic recession', *Journal of Democracy*, 26 (2015) 45–58.

19 Michael Ignatieff, intervention at King's College London, Yeoh Tiong Lay Centre, 28 October 2016.

20 Michael Ignatieff, 'Human rights as politics / human rights as idolatry', The Tanner Lectures, Princeton University, 4–7 April 2000, available at <http://tannerlectures.utah.edu/_documents/a-to-z/i/Ignatieff_01.pdf>, at p. 6 [last accessed 10 November 2016].

21 Kerry Brown, *What's Wrong with Diplomacy?: The Future of Diplomacy and the Case of China and the UK* (London: Penguin Specials, 2015).

22 Discussed in chapter 6.

23 Discussed in chapter 6.

24 Hannah Beech, 'China's search for dissidents has now expanded to foreign countries', *Time Magazine*, 18 January 2016, available at <http://time.com/4184324/gui-minhai-dissident-search/> [last accessed 11 April 2017]; Hong Kong Free Press, 'Returned bookseller says he was detained by "special unit" in China, TV "confession" was scripted', 16 June 2016, available at

<https://www.hongkongfp.com/2016/06/16/breaking-returned-bookseller-says-he-was-detained-by-a-special-unit-in-china-confession-was-scripted/> [last accessed 12 November 2016].

25 Isaac Stone Fish, 'You have the right to remain silent. Inside the fight over the American Bar Association's tepid condemnation of Beijing's crackdown on lawyers and activists', *Foreign Policy*, 23 November 2015, available at <http://foreignpolicy.com/2015/11/23/china_american_bar_association_crackdown_human_rights/> [last accessed 11 April 2017].

26 Jerome A. Cohen, 'More on rights lawyer Wang Yu's "confession and release" and China's revival of "brainwashing" practice', *Jerry's Blog on recent developments in the rule of law in Asia and China*, 3 August 2016, available at <http://www.jeromecohen.net/jerrys-blog/2016/8/3/more-on-rights-lawyer-wang-yus-confession-and-release-and-chinas-revival-of-brainwashing-practice> [last accessed 17 April 2017].

27 For example, in chapter 6 in lawyer Liu Wei's account of her defence of a Falun Gong defendant.

Index ————————————

ABA (American Bar
      Association) 151–2
abortion 129–30
ACFTU (All China Trade Union
      Federation) 128, 129
ACLA (All China Lawyers
      Association) 128, 129
ACWF (All China Women's
      Federation) 128–9, 129–30,
      141
administrative detention 60–1, 63,
      109
adversarial rights claims 24
advertising 77
advocacy 3, 6, 18, 32–54, 99, 145,
      147
   and environmental pollution 116
   and household registration–based
      discrimination 113–14
   the judiciary 36–7, 43–7
   'letters and visits' system 14, 33,
      47–51
   as resistance 51–4
   for the right of personal liberty
      63
   and rights–violating norms
      37–40
   transnational 122, 131, 149–52
   see also petitioners; rights defenders

Africa Charter on Human and
      People's Rights 114
Ahl, Björn 36
air pollution 114–15, 116, 117, 121
Ai Weiwei 93–4
All China Lawyers Association
      (ACLA) 128, 129
All China Trade Union Federation
      (ACFTU) 128, 129
All China Women's Federation
      (ACWF) 128–9, 129–30,
      141
American Bar Association (ABA)
      151–2
Amnesty International 32
'anaconda in the chandelier'
      image 87, 122
Arendt, Hannah 8
Armstrong, Thomas D. 108
arts, role of in China 94
assembly, freedom of 35
association, freedom of 35, 102
authoritarianism 6, 7–8
   and arguments against human
      rights 21
   arguments for 3
   consequences of authoritarian
      revival 135–43, 143–4, 150
   global revival of 13

authoritarianism (cont.)
    and legal mechanisms   145–6
    and liberal democracy   7, 148
    re–conceptions of 'law'   28–31
    and rights–based quests for
        justice   19

Bakken, Borge   71
Bandurski, David   88, 93
Bao Longjun   137
Bao Zhuoxuan   137
Beccaria, Cesare   71
Beijing
    Democracy Wall   79
Bentham, Jeremy   71
'birth planning' policies   1, 129–30
Bodde, Derk   22
bottom–up dynamic of human
    rights   3–4
Brown, Kerry   149
Brzezinski, Marina   7

Cao Shunli   33
CAT (Convention Against
    Torture)   35, 64–5
censorship
    and freedom of expression   78,
        82–7, 89–92
    self–censorship   87, 151–2
CERD (Convention on the
    Elimination of All Forms of
    Racial Discrimination)   35,
    102
Chai Jing   117, 121
Chang Wejen   23
charities as rights defenders   122
Charter '08   79, 80, 83, 85, 121,
    133
Chen Duanhong   30
Chen Youxi   66

children
    in 'cancer villages'   115–16
    education discrimination and
        migrant children   110–14,
        133
    left–behind rural children   111
China Against Death Penalty   73,
    75, 132
circumvention technology   90–1
citizen journalism   89
citizenship
    and rights defenders   133
    and the rights tradition   19
citizens' society (*gongmin shehui*)
    127
civic meals   133, 134
civil rights
    and socio–economic rights   100,
        120
civil society
    in China   8
    classical liberal conception
        of   127–8
    emergence of advocates   123–35
    organizations of rights
        defenders   123, 127–32
    transnational   149, 150–1, 152
Color Revolution (video)   95–6
communication technologies
    and freedom of
        expression   87–92
Communist Party
    Charter   95
    Discipline and Inspection
        Committee   62
    members
        restrictions on personal liberty
        58
        shuanggui detention of   41–2,
        62, 64

and *minquan* (people power) 18
official organizations 128–30
see also Party–State
compensation payments
  and the death penalty 73–4
complainants *see* petitioners
Confucianism
  and the concept of *yuan* 15
  and freedom of expression 79
  and the rights tradition 17–18
Confucian–Legalist counterdiscourse
    21–5, 30–1
Constitution
  and Charter '08 79, 80, 83, 85,
    121, 133
  draft 1908 Constitution 18, 79
  and extra–legal detention 60
  and freedom of expression 78,
    79–81, 82, 87, 146
  human rights protection 1, 5
  and the law 27, 34
  normative framework of human
    rights 35, 36, 37, 38–9, 40,
    42–3
  and petitioning 48
  and the right to liberty 58
  and socio–economic rights 102
  on torture 65
corruption
  and rights defenders 133
  and socio–economic rights 119
counterdiscourses of human
    rights 12–13, 20–31
  Confucian–Legalist 21–5, 30–1
  Maoist–Leninist 21, 25–8
  Party–State 21, 23–5, 27–8,
    28–31
crimes of expression 78, 82–7
criminal investigation detention
    (*xingshi juliu*) 59–60

criminal justice system 1, 148
  and the death penalty 73–4
  and human rights advocacy 122,
    124, 139
  and the right of freedom of
    expression 81
  and torture 66–7
  see also judiciary; lawyers
criminal law
  censorship and crimes of
    expression 82–5
Criminal Procedure Law (CPL) 37,
    38, 58–9, 59–60, 63–4
  reforms (2012) 138
  and torture 65
Cultural Revolution 25, 26, 123,
    143
Custody and Repatriation system
    40

Dahlin, Peter 138–9, 150
death penalty 56, 69–75, 76, 145–6
  arguments defending continued use
    of 71–2
  and compensation payments
    73–4
  crimes carrying the death penalty
    70
  and the criminal justice system
    73–4
  execution methods 70
  and international human rights
    law 70, 72
  organ transplants and executed
    prisoners 74–5
  public opinion on 71, 72, 73, 74
  reprieves 72
  and the right to freedom of
    expression 81
defamation law 82

democratic dictatorship
  and rights–violating norms   38
demonstrations, flash mob   133–4
Deng Xiaoping   104, 111
detention   57, 59–64, 75, 76, 148
  administrative detention   60–1,
    63, 109
  'black' prisons   50, 58, 62
  and law enforcement   145–6
  of lawyers   56, 63–4, 95,
    136–9
  of petitioners   50, 51
  restrictions on liberty and places
    of   58
  of rights defenders   50, 51,
    126–7, 134, 137–9
  and the right to freedom of
    expression   81
  for subversion crimes   83
  and thought work   97–8
development goals
  and socio–economic
    rights   100–1
disability discrimination   1–2
Disbarment (film)   126
discrimination   1–2
  anti–discrimination groups
    130–1
  anti–discrimination rights   3–4,
    100, 101, 102, 108, 118, 119,
    122–3
  and conflicts over pollution
    115–16
  household registration–based   41,
    111–14
  laws protecting against   37
domestic violence   131
drug addicts   61
Duan Yi   130

economic growth
  and rural–urban migration   109
  and socio–economic rights
    100–1, 118
  and urbanization   103–4
education rights   35, 36, 37, 102,
    119
  and the New Citizen Movement
    133
  rights defenders   121
  and rural–urban migration
    110–14
Emergency Shelter (film)
    9–11, 13–14, 16, 20, 25,
    106
employment discrimination   113,
    130–1
enemy–friend distinction
  Schmitt's political theory of
    30–1
enforced disappearances   35, 61
engagement
  and the incremental reform
    argument   2–3
enmity
  and the concept of yuan   15
environmental degradation
  human rights effects of   114–17,
    119
environmental NGOs   131
equality
  and the rights tradition   19
equality before the law
  and 'socialist' discourses   2
    6, 27
ethnic minorities
  rights defenders of   130
Europe
  speech crimes   83

evictions
  and land rights   104, 105–7, 116,
    146
excess children
  household registration
    for   112–14
expression, right of   3, 77–99, 146
  censorship and crimes of
    expression   82–7
  and the Constitution   78, 79–81,
    82, 87, 146
  and housing rights   107
  limits of the right of free
    expression   78, 79–82
  modern public expression   77–8
  and 'smart' technologies   87–92
  see also speech, freedom of
extra–legal detention   60–1, 62–3

Falun Gong practitioners   43–4, 46,
    51, 55, 62–3, 65, 74, 126,
    130, 152
Fan Qihang   73
farmland, polluted   115
fascism   8
fear, algorithms of   98
Feminist Five   136
Fengrui law firm   137
fifty–centers (*wumaodang*)   93–4
flash mob demonstrations   133–4
food safety and pollution   115
forced disappearances   63–4, 98,
    126, 132, 136–7
Fraenkel, Ernst   147
freedom of expression *see* expression,
    right of
Freedom House   32, 78, 92
freedom of movement, right to
    102

friend–enemy distinction
  Schmitt's political theory
    of   30–1
Fu Hualing   57, 59
Fukuyama, F.   148

Gao Zhisheng   126–7
Goldman, Merle
  From Comrade to Citizen   141–2
Gongmeng (Open Constitution
    Initiative)   131–2, 133
GONGOs (government–organized
    NGOs)   2
Goodburn, Charlotte   110
Google   90
Great Firewall of China   89–90
Great Qing Code   22–3
Guo Feixiong   85, 134
Guo Jianmei   131, 132, 136
Guo Yushan   132

Hala, Martin   88
Halliday, Terence C.   124
Hanqing, Guan
  The Injustice to Dou'E   13, 14, 15
Havel, Václav   11, 128, 142, 144
healthcare rights   102, 110
health rights   35
  and pollution   114–15
Hepatitis B   113, 131
He Weifang   20
He Yang   20, 126
Hong Kong   150
house arrest   56, 61, 126–7
household registration system   40,
    41, 57, 102
  and pollution in rural areas   115
  and rural–urban migration
    108–14

housing rights   102, 103–8, 118
  defenders   121
  Emergency Shelter (film)   9–11,
    13–14, 16, 20, 25, 106
  house demolitions   40, 104, 106,
    107
Huang Songyou   36, 51–2
Hu Jia   61
Hu Jintao   24
human rights
  Chinese words for   17
  Nickel's definition of   3, 4
Human Rights Action Plans   1
human rights advocacy *see* advocacy;
    rights defenders
Human Rights Watch   32
Hungary   148
hunger–strikes   55, 63
Hu Shigen   137

ICCPR (International Covenant on
    Civil and Political Rights)
    35, 59, 65, 70, 79, 134
  and free expression   80
  and internet access   91
  and socio–economic rights   102
ICESCR (International Covenant on
    Economic, Social and
    Cultural Rights)   35, 100,
    102, 114
Ignatieff, Michael   16, 149
ILO (International Labour
    Organization)   35
incremental reform argument   2–3
individual rights
  and state interest considerations
    40
individuals
  and the rights tradition   16–20

inequality
  and education rights   102
  and rural migrants   111–14
  see also socio–economic rights
interest theory of rights   6
international human rights
    movement   20
International Labour Organization
    (ILO)   35
international law   54
  and the death penalty   70, 72
  and land rights   105
  and the right of freedom of
    expression   78, 79–80, 81
  and rights–protective norms   36
  and the right to life and liberty
    57
  and socio–economic rights
    101–2
international treaties   1, 4, 27, 35
  and rights defenders   122
  on socio–economic rights   102
  on torture   35, 64–5
internet   1, 77–8
  censorship   82
  fifty–centers (*wumaodang*)   93–4
  and freedom of expression
    88–92
  see also social media
investigative journalism   122, 124–5

Jasmine protests   85
Jiang Shigong   30, 135
Jiang Tianyong   55–6, 63, 66
Jiansanjiang Incident   55–6, 58,
    62–3, 69–70, 75, 121
journalists   149
  and freedom of expression   87–8
  rights defenders   122, 124–5, 135

judiciary   29, 43–7
   and advocacy as resistance
      51–3
   complainants and the
      authorities   46–7
   and criminal trials   29, 45–6
   lack of independence   45–6
   People's Procurators   45, 60
   and rights–protective
      norms   36–7
   selection of judges   44–5
June Fourth Movement for
      Democracy   1, 83, 152
justice
   and human rights   6
   right of access to   108
   rights tradition of   16–20
   yuan tradition of   12, 13, 13–16,
      19, 31
   see also criminal justice system

Kang Youwei   79

labour rights   1, 35, 37, 40, 102
   crackdown on   136
   violations of   41
land–grabs   40, 47, 106, 119
   petitioners   47–9
   and pollution   116–17
land rights   1, 103–8, 118
   rights defenders   121
   see also housing rights
law enforcement
   attitudes of officials to   28–9
   and the authoritarian
      system   145–6
lawyers
   authoritarian control over
      139–41

   and civil society organizations
      130
   and human rights advocacy   33,
      43–4, 121, 122, 123–4,
      125–7
   Party–State control of   125–6
   and the right of freedom of
      expression   81
   rights defenders   33, 43–4, 121,
      122, 123–4, 125–7
   7–09 Crackdown on (2015)   56,
      63–4, 95, 136–9, 142, 143,
      151
   see also criminal justice system
left–behind rural children   111
Legal Education Bases   62–3
legalist counterdiscourse   21–5
Legislation Law (2000)   34, 38–9,
      39–40, 60
Leninism   26, 33
Leping case   66, 67, 69, 73
Letters and Visits Regulation
      (2005)   48
'letters and visits' system   14, 33,
      47–51
Liang Qichao   17–18
liberal democracy
   and authoritarianism in China   7,
      148
liberal tradition
   of rights in China   17–18
liberty, right of   3, 55–69
   formal and informal deprivations
      of liberty   58–64
   freedom of the mind and the
      freedom of the person   75–6
   and housing rights   107
   and the Jiansanjiang Incident
      55–6, 58, 62–3

liberty, right of (cont.)
  and the Party–State 56–7, 145
  restrictions of personal liberty
    57–64
  see also torture
Li Buyun 19
Li Chunfu 139
life expectancy
  and air pollution 115
life, right to 3, 145
  and the death penalty 56, 69–75
  and housing rights 107
  and the Party–State 56–7
  see also liberty, right of
Li Ling 45
Link, Perry 87
Linz, Juan 7
Litigation Law (2000) 81
Liu, Sida 124
Liu Wei 43–4, 51, 126
Liu Xiaobo 83, 84–5, 86, 87, 89,
  121
Liu Xiaofeng 30
Liu Zhengyou 33, 46, 47–9, 51,
  105, 106, 121
living standards
  and land grabs 106
local authorities
  and rights–violating norms
    38–40

McConville, Mike 66
Mao era
  Maoist–Leninist counterdiscourse
    19, 21, 25–8, 30
  and subversion crimes 83
  see also post–Mao reform era
Mao Zedong 12, 25–6
Marxism 26, 96

media 1, 2
  online news reporting 89
  and the Party–State 92–7
  and the petitioning system 49
  press freedom 78, 79, 81
  print media and freedom of
    expression 76–8, 78, 79, 81
  and public expression 77
  see also social media
Michnik, Adam 128
migrant workers
  rights defenders 130–1
  and rights–undermining norms
    41
  see also rural–urban migration
Mill, J.S. 56, 69
minquan (people power) 18
Minzner, Carl 49
mobile phones 78, 88
moral duty counterdiscourse 22–3,
  30–1
Morris, Clarence 22

Nationalist (Kuomintang) Party
  and *minquan* (people power) 18
National People's Congress
  (NPC) 34, 35, 38–9
National Security Law (2015) 27,
  140
networks
  and victims/survivors of rights
    violations 3
New Citizen Movement 18, 85,
  114, 132–4
NGOs (non–governmental
  organizations)
  and the authoritarian revival 136,
    140
  environmental 131

reports on human rights in
China 2
transnational advocacy 122, 131,
132, 133, 149–51
Nickel, James 3, 4
Ni Yulan 9, 10, 106, 121

officials
attitudes to law enforcement 28
and the petitioning system
49–50
and the *yuan* tradition of righting
wrongs 14–15
Open Constitution Initiative
(Gongmeng) 131–2, 133
Opium Wars 17
organ transplants
and executed prisoners 74–5

Party–State 145–7
authoritarian revival 7, 135–43,
143–4
and the concept of human
rights 19
counterdiscourses 21, 23–5,
27–8, 28–31
and freedom of expression 78,
81, 82, 86–7
and freedom of thought 92–8
and household registration–based
discrimination 113
and human rights advocacy 5, 6,
54, 122–3, 125–6, 130
human rights in the normative
framework 33–4
and the incremental reform
argument 1
internet control 91
and the judiciary 45, 47

and land and housing rights 104,
107
and legal institutions to protect
human rights 33
and the media 92–7
and the normative framework of
human rights 43
and petitioning 6, 48
and pollution 116–17
positions on human rights 6
and poverty reduction 117–18
recognition of rights 19–20
and rights of liberty 56–7, 76,
145
Social Credit Governance 97
and social media 53–4
and socio–economic rights
100–1, 118, 146–7
and subversion crimes 83–4
and torture 68–9
see also Communist Party
Peng Chun 107
petitioners 134, 135
and advocacy as resistance 52
in *Emergency Shelter* 9–11,
13–14, 16, 20, 25, 106, 121
lawyer–volunteers and petitioning
work 140–1
'letters and visits' system 14, 33,
47–51
restrictions on personal liberty
58
roles of complainants in responses
to injustice 121–2
and the *yuan* tradition 14–15
police
attitudes to law enforcement 28
and the authoritarian revival 140
brutality 9–10

police (cont.)
  detention centres   60
  and restrictions on personal
      liberty   57–8
  and 'soft restraint' (*ruanjin*)   61
  and torture   66
Polish Constitution (1952)   42
political change
  and human rights   149
political justification of human
      rights   5
political reform advocacy   18
political rights   100, 120
pollution, human rights effects of
      114–17
population control policies
  and excess children   112–14
post–Mao reform era
  and arbitrary detention and
      torture   75
  and freedom of thought   93,
      146
  household registration system
      109
  human rights advocacy   32–3, 54,
      134–5
  and human rights discourse   19
  and justice   12
  and land rights   104
  lawyers   123
  rights–protective norms   34–7
  and the right to free
      expression   78
  and the rule of law   141
  and socio–economic
      rights   100–1, 104
  and subversion crimes   83
  and victims/survivors of rights
      violations   3

poverty
  and human rights goals   1
  and socio–economic rights   100,
      101, 117–18
power–based conceptions of law   21,
      28–31
principles of human rights   3–4
print media
  and freedom of expression   76–8,
      78, 79, 81
prisons see detention
property developers
  and land rights   104–6
property rights   108
prostitutes   60, 61
proto–rights
  yuan as   16
Przeworski, Adam   42
psychiatric incarceration   126
public opinion
  on human rights   11
  and rights defenders   127
public–private divide
  and the rights tradition   19
public protest
  and advocacy as resistance   52–3
  Party–State responses to   7–8
punishment
  Administrative Punishment Law
      63
  and Confucianism   15
  Confucian–Legalist perspective
      on   23–4
  petitioners and protests against
      48
  and redress of rights violations
      17
  see also death penalty; detention;
      torture

Qing Dynasty   17
Qi Yuling   33, 34–5, 36, 37, 51–2
quanli (rights)   17

Rawls, John   98
red envelope journalism   88
Re-education Through Labour
    (RTL) system   57, 60
reform and opening era *see* post–Mao
    reform era
religion, freedom of   35
renquan (human rights)   17
Ren, Xuefei   108
residential surveillance   38, 75, 138,
    139
resistance
    advocacy as   51–4
    right of   5
    and *yuan* discourse   15–16
rights–based conceptions of justice
    and *yuan*   16
rights defenders   120, 121–44
    achievements of   144
    arguments   6
    and the authoritarian revival
        135–43
    civil society organizations   123,
        127–32
    claims   5
    coordinated actions and
        initiatives   123, 132–5
    and the death penalty   69–70
    emergence of civil society
        advocates   123–35
    New Citizen Movement   18, 85,
        114, 132–4
    and the Party–State   122–3,
        144
    persecution of   20
    renunciation of former
        advocacy   138
    see also advocacy; lawyers
rights–protective norms   34–7, 42
the rights tradition   16–20
rights–undermining norms   40–3
rights–violating norms   37–40, 42
Rosenzweig, Joshua   74
rule of law   147–8
    and the incremental reform
        argument   2–3
    and the judiciary   47
    and the post–Mao era   141
    and transnational advocacy   151
rural areas
    'cancer villages' and
        pollution   115–16, 116–17
    land expropriations   104
rural–urban migration   104
    and education rights   108–14
    see also migrant workers
Russia   148

Saether, Elin   88
Schmitt, Carl   29–30, 64, 142
self–censorship   87, 151–2
7–09 Crackdown on lawyers (2015)
        56, 63–4, 95, 136–9, 142,
        143, 151
Shang Yang   23
Shirky, Clay   132
shuanggui detention of Party
        members   41–2, 62, 64
Shue, Henry   101
Shunli, Cao   50–1
Simmons, Beth A.   54
Sino–Japanese War (1895)   17
Smog Journeys (documentary)   116
Social Credit Governance   97

socialist tradition
    counterdiscourses   25–8
social media   11
    and advocacy as resistance   52–3
    complainants   47
    and freedom of expression   85–6,
        88, 89, 90
    and public expression   77
    and rights defenders   125, 134
    and thought reform   96–7
socio–economic rights   3–4, 21,
    100–20, 146–7, 148–9
    and civil and political rights   100,
        120
    and environmental
        degradation   114–17
    and international law   101–2
    land and housing rights   1, 102,
        103–8
    and poverty reduction   100, 101,
        117–18
    and the 'sacrifice' theory   118, 120
    see also education rights
'soft restraint' (*ruanjin*)   61
Southern Metropolitan news
    group   87, 96
Southern Street Movement   85
sovereignty
    and arguments against human
        rights   21
    and the law   30
SPC *see* Supreme People's Court
    (SPC)
Special Rapporteur on
    Torture   74–5
speech, freedom of   35, 40, 80, 81,
    98–9, 146
    censorship and speech
        crimes   83–6
    and the internet   88–92

Spires, Anthony   130
State Council
    Human Rights Action Plan   100
    and petitioners   48
    Regulation on excess
        children   112
strike, right to   102
subsistence rights   35, 119
subversion crimes   83–5
Sun Zhigang Incident   33, 37–8, 39,
    40, 41, 51, 59, 60, 87, 121,
    135
Sun Zhongshan (Sun Yat–sen)   18
Supreme People's Court (SPC)   34,
    36, 48
    and the death penalty   72, 74
    Letters and Visits Office   48–9
Supreme People's Procuracy   34
Svensson, Marina   88

Taiwan   88
Tang Fuzhen   107
Tang Jingling   85, 134
Tang Jitian   43–4, 51, 55–6, 63, 126
televised 'confessions'   138
Teng Biao   28, 39, 51, 74, 75, 132
    on subversion crimes   83, 85
terrorism, fears of   28
thought, freedom of   3, 79, 81,
    92–8, 99, 146
thought reform (*sixiang gaizao*)   68,
    97–8
Tibetan activists   130
Tocqueville, Alexis de   127–8
top–down reform   2–3
torture   1, 28, 55, 63, 64–9, 75, 76,
    145
    attitudes to   67–9
    and coerced confessions   37, 46,
        66–7

Convention Against (CAT)   35,
       64–5
and criminal convictions   46
and the Criminal Procedure Law
       (CPL)   37
and the death penalty   70, 73
definition of   64–5
and housing rights   106, 107
in the Jiansanjiang case   63
methods of   64, 67–8
purposes of   65–6
of rights defenders   126–7, 132,
       138–9
and rights–violating norms
       38
and the right to freedom of
       expression   81
and the right to life and
       liberty   57
and *shuanggui* detention of Party
       members   41
and thought work   97–8
victims of   66–7
totalitarianism
and civil society   128
move towards neo–totalitarian
       political model   141–3
and present–day China   7–8
re–conceptions of 'law'   28–31
Transition Institute   132
transnational advocacy   122, 131,
       149–52
Turkey   148

Uighurs   130
Under the Dome (film)   117, 121
United Nations (UN)
Basic Principles on the Role of
       Lawyers   122, 141
Committee Against Torture   32

Declaration on Human Rights
       Defenders   122
Human Rights Council   80, 91
human rights reporting   2, 50
and rights–protective norms   36
Special Rapporteur on Extreme
       Poverty and Human
       Rights   118
Special Rapporteur on Human
       Rights and the
       Environment   114
see also international treaties
United States
Civil Society   127
and rights defenders   138
speech crimes   84
Universal Declaration of Human
       Rights (UDHR)   79–80
Universal Periodic Review (UPR)
       process   1
universities   57, 77, 131, 149
urbanization
and environmental degradation
       114–15, 116, 117
impact on land and housing
       rights   103–8, 118

'vernacular' human rights
       discourse   5, 118, 149
vernacularization of rights   20
violation–enabling norms   40–3
violations of rights   1–2, 5, 6, 20,
       152
and the concept of *yuan*   16
and the death penalty   70
international organizations
       on   32
land and housing rights   105,
       106–7, 108
and legal mechanisms   146

violations of rights (cont.)
   and the Party–State
      authority 147
   Party–State justification of 28
   redress for 16–17
   and rights lawyers 124
   rights–violating norms 37–40
   socio–economic rights 100–1,
      118, 119
   suppression of criticism of 32
   to liberty and life 75, 76
   victims of 3, 9–11
   women's rights 130
   and *yuan* 16
VPNs (virtual private
   networks) 90–1

Waldron, Jeremy 69
Wang Canfa 131
Wang Cheng 55–6, 63
Wang Guihua 9–10, 11, 14, 16, 20,
   24, 25, 28
Wang Shaoguang 30
Wang Yu 137–8, 151–2
Weatherly, Robert 17
weiquan (rights defence) 19
welfare increases
   and socio–economic
      rights 118–19
Wen Jiabao 24
Western influences
   on the Chinese rights
      tradition 17–18
White Book on Human Rights 1,
   100

'Who Am I?' propaganda
   video 94–5
women's rights 123, 129–30
   defenders 131
Women's Rights Centre 131
workers
   restrictions on personal liberty
      57

Xia Junfeng (executed street
   vendor) 74, 75
Xiao Han 19
Xie Yang 139
Xi Jinping 92–3, 94, 96, 123
   and the authoritarian revival 135,
      136, 141, 143–4
   and Party organizations 128,
      129
Xu Zhiyong 85, 132, 133, 134

Yang Hui 12, 85–6, 89, 92
Ye Guozhu 10, 11, 13–14, 16, 28
Yirenping 130–1, 136
yuan tradition of righting wrongs
   12, 13, 13–16, 19, 22–3, 31
Yu Jianrong 49, 77–8, 107
Yu Yingshi 24, 90

Zeng Jinyan 61
Zhang Aixiang 9, 10, 11, 14, 16, 20,
   25, 28
Zhang Jiake 116
Zhang Junjie 55–6, 63
Zhang Qianfan 20
Zigong land–grab case 47–9